THE CONTRIBUTIONS OF THE SOCIAL SCIENCES TO EDUCATIONAL POLICY AND PRACTICE: 1965-1985

◆

Edited by

JANE HANNAWAY
Princeton University

and

MARLAINE E. LOCKHEED
Educational Testing Service

◆

McCutchan Publishing Corporation
2526 Martin Luther King Jr. Way
Berkeley, California 94704

ISBN 0–8211–0771–2
Library of Congress Catalog Card Number 85–63433

Printed in the United States of America

Contents

Contributors

Gary J. Bekker, Michigan State University
Charles E. Bidwell, University of Chicago
Mary Jean Bowman, University of Chicago
Geraldine Jonçich Clifford, University of California, Berkeley
Elizabeth G. Cohen, Stanford University
Ruth B. Ekstrom, Educational Testing Service
Doris R. Entwisle, Johns Hopkins University
Frederick D. Erickson, Michigan State University
Bruce Fuller, The World Bank
Margaret E. Goertz, Educational Testing Service
Maxine Greene, Teachers College, Columbia University
Jane Hannaway, Princeton University
Marlaine E. Lockheed, Educational Testing Service
Paul E. Peterson, The Brookings Institution
Donald A. Rock, Educational Testing Service
Diane Scott-Jones, North Carolina State University
Brenda J. Turnbull, Policy Studies Associates

1

Introduction: The Social Sciences and Education

Jane Hannaway and Marlaine E. Lockheed

The mid-sixties were watershed years for education in the United States. Up until that time educational research had been dominated by psychologists, who were mainly concerned with the cognitive development of individuals and with issues of tests and measurement. The events of the mid-sixties led to a broader perspective. The Coleman Report found that family background—a social factor—was a critical determinant of student achievement (Coleman et al. 1966). Economists, such as Theodore Schultz, recognized that investment in education was an important factor affecting economic, in addition to individual, growth (Schultz 1963). The passage of the Elementary and Secondary Education Act of 1965 introduced new political actors and brought new policy instruments into the picture. And major court decisions, such as *Brown v. Board of Education* and *Lau v. Nichols*, forced rethinking of the principles on which education in our society should be based.

These changes were accompanied by one of the largest proportionate increases in federal research funding for education programs, with millions of additional dollars appropriated for evaluating the education programs of the Great Society. They were heyday years. The scientific method was being harnessed to improve the social and economic lives of people, and scholars responded to the opportunity and to the challenge. A new division—Division G: The Social Context

1

of Education—was established for the American Educational Research Association in 1968; its mission was to provide an intellectual home for the growing numbers of social scientists concerned with education.

It is now twenty years later. The researchers of the sixties are older, more knowledgeable, and more sober. Although easy answers did not emerge, and research funding never met expectations, much productive work was accomplished. This book reviews the contributions that social scientists have made to educational policy and educational practice over the last twenty years. It is an appropriate time to take stock, not only because twenty years represents a generation of effort, but also because the country is now riding a new wave of education reform. Some of the things that we have learned might be useful to reformers and researchers of the eighties.

Two principles guided our thinking in putting this book together. First, we intend the book to be practical, and to reflect upon real issues in education. That is, we have consciously addressed this book toward the current social context of education by reviewing the changing environment in which education has been operating since the mid-sixties. The chapters in Part One describe these changes. Second, the book is organized around the major social science disciplines, which provide a structure for assessing cumulative gains in knowledge. Part Two of this book grew out of two specially invited Division G vice-presidential symposia at the 1984 and 1985 AERA meetings in which noted scholars assessed the work of their particular discipline and its contribution to a better understanding of the educational enterprise.

THE SOCIAL CONTEXT

Education as a social institution is inextricably bound to its environment. Its policies, practices and, indeed, views of its productivity are directly affected by its social context. The four chapters that compose Part One of this book chronicle major changes in the social environment that not only have affected education over the last two decades but are also critically important today.

We begin with Diane Scott Jones's chapter on the family in which she describes the dramatic changes that have taken place in family structure and child-care practices in the United States and the implications these changes have for education. Tremendous increases in the number of working mothers, single-parent families, and teenage mothers pose significant new challenges for educators and the educational system in general.

In the next chapter Bruce Fuller reviews the ways in which we have viewed school quality in the twenty years since the Coleman Report. These changing views affect how researchers frame their research questions, how communities judge the quality of their schools, and what criteria policymakers use to design and to evaluate educational policies.

The chapter by Ruth Ekstrom, Margaret Goertz, and Donald Rock is also concerned with school quality but focuses on the performance of students. The authors describe the decline in the performance of American high school students as measured by standard achievement tests and then evaluate reasons for the decline. Specifically, the authors consider the effects of changes in the demographic characteristics of students, in their homes and families, in the schools they attend, and in their attitudes and behaviors. After taking a close look at the impact of school-based factors on achievement by using longitudinal data, they conclude that schools *can* make a difference. In the last part of the chapter they discuss the policy implications of their findings.

In the final chapter of Part One, Brenda Turnbull reviews the changing policy context affecting education. Her main focus is on federal policy. In the sixties the federal government began to move from its position as nearly a nonparticipant in primary and secondary education, to a major aggressive force in the seventies, and then once again to a minor player in the reforms of the eighties. Turnbull discusses the effects of the federal initiatives of the sixties and seventies and the ways in which their objectives and instruments differ from the current state-based reforms.

THE DISCIPLINES

In the second part of the book we turn to the disciplines for their theoretical orientations, not because we are interested in theory for theory's sake alone, but because we are interested in using theory to delineate educational issues in ways that are constructive for the long term and to formulate solutions that are thought through systematically. We believe that the systematic application of theoretical constructs to a set of problems moves a field forward. It encourages the development of new questions by conceiving them in more general terms. Taking this step back from the concrete can often generate new slants on old problems. Applying theory to practical problems permits us to accumulate knowledge because it offers a structure on which to hang our insights and findings.

Theory provides abstract constructs that specify relationships. From a practical point of view, theory helps us to determine which of many variables are worthy of investigation. This is especially important in a field such as education, where the possible number of variables is legion. While the capabilities of computers to manage large numbers of variables makes undirected investigations quite manageable, a sharp distinction must be drawn between analyses that simply correlate everything with everything else, in an attempt to find or establish some order, and analyses that select questions carefully, guided by theoretical principles. In the former case, the relevance of the finding is specific to the one instance only; it has no claim to generalizability. In the latter case, generalizability is achieved through the careful specification of the conditions under which the relationships hold. The ability to accumulate knowledge through the testing of hypotheses derived from theories is, perhaps, the most important advantage of scientific endeavors.

Theories also provide a mechanism by which knowledge gained from one domain may be transferred to another. If both schools and hospitals, for example, are analyzed as formal organizations, then findings about organizational processes that emerge from studies of hospitals can be applied to schools, and the converse. Moreover, techniques that are used in studying hospitals may be applicable to the study of schools, given that both are conceived of as formal organizations. Theory enhances the entire process of conducting research, from conceptualizing the problem, to selecting data, to interpreting findings, and then to developing the next set of research questions.

Not all disciplines, of course, proceed in a theoretically deductive manner. Anthropology and historiography provide invaluable contributions by staying close to the messiness of real life and applying highly disciplined methods of inquiry. The historiographer does this by analyzing the past and its interpretation; the educational anthropologist does it by looking closely at the present and identifying processes often overlooked by others.

No one discipline alone is sufficient for gaining a realistic understanding of an applied area like education. Applied enterprises are complicated by their very nature. They are affected by a number of different factors and they themselves have multiple effects. Each discipline has its own vantage point; this is its advantage. But this is also its limitation. Multiple perspectives are needed in order to identify and compare different avenues to improving practice—which, of course, is the final objective for applied research. The chapters in Part Two show the lenses that different disciplines use and the insights that they provide, although the boundaries between disciplines are not always rigid. Readers might find particularly stimulating the chapters on perspectives that are very different from their own. In every chapter, the institution under study is the same—education—but the questions of interest, the variables analyzed, and the findings that they yield are often very different.

The eight chapters in the second part of this book look at education from the viewpoints of major social science fields. Covered are social psychology, sociology, anthropology, organizational studies, historiography, economics, and political science; an afterword from philosophy completes the group. In these chapters a convergent set of themes emerges: social stratification, equity and efficiency, life-course development, and—most significantly—a growing recognition of the dynamic and interactive nature of the educational processes in question. The underlying vision that dominates these chapters is that the individual development encouraged by education does not take place in a vacuum but is largely influenced by and influences the social contexts in which it occurs.

The first chapter in Part Two is Doris Entwisle's discussion of constructs closest to the individual: cognitive development and development of self-concept. She introduces the concept of interactivity among elements of the social structure, developmental stages of achievement, and self-concept. Recognizing that the empirical investigation of such interactivity is difficult, she acknowledges that modeling the interactions between the social context and cognitive and social development has been vastly simplified by sophisticated statistical methodologies, enhanced by the capabilities of high-speed computers.

Elizabeth Cohen's chapter further elaborates this developmental theme by identifying specific elements of the classroom social context that affect achievement and student perception of their ability; these include the structure of the learning task, the evaluation processes in the classroom, and the status order of the classroom. She introduces the idea that these elements of classroom organization and control can easily result in the children's social structure replicating the social structure of the larger society. She then elaborates on how deliberate change in the social organization of classrooms can minimize such social reproduction and thus provide a learning environment in which the social status of the students does not come to determine their learning outcomes.

While most anthropology of education also takes classrooms and corridors as the venue of inquiry, Frederick Erickson and Gary Bekker describe in their chapter how the concern of anthropology of education has shifted over time from the study of how children are passively socialized to the study of the dynamic interplay between children and agents of socialization. First, anthropology of education looked at childrearing practices outside schools; then it looked at cultural differences as explanations of failure in school; today it examines the ways in which schools create symbolic, interactional resources for the production of social inequality.

In Charles Bidwell's chapter the scope widens from the classroom to the larger organization of the school and the administrative unit. Here the concern is with describing theoretical models of organizations and the change in these models over the past twenty years. Bidwell describes early conceptualizations of organizations as machines, operating with given objectives and resources in a closed system; he then discusses how subsequent formulations chipped away at this framework by viewing the system as open in various ways to environmental influences. He argues that the separate lines of research that have investigated environmental relationships should now be integrated and that control should be viewed as a system function, not only a management function, since the environment has effects over and above those transmitted by the formal management system.

Geraldine Clifford makes explicit in her chapter on historiography the change in the social context of education over the past twenty years; it has been a change from liberal to radical themes in which the expectation that schools could serve as homogenizing agents was replaced by a realization that interactions among home, school, and community served to create schools that differentiated among students on the basis of social class. While the debate among historians continues, this chapter raises the important consideration of the relationship between education and employment.

The theme of education and its importance for economic production is expanded in the chapter by Mary Jean Bowman. Economists have long recognized the importance of education in creating human capital. At first, it was thought that education provided specific professional skills, and attention was paid to comparisons between the rates of return to specific training programs. Then, attention shifted to examining general transferable skills acquired through education, particularly those that enabled individuals to respond to conditions of changing technology.Currently, education is considered as a producer of change, with the educated creating the new technologies.

The study of the political context of education has also profoundly changed over the past twenty years, and the chapter by Paul Peterson describes some of these changes. While two decades ago researchers were studying educational decision makers and the social-psychological concepts that were the foundation of decision theory, the politics of education today is attuned to a broader set of elements in the context of decision making and policy implementation.

In some sense, the change in studying education over the past two decades has been that of breaking through disciplinary boundaries. Each discipline has begun to examine the assumptions of its field and to move toward a theory of interaction between actor and environment. In the afterword by Maxine Greene, the philosopher's penchant for making the explicit the implicit and for questioning assumptions is turned to education. This final piece poses the profound question that lies below the surface: How do we know what is knowledge? Clearly the work in social science over the past two decades has been influenced by growing recognition of different perspectives, different languages, and clearly different "lived lives" for the poor, immigrants, women, blacks, religious fundamentalists . . . the list is endless. These perspectives are the culture that children bring with them to school and to the learning environment wherever they encounter it.

REFERENCES

Coleman, James S.; Campbell, E. O.; Hobson, C. J.; Mood, A. M.; Weinfeld, F. Z.; and York, R. L. *Equality of Educational Opportunity*. U.S. Department of Health, Education, and Welfare, U.S. Office of Education. Washington, D.C.: Government Printing Office, 1966.

Schultz, Theodore W. *The Economic Value of Education*. New York: Columbia University Press, 1963.

PART I

Twenty-Year Trends in the Social Context

2

The Family

Diane Scott-Jones

Families and schools are major social institutions that provide contexts for children's development. Because these institutions interact with and affect one another, education is likely to be most effective when characteristics of families are explicitly considered in the formulation of educational policy and in daily educational practice.

Families have changed dramatically between 1965 and 1985, prompting some researchers as well as the popular press to lament the demise of the traditional American family. The family unit composed of an employed father, a mother who does not work outside the home, and two or more school-aged children has virtually disappeared. Such families composed 60 percent of households in the United States in 1955 but constituted a mere 7 percent in 1985 (Hodgkinson 1985). In the mid-fifties the process of family formation followed a prescribed course during an individual's life span (Furstenberg 1984). Marriage occurred soon after schooling ended and pregnancy occurred shortly after marriage, if not before. The male entered the labor force, if he was not already working, and the female left the labor force, if she had worked, to become a full-time homemaker. Leaving the family of origin and setting up one's own household coincided with marriage. This "typical" mid-twentieth-century pattern of family formation was actually more rigid than was the nineteenth-century pattern, and it followed a period, during and immediately after World War II, when the divorce rate soared and then declined sharply (Furstenberg 1984).

Since the mid-sixties individuals in American society have varied greatly in the timing and sequencing of those events that formerly composed a fairly regular process of family formation. Many young adults now set up their own households before marrying; they might live alone, with roommates, or as unmarried couples. Marriage and pregnancy no longer occur only in tandem; single women bear children, whether by choice or by accident, and married women delay childbearing for several years after marriage or choose not to have children at all. In record numbers married women who are raising children are also working. Rates of divorce and subsequent remarriage are high, so that the pattern of marital relations might be described as serial monogamy.

This chapter attempts to summarize major changes in families and to discuss the implications of these changes for the educational system. Family patterns to be discussed include childless families, dual-earner families, single-parent families, blended families, and adolescent parents. These family forms may differ according to economic status and race or ethnicity; therefore, the increase in children who live in poverty and the increase in the proportion of minority families in American society will also be discussed.

CHILDLESS FAMILIES

Today, a relatively high proportion of households does not have children, and more of the population is elderly than in the past. In 1983 adults over 65 years outnumbered teen-agers (Hodgkinson 1985). Many older adults live in "empty-nest" households, without dependent children. In addition, some younger couples decide to remain childless or delay childbearing much longer than was thought desirable in the past. Of wives aged twenty to twenty-four, the percentage remaining childless increased from 25 percent in 1960 to 45 percent in 1975. Similarly, for wives aged twenty-five to twenty-nine, childless rates increased from 12 percent in 1960 to 22 percent in 1975 (Veevers 1979). The continuing shift toward later childbearing is indicated by the fact that between 1980 and 1983 the only age group to show a significant increase in birth rate was women thirty to thirty-four years (Current Population Reports 1984). Higher educational levels, occupational levels, and family incomes are found for women over thirty years who give birth, compared to those who give birth between ages eighteen and twenty-nine (Current Population Reports 1984). Higher educational, occupational, and income levels are also found for women in intentionally childless couples, compared to women of the same age in couples that have recently had a first birth (Feldman 1981).

The increasing number of childless families has two major implications for education. First, public support for education may erode if many members of society perceive that they do not derive benefits from the educational system. For example, elderly couples on fixed incomes and young childless couples seeking economic and career advancement may not believe that public spending for education benefits them. They may need to be convinced that a strong educational system affects more than the individuals directly involved in it.

A second implication of this demographic trend is the expected growth of adult and continuing education in the next decade. In addition, it is estimated that by 1992, 50 percent of college students will be over twenty-five years and 20 percent will be over thirty-five years (Hodgkinson 1985). Thus, educational institutions will need to accommodate an increasingly older student body.

DUAL-EARNER FAMILIES

A major change in the United States in this century has been the increase in the number of women who work outside the home. Earlier in this century, working women were likely to be unmarried (Weiner 1985). Currently, a high proportion of wives and mothers work, and the increase is much more dramatic for white than for Black women, who have always worked in relatively high numbers. In 1890 only 2 percent of white wives worked, in contrast to 23 percent of Black wives. By 1970, 39 percent of white wives and 51 percent of Black wives were employed (Weiner 1985). Today, 48 percent of white wives and 60 percent of Black wives work (Jones 1985). Women are more likely to work after their children enter school. In 1980, 62 percent of mothers with school-age children worked outside the home, compared with 45 percent of mothers with children younger than six years (U.S. Census Bureau 1981). However, even substantial numbers of mothers with infants work; in 1982, 40.8 percent of mothers of children under one year worked outside the home (Klein 1985). The amount of time women work is variable. Compared to men, employed women are more likely to work part time, to work less than twelve months a year, and to leave the work force periodically (Hoffman 1984). For many married women, staying at home is not a viable choice. Economic necessity is the foremost reason married women give for working; self-fulfillment is only secondary and is the reason more commonly given by highly educated women than by working-class women (Gordon and Kammeyer 1980).

Mothers' employment does not appear to have negative effects on their children's development. On the contrary, as Lois Hoffman (1980) proposes, mothers who do not work may invest more time and energy in the mothering role than is beneficial to the child. Research suggests that working mothers and full-time homemakers do not differ, for the most part, in communication patterns with their fifteen- to seventeen-month-old infants (Schubert, Bradley-Johnson, and Nuttal 1980). Toddlers with working mothers and those with non-employed mothers do not differ in security of attachment, problem-solving behavior (Easterbrooks and Goldberg 1985), or language development (Schachter 1981). Intelligence test scores were significantly lower for toddlers with working mothers, although the means for both groups were in the average range (Schachter 1981). The difference may represent a performance rather than a competence difference, because children of nonworking mothers were more adult-oriented and may have responded more positively to the test-giver than did children of working mothers, who were more peer-oriented and self-sufficient (Schachter 1981). Anita Farel (1980) found no differences on measures of intelligence and school adjustment between kindergarten children with working mothers and those with non-working mothers, when education, income and race were controlled. For middle-class white, two-parent families, maternal employment appears to be associated with higher school achievement for girls but may be associated with lower achievement for boys (Hoffman 1980). For low-income Black families, including some single-parent families, maternal employment is associated with enhanced school achievement (Hoffman 1980).

The fact that many mothers work outside the home has four major implications for education. First, patterns of involving families in school activities must change. Schools can no longer assume that mothers have leisure time during the day to attend meetings and programs, or that only mothers are actively involved in childrearing. Varied means of reaching and involving mothers and fathers will be required (see Scott-Jones and Peebles-Wilkins, in press).

Second, educational institutions will need to address the needs of children younger than five or six years. In 1964, 9.5 percent of three- and four-year-olds were enrolled in some form of schooling. By 1983 that figure had almost quadrupled: 37.5 percent of three- and four-year-old children were enrolled in a school (National Center for Education Statistics 1985). The majority of children in this age group attend private nursery schools or day-care centers. In contrast, infants tend to be cared for by mothers' relatives; in 1982 fewer than 10 percent of infants of working mothers were in center-based care (Klein 1985). The need for child care far exceeds available resources. It is estimated that 1.8 million children care for themselves while their parents work and that more than 2 million women would increase their working hours or seek employment if affordable child care were available (Marx 1985).

Because of the public's concern about the availability, quality, and cost of day care, increasing pressure may be brought on the public education system to provide prekindergarten programs. Some states now have public programs for three- and four-year-olds, but these programs typically are half-day only, limited to poor children, and not extensive enough to accommodate all eligible children. Head Start, for example, may serve as little as 13 percent of the eligible children. Because of the cost of high-quality day care and the limited eligibility for public programs, the educational experiences of three- and four-year-olds may be marked by segregation of poor and affluent children. In 1981 an equal percentage, 36 percent, of Black and white three- and four-year-old children were enrolled in some form of schooling. A slightly lower proportion, 25 percent, of Hispanic three- and four-year-old children were enrolled in school programs (Grant and Snyder 1983). However, the proportions of Black and white children attending public and private programs differ. In 1982, when 61 percent of three- and four-year-olds in school were in private programs, more than 70 percent of white children but only 33 percent of Black children were in private programs. Inequities in the educational system may begin at this early age.

A third and related issue is the before- and after-school care of children of working parents. Private day-care centers often provide such care. Some public schools have extended day programs to accommodate working parents. The lack of appropriate supervised care for elementary school children has resulted in increasing numbers of "latch-key" or "self-care" children. Because parents' work hours do not coincide with the school day, some children take care of themselves in homes without adult supervision for part of each day. In 1976 an estimated 13 percent, or 1.8 million, of seven- to thirteen-year-old children were self-care children. By 1983 that figure had increased to 5.2 million children. It is popularly believed that self-care arrangements are negative for children; in particular, fearfulness is thought to characterize self-care children. Little research has been conducted on the effects of self-care on children, probably because subjects are not as readily accessible as they are in more formal care arrangements. Hyman Rodman, David Pratto, and Rosemary Nelson (1985) found no differences between matched groups of self-care and adult-care children on measures of social and psychological functioning, including a self-esteem inventory, a locus-of-control scale, and a teacher rating scale. Some self-care children may follow a prescribed set of activities and guidelines for behavior, so that parents are indirectly supervising children's behavior. It is likely, however, that there will be increasing demands for supervised before- and after-school care for children, and schools may need to revise their programs to meet this need.

The fourth issue is the differential experiences of boys and girls in the educational system. Because it is now the norm that women work outside the home rather than engage in full-time housekeeping and childrearing, the educational system needs to prepare both boys and girls to perform competently in both work and home settings. Girls' education must emphasize skills that lead to occupations more lucrative than the traditional "pink-collar ghetto" jobs. Females are making inroads in mathematics and science, but their progress is slow. Earlier educational experiences, especially in mathematics, may act as a "critical filter" for later careers. Although differences are not found as consistently as in the past, there is still some evidence of higher science and mathematics achievement for boys than for girls, especially in high school (Stage, Kreinberg, Eccles, and Becker 1985). Taking different courses may account for differences in mathematics achievement between male and female high school students (Jones 1983). Girls will need to be actively encouraged to study mathematics and science and to pursue related careers. Elizabeth Stage and colleagues (1985) describe several programs aimed at increasing females' participation in science and mathematics.

SINGLE-PARENT FAMILIES

Although the divorce rate now appears to have stabilized, it has risen steadily since the mid-sixties, and divorce occurs earlier in the marriage than it had in the past (Furstenburg 1984). Researchers predict that approximately one-half of all recent marriages will end in divorce (Furstenburg 1984; Hetherington and Camara 1984). Many of these dissolved families include children; it is estimated that between one-third and one-half of children born in the 1970s will live some portion of their lives with only one parent (Hetherington, Camara, and Featherman 1981; Svanum, Bringle, and McLaughlin 1982). A number of reasons have been proposed for the current high divorce rate. Because of the increase in women's gainful employment, wives are less economically dependent on husbands and may value their work roles as much as their roles as wives and mothers. Welfare dependency has increased as an alternative to marital dependency. Personal fulfillment has become more accepted as a life goal, and thus individuals expect more of marriage and experience fewer legal and social constraints on ending an unhappy marriage (Furstenburg 1984).

Although custody laws are no longer biased in favor of mothers, mothers still are more likely than fathers to be granted custody of their children. Approximately 90 percent of children involved in divorces remain with their mothers. Fathers are more likely to obtain custody of boys than of girls and are not likely to gain custody of all the children from the previous marriage (Furstenburg and Spanier 1984). Within two years of the divorce, many fathers rarely see their children. Fathers who have joint custody, rather than visitation rights only, are much more likely to be involved with their children. Fathers' relationships with their children prior to the divorce appear to be unrelated to the relationship that develops after the divorce (Hetherington and Camara 1984).

The number of families headed by single females increased by 51 percent between 1970 and 1979; the total number of families increased by only 12 percent during that time period (Rawlings 1980). The numbers of Black and white children reared by single parents differ markedly. By age 16, 38 percent of white children and 75 percent of Black children will experience the disruption of their families. The majority of single-parent families, however, are white; Black children compose 35 percent of all children in single-parent homes (Hetherington and Camara 1984).

One outcome of the single-parent family is the higher likelihood of poverty. The income of the family is almost always lowered with the absence of a spouse (Duncan and Morgan 1981). The majority of single mothers do not receive regular child-support payments and do not have adequate incomes (Everett 1985). Single mothers work at slightly higher rates than do married mothers. Approximately 67 percent of single mothers with school-age children, 54 percent with preschoolers, and 45 percent with toddlers and infants are employed (Lamb, Chase-Lansdale, and Owen 1979). In addition to socioeconomic status, other factors that mediate the effects of divorce on children are the amount of conflict prior to, during, and after the divorce; the quality of the child's relationship with the noncustodial parent; the quality of the child's relationship with the custodial parent; the simultaneous occurrence of other stressful life events; and the availability of support networks. Boys may be more negatively affected than girls. Many of the negative effects of divorce do not persist for more than two years; families appear to adjust to their changed situations (Hetherington 1984; Hetherington and Camara 1984).

The major cause of single-parent families is separation and divorce. In addition to those children who live in single-parent homes because of their parents' divorce are children who are born to unmarried women. The majority of unwed mothers, 62 percent, are over twenty years (Children's Defense Fund 1985); they are not teen-agers as might be assumed. Although contraceptive methods have become highly effective and are widely available, births to unmarried women have increased. Between 1970 and 1982 both the number of births and the rate of births decreased for married women but increased for unmarried women. During that time period the birth rate for never-married women rose from .8 percent to 4.4 percent (Hetherington and Camara 1984); the proportion of all births to unmarried women increased from 11 percent to 19 percent (Ventura 1985). Although the nonmarital birth rate declined for Black women and increased for white women between 1970 and 1982, the rate for Black women, 7.96 percent, is four times that of white women, which is 1.88 percent (Ventura 1985).

One factor associated with the rise in nonmarital births is the increase in the number of women between twenty and forty years—the childbearing years. Because women born during the post–World War II baby boom are now in this age group, the percentage of women of childbearing age increased by 28 percent between 1970 and 1982. A second and more important factor is the increase in the proportion of women of childbearing age who remain unmarried. With many women of childbearing age remaining unmarried and, presumably, sexually active, the likelihood of births outside marriage, by choice or by chance, increases. Ventura (1985) estimates that 61 percent of the increase in nonmarital births between 1970 and 1982 is due simply to the increase in the number of women who are unmarried. The proportion of nonmarital conceptions ending in marital births has not changed substantially. In 1980, 40 percent of all first births were conceived outside marriage, compared to 29 percent in 1972. In both 1980 and 1972 approximately one-third of the mothers married before the child's birth (Ventura 1985).

Research findings on the differential school performance of children in single- and two-parent families are inconsistent. Some researchers have concluded that academic achievement is lower for children from single-parent homes, particularly in the early elementary years (Hetherington, Camara, and Featherman 1981; Shinn 1978). Others found no significant differences between children from single- and two-parent families (Herzog and Sudia 1973; Svanum, Bringle, and McLaughlin 1982). Some of the differences found are quite small, and others disappear when socioeconomic status is controlled (Svanum, Bringle, and McLaughlin 1982). The home environments of preschool children from divorced families have been found to be less cognitively and socially stimulating than those of preschoolers from two-parent families (MacKinnon, Brody, and Stoneman 1982). When noncustodial parents interact with their children, they are more likely to engage in social activities, such as going out to dinner, than in activities such as helping with homework (Furstenburg and Spanier 1984).

Because many single parents work, educational issues related to single-parent families are similar to those raised in the previous section concerning families with working mothers. In addition, schools may need to acknowledge children's family structures by sending communications regarding student performance and school activities to both the noncustodial and custodial parents. Teachers and counselors need to be prepared to handle possible changes in children's behavior during the time of separation and divorce. A school environment that includes explicit rules, warm and consistent discipline, and expectations for mature behavior is associated with enhanced cognitive and social development for young children in the two years following divorce. Boys may get less support from teachers and peers than do girls (Hetherington and Camara 1984).

BLENDED FAMILIES

For some children, living in a single-parent home is a transitional state. Approximately 80 percent of divorced parents eventually remarry (Glick 1979). Of these remarriages, approximately one-half occur within three years of the divorce (Hetherington and Camara 1984). Divorced men are more likely than divorced women to remarry (Furstenburg and Spanier 1984).

Approximately one-sixth of American children live in households where their parent has remarried (Furstenburg and Spanier 1984). Remarriages result in reconstituted or blended families. Blended families are potentially complex structures composed of children living with biological parents and stepparents, with varying relationships with noncustodial parents and their kin. Children's relationships can become exceedingly complicated when the noncustodial parent also remarries or when second and third divorces and remarriages occur. Few norms exist for the various roles that may occur in blended families, and little empirical research has been conducted on the process of remarriage and family reconstitution.

Although remarriage may be a positive event for many adults and may reduce some of the stress associated with financial difficulty and household management for custodial parents, remarriage may require difficult adjustments for the children involved (Hetherington and Camara 1984). Noncustodial fathers who remarry decrease their involvement with children from their first marriage. Adolescents have greater difficulty than do children of other age groups in accepting a stepparent. Stepfathers tend to be either uninvolved with children or extremely involved, to the point of being restrictive. The most positive outcomes for children occur when the stepfather supports the mother's disciplinary efforts, rather than remains uninvolved or extremely involved, and when the noncustodial father maintains regular contact. Because most children live with their biological mothers, even less is known about stepmothers living in the household with stepchildren and about noncustodial mothers.

Six to eleven-year-old children who had lived in families with stepfathers for at least eighteen months were compared in an observational study with children who had lived with divorced mothers and with both biological parents; this study indicated positive outcomes for children in families with stepfathers (Santrock, Warshak, Lindbergh, and Meadows 1982). Boys in families with stepfathers exhibited more competent social behavior than did boys in two-parent families. Girls in families with stepfathers, however, showed more anxiety than did girls in two-parent families. No differences were found between divorced and two-parent families.

For some children the amount of time spent in a single-parent family may be substantial. Blacks are less likely than whites to remarry. When Blacks do remarry, they experience a longer period of time between first and second marriages than do whites (Hetherington and Camara 1984). The average length of time in a single-parent household following a first marital disruption is three years for white children and ten years for Black children. After their parent remarries, 40 percent of white children and 60 percent of Black children experience a second disruption (Cherlin 1981; Glick 1980; Spanier and Glick 1980). The issues that blended families present for schools are similar to those presented by the divorce of children's parents. Teachers and counselors need to be aware of the potential adjustment problems children might have following their parents' remarriage. Schools may also need to communicate with parents in more than one household.

ADOLESCENT PARENTS

In 1980, 16 percent of all births and 28 percent of first births were to adolescent mothers (Moore 1983). Those teens giving birth in 1980 composed 5.2 percent of all female adolescents (Mecklenburg and Thompson 1983). Birth rates are higher for minority than for white teens. In 1980, 9.5 percent of minority teens and 4.5 percent of white teens gave birth (Moore 1983). The rates for the United States are higher than the rates of most other developed nations and of many developing nations (Alan Guttmacher Institute 1981).

Although the current birth rate for teenagers is commonly viewed as an "epidemic," adolescent birth rates have been higher in the past. For teens aged sixteen to nineteen years, the highest rates occurred in 1957 (4.57 percent, 8.58 percent, 13.62 percent, and 18.47 percent by age respectively) and for teens fourteen to fifteen years, the highest rates occurred in 1973 (.074 percent and 2.02 percent respectively). Comparable figures in 1981 for each successive age beginning with fourteen years were .054 percent; 1.41 percent, 3.04 percent, 4.98 percent, 7.10 percent, and 9.2 percent (Baldwin 1984). In contrast to the 1950s, however, when many of the relatively numerous teenage mothers were married and remained in stable families, today nearly half of the adolescent mothers are single, and many live in dire poverty (Children's Defense Fund 1985). Between 1970 and 1982, the birth rate for unmarried white teens increased as the rate for unmarried Black teens decreased (Ventura 1985).

The actual number of births to adolescents is dependent on both the birth rate and the number of adolescents in the population.

Because the largest cohort of the post–World War II baby-boom children reached nineteen years of age in 1976 (Baldwin 1984), the number of adolescents in the population had declined. Declines both in the numbers of adolescents and in their childbearing rates should lead to fewer births to adolescents. From 1960 to 1970 both the *percentage* of all births to adolescents and the *number* of births to adolescents rose, and then they both declined between 1970 and 1980. Only the rate of births to *older* adolescents (those eighteen to nineteen years), however, dropped below the 1960 rates for this age group. Thus, the age distribution of adolescent mothers has shifted downward slightly. The majority of adolescent births are still to older adolescents, many of whom have finished high school and for whom pregnancy has no significant adverse effects.

The number of births to younger adolescents, however, is cause for concern. The consequences of pregnancy for the development of both a young adolescent and her child are likely to be quite negative (Baldwin 1983). Because of their physiological immaturity, very young adolescents may have complications of pregnancy not totally accounted for by lack of or poor prenatal care (Children's Defense Fund 1985; Dott and Fort 1976). A fact sometimes overlooked in discussions of adolescent pregnancy is that the average age for the onset of puberty has declined (Roche 1979). Girls now reach puberty at an average age of twelve-and-a-half years, and the normal range of onset is ten to fifteen-and-a-half years (Tanner 1975). Boys reach puberty at an average of fourteen years, within a range of twelve to sixteen years (Tanner 1970). A conscious effort must be made to prevent pregnancy among adolescents who are capable of conceiving but are not ready for childbearing and childrearing.

Adolescent pregnancy disrupts the mothers' and, to a lesser extent, fathers' lives. Of adolescent females who give birth, the majority—86 percent in 1971 and 93 percent in 1976—keep their infants rather than give them up for adoption (Zelnik and Kantner 1978). Only half of teenage fathers have contact with the child or mother in the first two years after the birth, and a smaller percentage maintain contact after the second year (Earls and Siegel 1980). Not every adolescent pregnancy involves a teenage father; men older than twenty years father approximately half of the babies born to teenage women (Children's Defense Fund 1985). Although more than half of adolescent mothers eventually complete high school, the educational and occupational levels of both adolescent mothers and fathers are lower than those of their peers, and those who marry are more likely to have marital difficulty (Furstenberg 1976a, 1976b; Card and Wise 1978). In fact, educational and employment outcomes may be better for those who do not marry and who remain with their parents for five years after the child's birth than for those who marry (Baldwin 1983; Furstenberg and Crawford 1978).

With prenatal and follow-up health care, race, and socioeconomic status controlled, differences in physical health and later development of offspring born to adolescent and older mothers are not found (Chilman 1980, 1983). The academic achievement of children born to teenage mothers may not be different from that of children born to older mothers of the same socioeconomic status. Betty Morrow (1979) found no differences in academic achievement between low-income Black children born to women fifteen years and younger and those born to women twenty to twenty-four years old. Belmont and colleagues (1981) found a small linear relationship between maternal age and scores on the Wechsler Intelligence Scale for Children for Black children and white children, but the effect of maternal age could be accounted for by other factors related to the pregnancy. Sarah Broman (1981) found that four-year-old children who had been born to adolescent mothers scored lower on intelligence tests than did children who had been born to twenty- to twenty-nine-year-old mothers. The effect of socioeconomic status, however, was far greater than the effect of maternal age. The lack of differences clearly attributable to mother's age does not mean that adolescent pregnancy is a positive event. It may mean that adolescent pregnancy tends to occur in an already precarious situation.

In addition to some of the educational problems for working mothers and single mothers mentioned in the preceding sections of this chapter, teenage parenthood has implications for the dropout rate, the provision of special programs for pregnant teens, and the inclusion of sex education in school curricula. In a national study of the sophomore class of 1980, females cited pregnancy as one of the major reasons for dropping out of school (Whalen 1984). Among white females the most frequently cited reason (36.4 percent) was marriage or plans for marriage, which may have involved a pregnancy. An additional 20.5 percent of white girls cited pregnancy as a reason. Minority girls most frequently cited poor grades (30 percent), but pregnancy was a close second (29.2 percent); marriage or plans for marriage was cited by 19.2 percent.

Some schools and community organizations have developed special programs to help pregnant teens and teenage mothers to complete high school. An evaluation of a demonstration program indicated that after one year participating teens had more favorable educational and employment outcomes, were more likely to use contraceptives, and were less likely to have another pregnancy than were members of a comparison group. Some of the differences between the groups decreased after two years. The major features of the program were the use of community women as a support group, the use of peer-group sessions, and the development of an individualized program plan for each participant (Polit and Kahn 1985).

The provision of sex education programs in schools remains a controversial issue. Some parents fear that sex education actually leads to increased sexual activity among teens. There is no correlation between the two, however, and for sexually active teens, there is a negative correlation between attending a sex-education class and becoming pregnant (Zelnik and Kim 1982). Two recent public opinion polls found support for school-based sex education programs. A poll sponsored by Planned Parenthood (Harris, Kagay, and Leichenko 1985) found that 85 percent of adults believe that sex education should be taught in schools. In the annual survey of public perceptions of schools sponsored by Phi Delta Kappa (Gallup 1985), 75 percent of adults said that sex education should be part of the high school curriculum. In contrast, 52 percent believed sex education should be included in grades four through eight. For those who favored sex education, different topics were considered appropriate for elementary and high school. The biology of reproduction was considered appropriate for both levels, with 82 percent (of those who thought sex education should be taught) favoring that topic for high school and 89 percent favoring it for elementary school. More than 80 percent favored birth control and venereal disease as topics for high school but slightly less than half found these topics desirable for elementary school. Approximately 60 percent viewed the nature of intercourse, premarital sex, and abortion as appropriate topics for high school, but only 45 percent, 34 percent, and 28 percent favored these topics, respectively, for elementary school.

Parents appear to desire to communicate with their children about sex but seem to have ambiguous feelings about giving information. Although 76 percent of the parents participating in the Planned Parenthood poll talked with their children about sex, only one-third provided any information about birth control. More than 60 percent of adults believed that parents have little or no control over the sexual behavior of their teenage children. Some adults desire a strong and practical form of sex education; in the Planned Parenthood poll, 67 percent favored requiring a link between public schools and family-planning clinics, so that adolescents could learn about and obtain contraceptives. In schools that have allowed health clinics to be housed in their buildings, contraceptive use has increased and pregnancy rates have decreased (Edwards, Steinman, Arnold, and Hakanson 1981).

Many schools provide some sex education but often it is not extensive and does not reach the majority of students. In 1982, 80 percent of approximately two hundred urban school districts surveyed offered some form of sex education, but only 16 percent of senior high schools and 11 percent of junior high schools provided separate courses (Sonenstein and Pittman 1984). Between 31 percent and 43 percent of adolescents have attended formal sex-education programs (Alan Guttmacher Institute 1981) but only 10 percent have attended programs lasting more than forty hours (Kirby 1984).

POVERTY

An increasing number of American children now live in poverty. Between 1959 and 1969 childhood poverty fell from almost 26 percent to 14 percent (Hodgkinson 1985), but rates rose to 18.3 percent in 1980 and to 22 percent in 1983. Poverty levels vary greatly by state and region, ranging from 7.5 percent of the school-age population in Wyoming to 30.4 percent in Mississippi (U.S. Department of Education 1985). Childhood poverty varies also by race (40 percent for minorities and 14 percent for whites) and by family structure (50 percent for female-headed households and 12 percent for male-present households) (Hodgkinson 1985). Research on families does not always adequately assess or control for economic status. In addition, studies of the processes of family change generally are conducted with middle- rather than low-income populations (Hetherington and Camara 1984).

Because schools are typically middle-class in orientation, there is likely to be some incompatibility between home and school for children from poor families (Hoffman 1984). Compared to the middle-class child, the poor child is less likely to meet teachers' expectations regarding language, social behaviors, and dress. Poor parents are less likely than middle-class parents to feel comfortable attending school functions and communicating with teachers (Hoffman 1984).

Poor children may not have access to many resources needed for academic success. Schools must continue to be sensitive to the needs of poor children. For example, as computer technology is infused into the educational system, access to computers must be monitored in order to prevent an increase in achievement gaps between poor and affluent children. Middle-class children may have access to computers in their homes and at school, whereas poor children may have only limited access to an inadequate number of computers at school.

Children in poor families experience a higher level of stress and have more difficulty coping with new problems or crises (Hoffman 1984). For example, single-parent families and adolescent pregnancy more frequently occur among the poor; adverse effects on children may be exacerbated by poverty.

MINORITY FAMILIES

The proportion of minorities in the United States is expected to increase. Minorities composed 20 percent of the United States population in 1983; of this number, 11.6 percent were Black, 6.4 percent Hispanic, 1.4 percent Asian and Pacific Islander, and .6 percent Native American (Harrison, Serafica, and McAdoo 1984). The number of Hispanics is increasing more rapidly than is the population of other groups because of their young age, high fertility rate, and legal and illegal immigration (Harrison, Serafica, and McAdoo 1984). Currently, minorities compose 26.7 percent of students in public schools. Enrollment of minorities in public schools ranges dramatically from .9 percent in Maine to 96.4 percent in the District of Columbia (U.S. Department of Education 1985).

The changes in families just described differ for minority and white families, and various minorities differ from one another (see Harrison, Serafica, and McAdoo 1984; Scott-Jones and Nelson-Le Gall, 1986). A serious problem is the lack of appropriate research on minority families. For example, available research focuses on the incidence of divorce and remarriage in minority groups and on comparisons with whites. There are no studies of the *process* of divorce and remarriage among Blacks, Hispanics, and other minorities that are comparable to studies conducted with whites. Findings for whites cannot plausibly be generalized to other groups (Hetherington and Camara 1984).

Schools must continue to address the issue of equality of educational outcomes for minority students. Children's school experiences should reflect an acknowledgement of the racial and ethnic diversity of family experience in the population.

SUMMARY

Family forms that were considered aberrant in the past are now becoming the norm. The life course of the majority of adults no longer consists of a stable pattern of marriage, childbearing, childrearing, and remaining in that marriage until the death of a spouse. Individuals may remain unmarried and childless, they may have and rear children outside marriage, they may marry but choose to remain childless, or they may engage in serial marriages with complex patterns of relationships from various unions. Many of the changes in families are considered inherently negative. Some changes, however, may represent adaptations to social and economic conditions; others may reflect an acknowledgement of individual needs and individual choice.

Rather than mourn the death of old family forms, we must adjust to new and changing family structures. Changes in society's institutions need to occur in synchrony with one another. Schools cannot blame children's problems on changed family forms. The school experience must be altered to accommodate existing family structures, while at the same time society bolsters families in ways that will positively affect children's school achievement.

REFERENCES

Alan Guttmacher Institute. *Teen-age Pregnancy: The Problem that Hasn't Gone Away.* New York: Alan Guttmacher Institute, 1981.

Baldwin, W. H. "Statement." *Teen Parents and Their Children: Issues and Programs.* Hearings before the Select Committee on Children, Youth, and Families, U.S. House of Representatives. July 20, 1983. Washington, D.C.: U.S. Government Printing Office, 1983.

Baldwin, W. H. "Adolescent Pregnancy and Childbearing—Rates, Trends and Research Findings from the CPR, NICHD." Bethesda, Mary.: Demographic and Behavioral Sciences Branch, Center for Population Research, 1984.

Belmont, L.; Cohen, P.; Dryfoos, J.; Stein, Z; and Zayac, S. "Maternal Age and Children's Intelligence." In *Teenage Parents and Their Offspring*, edited by K. Scott, T. Field, and E. Robertson, pp. 177–194. New York: Grune and Stratton, 1981.

Broman, S. H. "Long-term Development of Children Born to Teenagers." In *Teenage Parents and Their Offspring*, edited by K. Scott, T. Field, and E. Robertson, pp. 195–224. New York: Grune and Stratton, 1981.

Card, J., and Wise, L. "Teenage Mothers and Teenage Fathers: The Impact of Early Childbearing on the Parents' Personal and Professional Lives." *Family Planning Perspectives* 10 (1978): 199–205.

Cherlin, A. J. *Marriage, Divorce, and Remarriage.* Cambridge, Mass.: Harvard University Press, 1981.

Children's Defense Fund. "Teen Pregnancy and Its Prevention."*Children Having Children*. Washington, D.C.: Children's Defense Fund, 1985.

Chilman, C. "Social and Psychological Research Concerning Adolescent Childbearing: 1970–1980." *Journal of Marriage and the Family* 42 (1980): 793–805.

Chilman, C. *Adolescent Sexuality in a Changing American Society*. New York: John Wiley and Sons, 1983.

Current Population Reports. "Fertility of American Women: June 1983." Bureau of the Census Series P-20, No. 386. Washington, D.C.: U.S. Government Printing Office, 1984.

Dott, A. B., and Fort, A. T. "Medical and Social Factors Affecting Early Teen-age Pregnancy." *American Journal of Obstetrics and Gynecology* 125 (1976): 532–536.

Duncan, G. J., and Morgan, J. N. "Persistence and Change in Economic Status and the Role of Changing Family Composition." In *Five Thousand American Families: Patterns of Economic Progress*, Volume 9, edited by M. S. Hill, D. H. Hill, and J. N. Morgan. Ann Arbor, Mich.: Institute for Social Research, 1981.

Earls, F., and Siegel, B. "Precocious Fathers." *American Journal of Orthopsychiatry* 50 (1980): 469–480.

Easterbrooks, M. A., and Goldberg, W. A. "Effects of Early Maternal Employment on Toddlers, Mothers, and Fathers." *Developmental Psychology* 21 (1985): 774–783.

Edwards, L. E.; Steinman, M. E.; Arnold, K. A.; and Hakanson, E. Y. "Adolescent Pregnancy Prevention Services in High School Clinics." In *Teenage Sexuality, Pregnancy, and Childbearing*, edited by F. F. Furstenberg, R. Lincoln, and J. Menken. Philadelphia: University Press, 1981.

Everett, J. E. "An Examination of Child Support Enforcement Issues." In *Services to Young Families*, edited by H. McAdoo and T. M. J. Parham, pp. 75-112. Washington, D.C.: American Public Welfare Association, 1985.

Farel, A. M. "Effects of Preferred Maternal Roles, Maternal Employment, and Sociodemographic Status on School Adjustment and Competence." *Child Development* 51 (1980): 1179–1186.

Feldman, H. "A Comparison of Intentional Parents and Intentionally Childless Couples." *Journal of Marriage and the Family* 43 (1981): 593–600.

Furstenberg, F. F. "The Social Consequences of Teenage Parenthood." *Family Planning Perspectives* 8 (1976): 148–164. (a)

Furstenberg, F. F. *Unplanned Parenthood: The Social Consequences of Teenage Childbearing*. New York: Free Press, 1976. (b)

Furstenberg, F. F. "Conjugal Succession: Reentering Marriage After Divorce." In *Life-span Development and Behavior, Volume 4*, edited by P. B. Baltes and O. G. Brim, pp. 107–146. New York: Academic Press, 1984.

Furstenberg, F. F., and Crawford, A. G. "Family Support: Helping Mothers to Cope." *Family Planning Perspectives* 10 (1978): 322–333.

Furstenberg, F. F., and Spanier, G. B. *Recycling the Family: Remarriage After Divorce*. Beverly Hills, Calif.: Sage, 1984.

Gallup, A. "The 17th Annual Gallup Poll of the Public's Attitudes Toward the Public Schools." *Phi Delta Kappan* 67 (1985): 35–47.

Glick, P. C. "Children of Divorced Parents in Demographic Perspective." *Journal of Social Issues*, 35 (1979): 170-182.

Glick, P. C. "Remarriage: Some Recent Changes and Variations." *Journal of Family Issues* 1 (1980): 455–498.

Gordon, H. A., and Kammeyer, K. C. "The Gainful Employment of Women with Small Children." *Journal of Marriage and the Family* 42 (1980): 327–336.

Grant, W. V., and Snyder, T. D. *Digest of Education Statistics 1983–84.* Washington, D.C.: U.S. Government Printing Office, 1983.

Harris, L.; Kagay, M. R.; and Leichenko, S. *Public Attitudes about Sex Education, Family Planning, and Abortion in the United States* (Study No. 854005). New York: Louis Harris and Associates, 1985.

Harrison, A.; Serafica, F.; and McAdoo, H. "Ethnic Families of Color." In *Review of Child Development Research. Vol. 7: The Family*, edited by R. D. Parke, pp. 329–371. Chicago: The University of Chicago Press, 1984.

Herzog, E., and Sudia, C. E. "Children in Fatherless Families." In *Review of Child Development Research*, Volume 3, edited by B. Caldwell and H. Ricciutti, pp. 141–232. Chicago: University of Chicago Press, 1973.

Hetherington, E. M. "Stress and Coping in Children and Families." In *Children in Families Under Stress. New Directions for Child Development, No. 24*, edited by A. Doyle, D. Gold, and D. S. Moskowitz, pp. 398–439. San Francisco: Jossey-Bass, 1984.

Hetherington, E. M., and Camara, K. A. "Families in Transition: The Processes of Dissolution and Reconstitution." In *Review of Child Development Research. Vol. 7: The Family*, edited by R. D. Parke. Chicago: The University of Chicago Press, 1984.

Hetherington, E. M.; Camara, K. A.; and Featherman, D. L. *Cognitive Performance, School Behavior and Achievement of Children from One-Parent Households.* Washington, D.C.: National Institute of Education, 1981.

Hodgkinson, H. L. *All One System: Demographics of Education, Kindergarten Through Graduate School.* Washington, D.C.: Institute for Educational Leadership, 1985.

Hoffman, L. W. "The Effects of Maternal Employment on the Academic Attitudes and Performance of School-Aged Children." *School Psychology Review* 9 (1980): 319–336.

Hoffman, L. W. "Work, Family, and the Socialization of the Child." In *Review of Child Development Research. Volume 7: The Family*, edited by R. D. Parke, pp. 223–282. Chicago: University of Chicago Press, 1984.

Jones, J. *Labor of Love, Labor of Sorrow: Black Women, Work, and the Family from Slavery to the Present.* New York: Basic Books, 1985.

Jones, L. V. "White-Black Achievement Differences: The Narrowing Gap." *American Psychologist* 39 (1984): 1207–1213.

Kirby, D. *Sexuality Education: An Evaluation of Programs and their Effects, An Executive Summary.* Arlington, Va.: Mathtech, Inc., 1984.

Klein, R. P. "Caregiving Arrangements by Employed Women with Children Under One Year of Age." *Developmental Psychology* 21 (1985): 403–406.

Lamb, M. E.; Chase-Lansdale, L.; and Owen, M. T. "The Changing American Family and Its Implications for Infant Social Development: The Sample Case of Maternal Employment." In *The Child and Its Family*, edited by M. Lewis and L. A. Rosenblum. New York: Plenum Press, 1979.

MacKinnon, C. E.; Brody, G. H.; and Stoneman, Z. "The Effects of Divorce and Maternal Employment on the Home Environments of Preschool Children." *Child Development* 53 (1982): 1392–1399.

Marx, F. "Child Care." In *Services to Young Families*, edited by H. McAdoo and T. M.

J. Parham, pp. 113–166. Washington, D.C.: American Public Welfare Association, 1985.

Mecklenburg, M. E., and Thompson, P. G. "The Adolescent Family Life Program as a Prevention Measure." *Public Health Reports* 98 (1983): 21–29.

Moore, K. A. *Facts at a Glance.* Washington, D.C.: The Urban Institute (Statistics compiled from the National Center for Health Statistics), 1983.

Morrow, B. H. "Elementary School Performance of Offspring of Young Adolescent Mothers." *American Educational Research Journal* 16 (1979): 423–429.

National Center for Education Statistics. *Indicators of Education Status and Trends.* Washington, D.C.: Department of Education, January 1985.

Polit, D. F., and Khan, J. R. "Project Redirection: Evaluation of a Comprehensive Program for Disadvantaged Teenage Mothers." *Family Planning Perspectives* 17 (1985): 150–154.

Rawlings, S. W. *Families Maintained by Female Householders 1970–1979.* Current Population Reports, Special Studies Series P-23, No. 107. Washington, D.C.: Bureau of the Census, 1980.

Rodman, H.; Pratto, D. J.; and Nelson, R. S. "Child Care Arrangements and Children's Functioning: A Comparison of Self-care and Adult-care Children." *Developmental Psychology* 21 (1985): 413–418.

Santrock, J. W.; Warshak, R.; Lindbergh, C.; and Meadows, L. "Children's and Parent's Observed Social Behaviors in Stepfather Families." *Child Development* 53 (1982): 472–480.

Schachter, F. F. "Toddlers with Employed Mothers." *Child Development* 52 (1981): 958–964.

Schubert, J. B.; Bradley-Johnson, S.; and Nuttal, J. "Mother-Infant Communication and Maternal Employment." *Child Development* 51 (1980): 246–249.

Scott-Jones, D.; and Nelson-Le Gall, S. A. "Defining Black Families: Past and Present." In *Redefining Social Problems,* edited by E. Seidman and J. Rappaport. New York: Plenum, 1986.

Scott-Jones, D., and Peebles-Wilkins, W. "Sex Equity in Parenting and Parent Education." *Theory Into Practice,* in press.

Shinn, M. "Father Absence and Children's Cognitive Development." *Psychological Bulletin* 85 (1978): 295–324.

Sonenstein, F. L., and Pittman, K. J. "The Availability of Sex Education in Large City School Districts." *Family Planning Perspectives* 16 (1984): 19–23.

Spanier, G. B. and P. C. Glick. "Paths to Remarriage." *Journal of Divorce* 3 (1980): 283–298.

Stage, E. K.; Kreinberg, N.; Eccles, J.; and Becker, J. R. "Increasing the Participation and Achievement of Girls and Women in Mathematics, Science, and Engineering." In *Handbook for Achieving Sex Equity Through Education,* edited by S. S. Klein, pp. 237-268. Baltimore: Johns Hopkins University Press, 1985.

Svanum, S.; Bringle, R. G.; and McLaughlin, J. E. "Father Absence and Cognitive Performance in a Large Sample of Six- to Eleven-Year-Old Children." *Child Development* 53 (1982): 136–143.

Tanner, J. M. "Physical Growth." In *Carmichael's Manual of Child Psychology.* (Vol. 1, 3rd. ed.), edited by P. H. Mussen. New York: Wiley Publishers, 1970.

Tanner, J. M. "Growth and Endocrinology of the Adolescent." In *Endocrine and Genetic Diseases of Childhood and Adolescence,* 2d ed., edited by L. J. Gardner. Philadelphia: W. B. Saunders, 1975.

U.S. Bureau of Census. *Statistical Abstract of the United States.* Washington, D.C.: U.S. Government Printing Office, 1981.

U.S. Department of Education. "State Education Statistics." Washington, D.C.: U.S. Government Printing Office, 1985.

Veevers, J. E. "Voluntary Childlessness: A Review of Issues and Evidence." *Marriage and Family Review* 2 (1979): 1–26.

Ventura, S. *Recent Trends and Variations in Births to Unmarried Women.* Paper presented at the meeting of the Society for Research in Child Development. Toronto, Canada, April 1985.

Weiner, L. Y. *From Working Girl to Working Mother: The Female Labor Force in the United States, 1820–1980.* Chapel Hill, N.C.: University of North Carolina Press, 1985.

Whalen, R. E. "Secondary Education: Student Flows, Course Participation, and State Requirements." In *The Condition of Education, 1984 Edition,* edited by V. W. Plisko. Washington, D.C.: U.S. Government Printing Office, 1984.

Zelnik, M., and Kantner, J. F. "First Pregnancies of Women Aged 15–19: 1976 and 1971." *Family Planning Perspectives* 10 (1978): 11–20.

Zelnik, M., and Kim, Y. J. "Sex Education and Its Association with Teenage Sexual Activity, Pregnancy and Contraceptive Use." *Family Planning Perspectives* 14 (1982): 117–126.

3

Defining School Quality

Bruce Fuller

OVERVIEW

Once upon a time, pointing out a good school seemed a rather simple task. A high-quality school was distinguished either by its proficient students or by its abundant material resources. But judging a school's specific effect by the achievement level of its pupils fails to take into account the independent effects of parents and community on students' long-term intellectual growth. Inferring that a school rich in material resources is of high quality is equally unfounded. Since the (not so) celebrated Coleman Report (1966), the empirical evidence shows no consistent relationship between a school's material resources and the performance of its students.

Exposing these naive definitions, however, has not dampened the search for clear signals of school quality. Parents want to find a good school for their children. Educators are under relentless pressure to improve school quality and effectiveness. Political leaders recurrently

This work was supported in part by a grant from the National Institute of Handicapped Research, U.S. Department of Education, to the University of Maryland (# G008435022). Conversations with my colleagues on this project—Peter Leone, Edison Trickett, and Susan Zlotlow—continue to be stimulating and fun. In addition, George Psacharopoulos and Stephen Heyneman at the World Bank have aided this research financially and intellectually.

express sincere worries and gain popular support by attacking this enigmatic social ill, called "low school quality."

This chapter reviews the various definitions of school quality that have emerged over the past two decades. A rather colorful spectrum of definitions has arisen as educators and school researchers have attempted to grasp the meaning of a "high-quality school." In the twenty years since the Coleman Report and the similar Plowden Report in Britain (Peaker 1971), educational interest groups have pursued several directions in trying to grasp those school characteristics that raise student achievement. First, the Coleman group assumed that "school quality" could be seen within the *technical production process* of schooling. This viewpoint argues that various levels and mixes of material inputs are combined to produce learning. These inputs include school facilities, teachers, books, and instructional materials. When the Coleman group found few effects of material inputs on achievement, other researchers spent the decade following 1966 retesting and adjusting this basic production-function model.

Second, *individual abilities and perceptions* of teachers or pupils are often viewed as valid indicators of school quality. Grounded in psychological theories of learning and motivation, this definition focuses on the behaviors of individual teachers as well as on students' perceptions of themselves and of the classroom climate. This definition of quality has prompted interventions aimed at treating or changing the individual within the classroom, such as individualizing instruction, attacking the low self-concept allegedly held by many children, and changing the form of interaction between the teacher and each student. The focus here remains on getting the proper inputs and the most efficient mix into a production model while emphasizing the human and behavioral ingredients, and not only the material inputs.

Third, as the general production-function metaphor has lost credibility, school quality has become associated more with the integrity of *the school and classroom organization*. Since the mid-1970s, this viewpoint has emphasized how instruction is organized within the classroom and the potential effects on learning of strong schoolwide management. Rather than specifying material or psychological variables within an additive model of production, this viewpoint emphasizes the social rules that pattern interaction and shared beliefs.

Fourth, the pursuit of school quality may simply be an exercise of *institutional signals*. Technical improvements in school may be less important than the symbolic role of initiatives aimed at improving school quality. Whether students learn more or not, the rhetoric and political battles that surround school reforms express a variety of social values. For example, when a United States President says that we must tighten discipline and work harder in the schools, is the social goal really to boost academic achievement? Or does the school organization provide a stage upon which cultural values are voiced and debated? This definition of school quality emphasizes not what goes on inside the school, but the school institution's centrality within the culture.

I will discuss in turn each of these four definitions, and I will review exemplary studies for each. I focus here on the underlying assumptions and implicit values that operate within each model. This chapter is not an exhaustive review of the empirical research on school quality or school effectiveness; recent and thorough reviews are available (see Barr and Dreeben 1983; Purkey and Smith 1983; Austin and Garber 1985). I conclude this chapter with some critical comments on how school quality and school effectiveness have been conceptualized and discuss how this twenty-year line of research relates to the important task of improving school quality in countries outside the United States and western Europe (where most of the research has been done). In brief, I argue that the Third World can avoid the pitfalls of earlier misconceptions of school quality.

TECHNICAL PRODUCTION OF STUDENT ACHIEVEMENT

The original Coleman and Plowden studies simply applied the production-function metaphor of economics to the manufacture of learning within the school. This form of analysis has been largely discarded by researchers in the United States and western Europe. However, the model's basic tenets continue to surface as underlying assumptions of current efforts to improve school quality. Advocates of the basic model propose that discrete school characteristics or inputs can be additively placed in the school to raise pupils' achievement. According to this logic, higher-quality schools have greater quantities of these various inputs. General proxies for material resources have been used to test this model, including expenditures for each student or the ratio of students to each teacher.

The Coleman Report in 1966 concluded that a school's overall level of material inputs was not related to student achievement. Into the mid-1970s this contention was retested in a variety of school settings. The production-function metaphor was also broadened to include human inputs, such as the amount of a teacher's preservice training or experience in the classroom. But whether the inputs were material or human, the emphasis of the production-function framework was to quantify levels of each ingredient of schooling that might be related to students' performance.

Table 3.1 provides an overview of this line of research from the United States and western Europe; I have simply compiled existing reviews of individual empirical studies to assess general patterns. Most of this work is grounded in the production-function model of school quality. Although this approach was giving way by the mid-1970s to studies that examined the influence of teacher behaviors and classroom organization, I want to concentrate for the moment on studies set in the production-function mold.

One important pattern is apparent in Table 3.1: The Coleman group's basic finding was not overturned by the decade of research that followed release of its report. Effects on achievement from the level of material inputs (Category A) were rarely observed, despite the fact that studies looked at a variety of schools and communities. Material inputs may influence achievement in certain subjects (such as science) and in particular nations. But in general, material inputs do not make a difference within industrialized countries. A very convincing review is offered by Eric Hanushek (1981). After reviewing 130 production-function studies, he found that the quality of a school's physical facilities was related to achievement in just seven analyses, to the student-teacher ratio in only nine, and to overall per-pupil expenditures in but five investigations (confirmed by Rutter 1983).

This dead end prompted greater interest in the characteristics or quality of teachers, who are the primary *human input* into educational production. The second set of school characteristics (Category B) in Table 3.1 includes features of teachers that could be easily surveyed. Here, too, concrete characteristics, including teachers' length of preservice training, amount of classroom experience, or salary level, were not found to be consistently related to pupils' achievement. One exception is important to emphasize: studies have repeatedly found that the verbal competence of teachers influences student achievement. This sole characteristic appears to validly indicate teacher quality. But the production-function method simply identified its efficacy; the research method does not help to explain *how* a teacher's verbal proficiency boosts achievement.

Table 3.1 also summarizes more recent findings on how aspects of school and classroom organization influence achievement, including classroom time spent on academic tasks, evaluation of student performance, and democratic management by school principals (Categories C and D). This work departs from the production-function approach by looking at the frequency and nature of social interaction, not at the addition of individual inputs. I will return to these school qualities in following sections of this chapter.

A fundamental contribution of the production-function approach to the study of school quality is the discovery that the material characteristics of school have little impact on students' learning. This body of work dispels much of the common wisdom about how to improve the effectiveness of schools. For example, communities and legislatures concerned with low performance by students often appropriate more funds to increase per-pupil expenditures and to lower the average class size. These material inputs, however, are not efficacious in raising achievement. In addition, simply requiring more teacher training or boosting salaries will not increase student achievement. These tangible and convenient definitions of "school quality" have proved to be unjustifiable—to the extent that indicators of quality should be linked empirically to higher student achievement. Research that follows the production-function tradition has contributed to destroying this conventional wisdom about what characteristics of schools and teachers actually contribute to achievement.

However, the production-function metaphor constrains our ability to more deeply explore classroom or school processes that may be more efficacious in boosting achievement. The production-function metaphor seems sensible intuitively. The school organization can be seen as a business firm, assembling various means of production to yield varying levels of achievement. Just as factories employ labor and technology (capital), so does the school. The level of capital and the "quality" of labor (that is, teachers) could be easily assessed across a large number of schools or classrooms with conventional analysis of existing school documents or through straightforward survey forms. But even firms devise social structures and rules for managing the process of combining discrete inputs. This is not captured by modeling production through the additive combination of capital, technology, and labor. The problem is clear in school organizations, where the majority of investment is in people, not in material inputs. And learning stems from the *social rules and kinds of interaction* that unfold in classrooms. Therefore, the level of learning that occurs may flow more

Table 3.1

School Quality and Student Achievement: Review of Research in the United States and Western Europe

School Characteristic	Hypothesis	Findings	Research Review
A. Material Inputs			
1. Expenditures per pupil	A higher level of resources will raise student achievement levels	*Mixed* effects found in three United States studies; *Positive* effects found in two other studies, with expenditures operating indirectly via the pupil-teacher ratio	Bridge, Judd, and Moock (1979)
		No or negative effects found in fifty of fifty-five United States studies	Hanushek (1981)
		Positive effects found for instructional expenditures, six models reported in four United States studies	Glasman and Biniaminov (1981)
		No effect found in four United States studies; *Positive* effect found in one United States study	Jamison, Suppes, and Wells (1974)
2. Class size	Fewer students per teacher will improve the quality of instruction	*Positive* effect of smaller class size found for science classes in Belgium, Germany, and the United States; *No effect* in six other industrial countries	Heyneman and Loxley (1983)

		Positive effects found in ten models estimated within five United States studies; *Negative* effect found in two models reported within the same studies	Glasman and Biniaminov (1981)
		No effect found in one hundred of one hundred nine United States studies reviewed	Hanushek (1981) Also reviewed in Averch et al. (1974)
		No effect found for class size difference within the twenty to forty students/teacher range within the United States and England; *Positive* effect for class size of less than twenty	Glass and Smith (1978) Rutter (1983)
		No effect found in comparing the class size of Japanese and United States classrooms	Stevenson et al. (in press)
3. School size	Smaller schools will increase the amount and quality of teacher-student interaction	*No effect* found in six United States studies	Bridge, Judd, and Moock (1979)
		Mixed effects found in six studies reviewed from England and the United States	Rutter (1983)

Table 3.1 (*Cont.*)

School Characteristic	Hypothesis	Findings	Research Review
A. Material Inputs			
4. Instructional materials	Higher availability of textbooks and instructional materials will boost the quality of learning activities	*Positive* effect found for expenditures on books in Germany and Hungary; *No effect* found for nine other countries	Heyneman and Loxley (1983)
5. Length of school day/year	More total hours spent in school on instructional activities will boost achievement	*Positive* and consistent effects found in four United States studies	Bridge, Judd, and Moock (1979)
6. Physical facilities	Better facilities provide more motivating conditions for learning	*No effect* found in sixty-four of seventy-one studies reviewed	Hanushek (1981)
7. Library	Libraries provide higher level and a greater variety of reading materials	*Mixed* effects found in all eight United States studies reviewed	Bridge, Judd, and Moock (1979)
B. Teacher Quality			
1. Preservice training	More years of college instruction will boost teaching effectiveness	*Positive* effect found for reading teachers in Hungary, New Zealand, and England; *No effect* found in ten other industrial nations	Heyneman and Loxley (1983)

	More years of graduate teacher-training will boost instructional skills	*No or negative* effects found in seven United States studies; *Positive* effect found in two studies	Bridge, Judd, and Moock (1979)
2. Teacher experience	Teachers with longer tenure will develop stronger instructional skills	*Positive* effects found in five United States studies; *Mixed* effects found in five other studies depending on the specific student achievement variable examined	Bridge, Judd, and Moock (1979)
		Positive effects found in a review of six United States studies; *no effect* in one additional study	Jamison, Suppes, and Wells (1974)
		Positive effects found in thirty United States studies; *No effect* reported in seventy-four other examinations of this factor	Hanushek (1981) Also reviewed in Averch et al. (1974)
		Positive effects found in all twenty-three analyses reported in eight United States studies	Glasman and Biniaminov (1981)
3. Teacher's verbal ability	Teachers with greater verbal skills will increase the quality of student-teacher interaction	*Positive* effects found in four United States studies; *Mixed* effects found in three other studies	Bridge, Judd, and Moock (1979)

Table 3.1 (*Cont.*)

School Characteristic	Hypothesis	Findings	Research Review
		Positive effects found for the teacher's verbal skill on pupil's achievement scores	Jamison, Suppes, and Wells (1974)
		Positive effects found for teachers' verbal achievement within all fifteen models reported in four United States studies	Glasman and Biniaminov (1981)
4. Teacher salary	Higher salaries will attract better qualified people and more strongly motivate teachers	*Mixed* effects found in six United States studies	Bridge, Judd, and Moock (1979)
		No effect found in fifty-one of sixty studies reviewed	Hanushek (1981)
		Positive effects found in two United States studies; *No or negative* effects found in five other studies	Jamison, Suppes, and Wells (1974) Also reviewed in Glasman and Biniaminov (1981)

C. Classroom Structure/Teaching Practices

1. Classroom time spent on instructional tasks	More time spent on concrete learning activities—versus time on disciplining students, managing records, or arranging lessons—will increase achievement	*Positive* effect found for amount of class time spent reading the science text in seven industrial nations; *No effect* found in five other countries	Heyneman and Loxley (1983)
		Positive effect found for hours of instruction spent per week on reading in Germany and Hungary	Heyneman and Loxley (1983)
		Positive effect found for the number of academic courses completed (versus vocational or elective courses) in a national sample of United States students	Walberg and Shanahan (1983)
	Assignment and close evaluation of homework will boost student learning	*Positive* effects found in two British studies	Rutter (1983)
2. Cooperative instructional tasks	Arrangement of and rewards for cooperative instructional tasks will increase interaction among students and subsequent learning	*Positive* effect found in twenty-nine evaluations of cooperative instructional tasks in the United States; *No effect* found in twenty-one other studies	Slavin (1983) Also reviewed in Webb (1982)

Table 3.1 (*Cont.*)

School Characteristic	Hypothesis	Findings	Research Review
3. High teacher expectations for student performance	Teachers who expect high standards of performance receive stronger commitment and achievement from students	*Positive* effects found when teacher expectations are matched with effective classroom management and active learning exercises, United States studies	Brophy (1979) Walberg (1984)
4. Active teaching and learning roles	The level of interaction between teacher and student (and with learning materials) will increase student achievement	*Positive* and consistent findings: the amount of time teachers spend interacting with the class, not only with individual students, is related to student achievement; efficacy of instructional materials in facilitating active learning remains unclear, based on British and United States studies	Brookover et al. (1979) Rutter (1983)
5. Tight evaluation of student achievement	A close contingency between student effort and rewards from the teacher will boost the student's motivation and achievement	*Positive* effect of students' perception of efficacy on achievement level in one study of 120 United States schools	Brookover et al. (1979)
		Positive effect found for the teacher's consistent recognition of high student performance	Walberg (1984)

		Positive effects found in four United States studies	Bridge, Judd, and Moock (1979)
6. Clarity of teacher's presentation	Clear explanations of material will raise student comprehension	*Positive* findings found in fifty studies reviewed from the United States	Rosenshine and Furst (1971) Also reviewed in Averch et al. (1974)
7. Individualized instruction	Curricula that allow each student to progress at his or her own pace will increase mastery of material and student motivation	*No effect* found in thirty-nine United States studies; *Positive* effects in ten reports	Bangert, Kulik, and Kulik (1983)
D. School Structure			
1. Academic versus vocational curriculum	Tracking students into a vocational curriculum—where academic achievement is not emphasized—will lower student performance	*Negative* effect of vocational track found in Scotland, New Zealand, Netherlands, and Austria; *No effect* found in nine other industrial nations	Heyneman and Loxley (1983)
2. Student tracking by competence level	Placing students in different tracks will hinder performance of students who are expected to perform at lower levels	*Mixed* effects found in nine studies from the United States and England	Rutter (1983)

Table 3.1 (Cont.)

School Characteristic	Hypothesis	Findings	Research Review
3. School selectivity	Admitting more able students will provide higher achievement standards	*Positive* effects found: a school's student composition moderately influences the individual student's achievement, after controlling on the latter's family background; findings from eight British and United States studies	Rutter (1983)
4. Democratic management	Greater involvement of teachers in school decision making will improve teacher motivation and commitment	*Positive* effects found in British and United States studies	Rutter (1983)
5. Size of administrative staff	An ample number of administrators will free time to improve the quality of teaching	*Mixed* effects found in six United States studies; *Positive* effects found in one study	Bridge, Judd, and Moock (1979)
	Administrators with more training and from higher-quality universities will utilize resources more efficiently	*No effect* found in fifty of fifty-four studies	Hanushek (1981)
6. Integration of school and work	More time spent in out-of-school work activities will lower school achievement	*Mixed* results from United States studies; moderate levels of work outside school may positively influence school commitment and achievement	D'Amico (1984)

from the management and organization of inputs than from their absolute level.

Production-function research has only rarely studied the interaction of different inputs. This is particularly important if one is trying to determine whether the existing combination of inputs are efficiently managed (technical efficiency) or whether the optimal mix of inputs is being approached (allocative efficiency). Inattention to the interaction of inputs can limit discovery of important relationships. Launor Carter (1984), for instance, found that a higher ratio of students to teachers was associated with poor achievement in low-income schools when a high ratio increased time spent by teachers on classroom management and not on academic tasks. That is, the ratio interacted with classroom management practices.

Second, reliance on large-scale surveys prompted researchers to come up with proxies for human inputs or teacher quality, such as a teacher's amount of preservice training or salary level. But the meaning of a particular proxy's effect is often unclear (Levin 1976). For instance, the consistent finding that a teacher's verbal competence influences student achievement is difficult to interpret. Does this measure simply substitute for the teacher's total amount of schooling or social-class background? And what is the process by which verbal proficiency influences students' cognition and learning? Large-scale surveys often provide data on a large number of covarying school characteristics. Therefore, effects often appear for the school characteristic that can be most unambiguously measured, even if the proxy measure's effect is difficult to interpret and impossible to attack from the educator's standpoint (Fuller 1986).

Third, production-function studies often fail to specify the conditions under which findings apply. Large-scale surveys invite inferences that certain school characteristics do or do not influence achievement across all settings. Little work has been done that clarifies when particular school characteristics shape pupil performance. The risk of claiming universal patterns is sharply illustrated by a well-known paper written by staff of the World Bank. John Simmons and Leigh Alexander (1978) studied the early production-function work conducted in North America and western Europe, and they inferred that the level of a Third World nation's investment in schooling would make little difference in raising student achievement. This inference was logical at the time, given that researchers in industrialized nations had failed to offer any scope conditions to confine their universal claims. Yet recent empirical evidence suggests that increasing the level of material inputs does contribute significantly to student achievement in developing countries where school quality and pupil performance remain quite low (Heyneman and Loxley 1983). This chapter's appendix augments Table 3.1 by summarizing this very different pattern; it was developed from a review of sixty-two production-function studies conducted in developing nations. Similarly, within industrialized countries material inputs and proxies for teacher quality may be associated with higher student achievement when the variation of school quality among low-income communities is examined (for example, see Coleman 1975).

School Quality and Efficiency

One contribution of the production-function metaphor lies in its formal modeling of how we define the specific influence of the school, net the influence of factors outside the school. Inputs into the schooling process include not only features of the school organization but also characteristics of students themselves, their families, and their local neighborhoods. The production-function metaphor helps to avoid naive use of unsound indicators of school quality, instead describing two elements of a more solid definition. First, high-quality schools should boost learning after accounting for the antecedent influence of preschool development and the ongoing demands of the child's environment. This *value-added* denotation of quality avoids the popular mistake of inferring the quality of a school from the performance of its pupils. This latter indicator of "quality" does not account for the student's skills prior to entering the school. Second, a high-quality school should efficiently transform a given level of material and human resources so as to maximize student achievement. Just as firms vary in how efficiently they manage and combine material factors of production, schools variably manage their resources. A school may squander its rich stock of instructional materials, new facilities, and high-salary teachers through the poor use of class time or through poor school management.

The production-function metaphor emphasizes variability in the efficiency with which schools influence achievement. The distinction between school quality versus school efficiency should be clarified. School A, for instance, may be of high quality and substantially increase the level of students' achievement. But the cost of providing

Table 3.2
United States Efficiency Study (Reading)

School-Quality Element	(a) Effect Size	(b) Cost Per Student	(c) Effect Size Per $100 in Cost
1. Lengthen instructional time	.07	$ 61	.12
2. Reduce class size (from 35 to 20 pupils)	.22	$201	.11
3. Peer tutoring	.48	$212	.22

Source: Levin, Glass, and Meister (1984)

this level of quality may be very high (linked to a wealth of instructional materials, ample in-service teacher training, or recruitment of the best principals). School B, however, may be of lower quality (that is, it holds less influence on students' achievement), but it may be more efficient. That is, the ratio of benefits (achievement gains) to costs (of quality) may be considerably higher for School B.

The production-function approach urges educators and researchers to look at (1) the costs associated with alternative strategies for improving school effectiveness, and (2) the magnitude of these different interventions. For example, Henry Levin, Gene Glass, and Gail Meister (1984) estimated the relative efficiency of three school-improvement initiatives. Table 3.2 summarizes their findings. Column A reports the *magnitude* of each intervention's influence on student achievement by standard deviations from the mean student score prior to introducing the intervention. For example, when the peer-tutoring program operated for one year, reading scores increased by almost one-half (.48) of a standard deviation. This program was considerably more costly for each student each year relative to decreasing class size or lengthening the school day (Column B). But the effect on achievement for each $100 dollars invested remained highest for the peer-tutoring program. Problems do exist with this type of analysis. Costs of school characteristics are often difficult to determine. In addition, schools are not in the business (at least not until recently) of only raising students' standardized test scores. Therefore, the relative value of increasing a child's reading score (as one form of benefit) against raising competence in working cooperatively is impossible to determine, and relative values vary across different parents and communities (Levin 1976). The central point, however, is that

recent work on school effectiveness focuses on only the statistical
significance of various school factors. Once these efficacious factors
are identified, little attention is paid to the magnitude of their effect,
the relative cost of increasing the inputs or practices, and the efficiency of alternative school-improvement strategies. In this case,
perhaps we should throw out the baby—the production-function per
se—but keep some of the bath water.

By the mid-1970s the production-function metaphor was over-
taken by two other frameworks that define the meaning of a "high-
quality school." Again, I speak here of only dominant thought within
industrialized countries. (Educational practice and research within
Third World schools generally remains stuck in the production-function
paradigm.) First, the *school-effectiveness movement* in the United States,
aided by a slight dose of empirical research, gained many advocates
among educators, legislators, and parents. Its thrust was to specify
what general characteristics of schools would help raise student
achievement. For example, Ronald Edmonds (1982) proclaimed that
an "effective school" possesses a strong academic mission, teachers
who expect high performance by students, a principal who is an
"academic leader," an orderly climate conducive to learning, and
procedures for frequently monitoring students' performance. These
articles of faith, while not always clearly explained nor empirically
tested, have also found their way into educational reform programs
advocated at local and statewide levels (Neufeld, Farrar, and Miles
1983; Fuller and Izu, in press). Second, *research on teaching* achieved a
substantial empirical base by the mid-1970s (for example, Gage and
Berliner 1975). A burgeoning amount of teaching materials and
research emerged at this point that specified effective teaching behaviors and models for organizing classroom instruction.

In an attempt to disentangle the assumptions underlying these
two sets of definitions of school quality, I will present pieces of each in
the following three sections. These approaches do not stem entirely
from independent streams of thought; therefore, I begin with the piece
that links most directly to the production-function metaphor: defining
school quality by the individual abilities and perceptions of teachers
or students. I then move to those elements of both the school-
effectiveness model and the research-on-teaching framework that
emphasize the structure of social interaction within the school, rather
than focus exclusively on individual-level characteristics or traits.

INDIVIDUAL ABILITIES AND PERCEPTIONS

The question of how the individual learns has been a major concern of research psychologists since the late nineteenth century. In the past two decades educational psychologists have taken this work on cognition and motivation into classrooms by stepping back to examine what behaviors of the individual teacher increase learning by the individual student. The *research-on-teaching* framework, therefore, attempts to improve school quality by addressing the interaction between this dyad—the teacher and the pupil. A second view of school quality has emerged from this concern with individual-level perception and motivation. The study of *school climate* stems from psychologists' concern with what perceptions are held by individual actors in the classroom, and how different types of social-emotional feelings influence the individual child's motivation. A wide range of perceptions is included in the study of classroom climate, from feelings of affiliation with other children to the perceived clarity of classroom rules (for example, Moos 1979). Both approaches stem from psychological views of the individual within the school, and they emphasize the nature of the child's learning and motivation.

Individual Learning and Teaching

Importantly, research on teaching takes the individual student— not characteristics of the school in general (as assumed by the production-function framework)—as the starting point in determining how to improve school quality. For example, an information-processing theory of learning demonstrates that vividly illustrated, concrete information is better retained by the individual. Nathaniel Gage and David Berliner (1975) describe ways in which the teacher can organize lessons, present information in graphic ways, and provide students an opportunity to discuss and exercise the material to boost rates of retention. Alternatively, a behavioral theory of cognition and learning emphasizes the need for external rewards and reinforcement. The research-on-teaching framework, therefore, articulates detailed ways in which the teacher can establish a reinforcement schedule attached to clear behavioral objectives (Dunkin and Biddle 1974). Overall, the practice of teaching is broken down into several steps, including choosing objectives, understanding and adapting to individual differences of students, choosing optimal teaching procedures, and designing tight procedures for evaluating

student progress. Each of these steps is then broken down into twenty
to thirty subtasks that teachers normatively are expected to perform.
These teaching behaviors are aimed at nurturing growth in twenty
distinct components of cognition, thirteen aspects of affective development, and fifteen psychomotor proficiencies (Gage and Berliner
1975).

Many of these individual teaching behaviors are associated empirically with higher levels of student achievement. However, this finding comes from correlational evidence for more than a hundred discrete
teaching actions. The model is far from parsimonious, and whether these
teaching behaviors actually cause higher achievement has not been
substantiated. It may be that the characteristics of the students or
schools allow the teacher to perform these careful behaviors; that is,
organizational features affect the behavior of the individual teacher
(Barr and Dreeben 1983). Proponents of this model have attempted to
group these many-faceted behaviors into a fewer number of patterns.
Good and Brophy (1973), for instance, argue that the teacher should
model social norms and act in a respectful and friendly way toward all
children. The teacher should be aware of which children infrequently
ask questions and rarely participate in class activities. Gage (1978)
summarizes this area by urging teachers to move around the classroom while they monitor seatwork and communicate an awareness of
pupils' behavior. And when students are working individually in the
classroom, the assignments should be interesting and at an appropriate level of difficulty. However, these summary statements tend to
blur any theoretical consistency that once may have existed within the
research-on-teaching area. For instance, some motivation theorists
argue that excessive levels of external monitoring and sanctioning of a
child's behavior will *lower*, not raise, motivation. This conflicts directly with the previous concern about the student's self-concept and
the alleged importance of praise by the teacher in shaping self-esteem
(Brophy 1981). Advocates from the research-on-teaching field fail to
build from a consistent theory of motivation. Some prescribed teaching behaviors suggest that making the classroom tighter and more
rationalized will boost achievement. Other prescribed teaching behaviors imply that giving the child an opportunity to be creative and to
develop intrinsic interests will be effective (Joyce and Weil 1980).

Simpler and more consistent models have attempted to identify a
key element of the pupil's (or teacher's) motivation and then ask,
What ways of organizing the classroom will boost the individual's
motivation? Susan Rosenholtz and Stephen Rosenholtz (1981), for

instance, found that devising diverse ways in which students can achieve will likely boost perceptions of their ability that are held by both the teacher and other students. Where a one-dimensional definition of achievement exists, such as proficiency in mathematics, pupils compare their status relative to others, then generalize this level of ability to other areas. But when students perform well on other activities, competitive comparison along a single criterion is difficult, and a perception of the student's "general ability" is impossible to formulate (for review, see Elizabeth Cohen's chapter in this volume). Given this straightforward principle, the teacher can then devise instructional tasks, grouping practices, and evaluation procedures designed to boost the child's view of his or her own ability and efficacy (Marshall and Weinstein 1984).

This focus on boosting a child's perception of efficacy stems, in part, from a seemingly small finding in the Coleman Report. After taking into account social-class background, the Coleman group found that students who believed they could control their own performance and success did better in school. Motivation theorists now more precisely define efficacy as the individual's perceived expectation of obtaining valued outcomes through personal effort. Wilbur Brookover and associates (1979) extended the Coleman finding when they discovered that students' perceived efficacy in performing well in school varied independently from their social class and strongly predicted their actual level of achievement. Interestingly, Paul Berman and Milbrey McLaughlin (1978) found that teachers who held higher levels of efficacy were more likely to undertake and persist in implementing school-improvement initiatives. Given the important relationship of individual efficacy to performance (for both teachers and students), some work has begun on what features of the school organization raise the individual's efficacy (for review, see Fuller et al. 1982).

School Climate

The quality of a school has also been defined by its overall climate or atmosphere. This line of thought de-emphasizes discrete behaviors of the individual teacher and instead tries to focus on the culture and normative beliefs that may be shared within a school or classroom. Research on school climate is grounded in Kurt Lewin's (1936) theory of personality, which postulated that motivation stems from both internal drives and situational cues exercised by other actors within the individual's perceptual field. John Withall (1949) defined school climate as the perceptual world of the individual, the *esprit de corps* of the group, the meaning of individual and group activities, and the type of norms that govern interpersonal communication (reviewed in Chavez 1984). By 1982 Carolyn Anderson could identify over two hundred empirical studies of school climate. These studies typically survey individual students and teachers, asking about their perception of involvement and affiliation with other students, trust and friendship between student and teacher, as well as levels of order, rule clarity, teacher control, and competition present in the classroom (for example, Trickett and Moos 1973; Moos 1979).

The school-effectiveness móvement has been heavily informed by research on school climate. For example, the usual checklist for an "effective school" includes items that speak to normative beliefs and the school's atmosphere: a feeling of trust among staff and students, a concern for strong academic achievement, a spirit of collaboration among teachers, and clear rules for how pupils should behave and perform. In addition, certain elements of a positive school climate are related to student achievement. After controlling for the school's social-class status, Brookover and associates (1979) found that variation across schools in teachers' expectations of pupils' achievement, the perceived commitment of teachers to improve the school, and feeling that one's own efforts would be recognized and rewarded (efficacy) did contribute to higher achievement. Michael Rutter (1983) reports similar findings for British schools.

Yet weaknesses do exist in how proponents of the school-climate field conceptualize educational quality. First, measures of climate confound the pupil's or the teacher's perception of their own involvement in a classroom with the rules or structure imposed by others. The student, for instance, reports his or her affiliation with other students and the teacher. Then the pupil assesses the clarity of rules and degree of competition among students. These latter features are properties of the organization, perhaps determined by the principal or parents, not socio-emotional elements of the particular student's own experience in the classroom. Second, an important strength of climate measures is that they tap the subjective meaning of classroom characteristics held by the individual. But the trade-off here is that actual behaviors are not observed. In the absence of clear descriptions of what behaviors create a positive climate, how can this research actually be used to improve teaching? Third, like research on teaching, the school-climate area fails to clarify its theory of organizing.

Are proponents arguing that a feeling of competition and individual-istic achievement (one subscale) contributes to achievement? If so, does not a high feeling of affiliation and trust (another subscale) contradict this competitive emphasis? In short, the climate model does not present a cohesive set of organizational features that can be behaviorally observed.

CLASSROOM AND SCHOOL ORGANIZATION

By concentrating on the abilities and perceptions of the individual teacher or student we lose sight of the underlying factors that pattern how the entire school organization actually works (Barr and Dreeben 1983). The production-function metaphor focuses on what material and human ingredients are placed within the school. Research on teaching and inquiry into school climate inform us about how individ-ual perception, motivation, and preferred teaching practices can help raise student achievement. But these definitions of quality fail to detail how students and school staff actually behave in the school organization and the underlying structures that may pattern individ-ual action. For instance, when the individual teacher fails to follow prescriptions on how to instruct effectively, do we conclude the teacher is just ignorant? Alternatively, do pressures emanating from the deeper structure of the entire school constrain the teacher or fail to encourage improvement?

Classroom Organization

Two elements of the classroom structure are especially important in defining educational quality. First, how students actually spend their time varies enormously among different classrooms. Nancy Karweit (1985), for instance, reports that in one classroom she observed the teacher spent almost 100 minutes of class time per week on managing student behavior and on setting up instructional tasks. In another classroom the teacher spent only 10 minutes per week on such activities. Among the twelve classrooms she observed, children spent (on average) between 100 and 240 minutes per week actually engaged in instructional tasks. This variation was far wider than the difference in the total length of the school day across the different schools. Charles Fisher and colleagues (1980) found that the amount of class time actually allocated to reading instruction by different fifth-grade teachers ranged from 60 to 140 minutes per day. The proportion of assigned time that students were actually engaged in reading tasks varied between 50 percent in the least-effective class-rooms and 90 percent in classrooms that showed higher levels of student achievement (also see Rosenshine 1980). Classroom observa-tions by Jean Carew and Sara Lawrence Lightfoot (1979) focused on variation among individual students within four classrooms. Here, too, great variation was observed in the proportion of time individual students spent working on academic tasks, relative to playing alone or talking with other students about something unrelated to the instruc-tional activity.

Looking across different cultural settings, Harold Stevenson and colleagues (in press) found that fifth-grade students in the United States spent 64 percent of class time engaged in academic tasks, versus 87 percent of class time spent by pupils in Japanese schools. These studies generally find that the amount of time students are engaged in instructional tasks covaries with achievement. However, only a subset of these time-on-task studies have controlled for pupils' competency levels prior to their entering the classroom. When this necessary accounting of prior proficiency occurs, effects of time-on-task on achievement do diminish, though they generally remain significant (Karweit 1985). Less work exists on the character of (not just time spent on) academic tasks. For instance, Penelope Peterson and colleagues (1984) found that students' own reports of attention to and understanding of instructional tasks were more valid indicators of actual learning than were observers' assessment of the time pupils spent on the same tasks.

Second, classroom organization can be described by the rules that govern social interaction. The teacher may stand before and lecture to a class in which the students sit neatly in rows. Or students may work collaboratively within small groups. A considerable amount of time is often spent with pupils sitting alone, engaged in worksheets or paper-and-pencil exercises. Variability across teachers and classrooms on these dimensions of structure is well documented. School quality is often inferred by the "tightness" of the classroom organization: the appearance of order and a strong teacher leading the class. For instance, the Stevenson group reported that students in the United States were observed to be working individually 47 percent of the time, whereas Japanese students work individually only three percent of the time. In Japan the teacher was explicitly leading the entire class 70 percent of the time, compared to less than half the time in those North American classrooms observed.

However, increasing the vertical tightness of the classroom may actually lower achievement. When the teacher is standing before the class, only one or two students can actively participate at any one time, even assuming the teacher is allowing discussion. But by delegating some authority and responsibility to small learning groups, all students can actively participate and the teacher can concentrate attention on lower-achieving students. By allocating some rewards directly to the work groups, not only to the individual pupil, cooperative skills and helping behaviors between students are also encouraged. Extensive empirical research on the relationship between such cooperative instructional groups and achievement now exists (for review, see Slavin 1983). Effects on achievement are not always observed across studies, but as Noreen Webb (1982) points out, one must recognize the specific steps required in implementing a cooperative instructional program effectively. This includes placing appropriate cognitive demands on students, creating a good mix of students in each group, and carefully rewarding children's cooperative and helping behaviors. When these aspects are taken into account, the link between cooperative instruction and achievement may become stronger.

This approach to improving school effectiveness also offers a more consistent model of how to organize tasks, roles, and authority within the classroom. The models of schooling described above usually confound rational-bureaucratic ways of tightening up versus a collective organizational model that calls for more democratic social relations (and an emotionally warmer school climate). The cooperative-instruction movement, however, builds on clearer conceptions of how the work of teaching and learning can be better organized. Normative values about desirable social rules are also confronted head on. Rather than implicitly accepting that learning should occur individualistically and be judged competitively, proponents of cooperative learning suggest an alternative set of social rules.

School Organization

School quality may have more to do with the structure of the entire school organization than with behavioral patterns found within individual classrooms. Indeed, classroom-level research leaves us with the question, What antecedent factors cause this enormous variation in teaching practices and classroom structures? The literature on effective schools explains that the actions and beliefs of the principal play an important role—especially in sharpening the school's academic mission, in building a feeling of camaraderie among teachers, in evaluating teachers' performance, and in pushing to improve teaching practices.

To this point, the definitions of school quality have assumed that the individual teacher works in a vacuum, attached only to his or her students. But as Susan Rosenholtz (1985) points out, the schoolwide structure first determines whether the individual teacher retains some degree of freedom to shape his or her own practice. For instance, school principals spend a lot of time buffering their teaching staff from the outside demands made by parents and government agencies. Second, whether the individual teacher feels a part of a schoolwide team and professional group depends largely on the structure and culture of the school, the tone of which is set by the principal and respected teachers at each school. For instance, assume that the teacher's sense of his or her own efficacy is a strong motivator and antecedent to effective teaching. Boosting the teacher's efficacy stems in part from the teacher's influence within the school structure, as well as from the interest of the principal and staff in collectively helping to improve his or her teaching skills. The conditions for improving the quality of instruction within the classroom lie within the expectations and capacities of the school staff as a whole, not with the static skills of the individual teacher.

Undoubtedly the principal plays a central role in creating a supportive and well-managed school structure. However, we know that principals often fail in this regard. For example, principals rarely evaluate the performance of their teachers, despite outside pressures for accountability or internal interest in improving teachers' skills (Dornbusch and Scott 1975). Initial evidence does show wide variability across schools in the degree of consensus among teachers about instructional priorities. Where teachers perceive that the principal is a strong instructional leader (not just an administrator) and where teachers' perceived efficacy is high, the degree of shared beliefs is higher within the school (Fuller and Izu, in press). In addition, abundant knowledge exists on what principals actually do day to day and on the strategies they employ to improve school quality (for review, see Leithwood and Montgomery 1982). Unfortunately, little evidence exists on how different behaviors of principals and school structures relate to actual achievement in schools. Descriptions of principals in effective and ineffective schools are available. But how much principals' actions and different organizational structures influence pupil achievement is not known.

The structure of the entire school is related to quality in another way. Different groups judge school quality by the institution's capacity to improve the student's eventual status in the outside world. For instance, schools are often called on to help reduce occupational and social inequalities experienced by minority groups. Evidence does indicate that ethnic minority and low-income students are differentially treated within schools through tracking policies and the complexity of the instructional tasks that are assigned to them (for example, Oakes 1982). Some constituencies demand different forms of instruction, say vocational versus academic schooling, in the belief that a particular type will advance their future opportunities and status. To address how these elements of school structure relate to achievement is beyond the scope of this chapter. But one should note that this is another way in which school structure defines "educational quality" in the eyes of many parents, teachers, and politicians.

INSTITUTIONAL SIGNALS

A fourth definition of school quality challenges the rational and material assumptions made by the three prior models. The starting point of the institutional view of quality is the conclusion reached by the Coleman group: Compared to the child's social-class background, differences in school quality do not make much of a difference in determining levels of achievement. Subsequent work extended this finding; it argued that variation in school quality did not influence the student's eventual occupational status, and it controlled for the force of the child's social-class background. John Meyer (1977) thus argues that despite improvements in how school characteristics are identified and measured, their collective impact on achievement and future adult status remains marginal. In addition, schools are loosely structured and remain very resistant to real change. But if the school is largely impotent in raising achievement, why do societies continue to invest heavily in formal education and recurrently express concern over low school quality?

The institutional model suggests that the school's impact rests not in its internal structure but through its role within the larger society and set of discrete organizations with which the school interacts. Schools are chartered by the society to produce graduates who are labeled in certain ways, depending on the type of school attended and its relative prestige. What is actually learned within the school is not important. The symbolic designation gained by the graduate, however, does hold currency as individuals seek status and income after they leave school. Formal schools designate individuals with roles that make sense to the outside world, such as technician, lawyer, or dropout. The material skills held by these individuals are secondary to the fact that the culture, especially employers, recognizes these labels or signals of competence.

But how do institutional signals relate to concern with school quality? First, the pursuit of improving school quality, in part, is a symbolic activity founded on a shared faith. For instance, the basic tenets of the school-effectiveness movement have not been substantiated by empirical evidence. But people have come to believe, for example, that "raising teachers' expectations for high pupil performance" is a potent method for actual boosting of achievement. And the fact that university researchers are making these claims—backed by thick reports and an occasional correlation matrix—gives the movement even greater legitimacy (Rowan 1984).

Second, when political leaders advocate school reform they are enhancing their own visibility and advancing fundamental cultural values—two agendas totally unrelated to improving school effectiveness. It is no coincidence, for instance, that a former governor of California championed the school reform cause the year immediately prior to his race for the United States senate. The recurrent political push to "improve school quality" can evoke symbols of moral virtue, hard work, equal opportunity, and competition. These signals help to legitimate the particular government that presently holds power; evoking these symbols also strengthens the popularity of local educators. Regardless of any material changes in the school organization, claims that schools must tighten discipline, expect excellence, and raise individualistic competition resonate to dominant cultural beliefs (at least within the United States and parts of western Europe).

Third, various signs associated with the improvement of quality emanate from school-reform programs funded by the state and operated by the local school. So, for instance, a local principal may brag of how pupils with learning disabilities now receive more individualized instruction from specialized teachers in fancy resource rooms. But is the actual quality of instruction any better? From a symbolic standpoint, this question is not important; the shift in school structure alone will signal an apparent improvement in school quality in the eyes of many (Rowan 1982). Similarly, governments and schools have broadened the decision-making process to involve teachers, parents, and occasionally students. This may be seen as a means for improving school quality; clearly this strategy helps to boost the legitimacy of the school. But it must be viewed as a symbolic improvement in quality, given the absence of any demonstrable impact on student achievement (Weiler 1983). In each case the attack on low school quality is advanced primarily to boost the institution's legitimacy. Precise means for improving teaching or raising learning are of secondary importance.

CONCLUSIONS

What have we learned about the nature of "school quality" over the past two decades? First, we have learned that it is not easy to pin down this slippery concept. Denotations of school quality began with material things: books, expenditures, and salaries. Then, discrete skills and behaviors of teachers seemed more important. But some persons pointed out that students hold varying perceptions of the action that unfolds in a classroom and the classroom's climate. And how the child perceives the teacher may shape his or her own concept of self. More recently, educators and researchers who are drawing images of school quality are describing features of the organization, the school's rules and culture that pattern behavior and shared commitments. Yet recurrent debates over school quality may simply involve symbolic rhetoric—as both political and school institutions seek to advance their own legitimacy and the school's apparent responsiveness to a society that often questions how its children are being socialized. Calls to improve school quality, in large part, may reflect an evangelical healing process aimed at restoring confidence in the school institution (Rowan 1984). In sum, the indicators of school quality have become more complex, more colorful, and less agreed on.

Second, many practitioners and scholars have become conscious of individual versus social definitions of school quality. The reductionist instincts of economists and psychologists have been moderated by a growing awareness of social rules and beliefs that connect material inputs and individuals. The book and the teacher are no longer seen as independent ingredients poured into a simple technological process. The rules that manage, combine, and mobilize these inputs form the social structure of the classroom and school. The discrete features of this social structure help to order our images of action in the school and better describe how good schools work. How are classrooms organized to maximize the time students actually spend on instructional tasks? Are students actively engaged in learning activities or passively listening to the teacher? What is the level of shared beliefs and camaraderie present among school staff? How does this sense of teamwork motivate teachers to improve their own skills? These are all questions about the structure of human interaction, not of individual attributes. These questions were not often asked twenty years ago.

Third, we are more conscious of *different forms of organization*. Earlier conceptions of school quality held prescriptions for tightening up the school's discipline, rules, and authority. Then the next paragraph in a text on teaching methods commonly would talk of building trust, solidarity, and a spirit of cooperation between teacher and student. Advances in cooperative types of classroom instruction at least have forced us to think about distinctions between rationalizing the classroom versus building more collective ways of organizing academic work. Teachers and principals can choose to make the classroom a more regulated and bureaucratic place within which to work, often emphasizing individual seatwork and traditional lectures. Or school staff can involve pupils more actively in learning through the use of cooperative groups. This calls for a different way of defining the teacher's authority and actions in the classroom—some of which remain hazy. But importantly, we are now aware of different ways of organizing work in the classroom.

All four images of school quality have failed to address two weaknesses. Most importantly, they all focus on improving the technical task of raising student achievement. The official structure of the school receives the full attention of most researchers. But why do students often resist the rules and expectations embedded in the school and classroom? The conflict between the teacher's will and the student's is very clear to the casual observer of any school. But only a few scholars have attempted to examine children's own social networks and how they conflict with, or enhance, the formal school structure (for important exceptions, see Everhart 1983; Hallinan and Smith 1985). Current models of school quality assume that the formal structure operates either independently of, or to explicitly confine, childrens' own commitments and interests. This is a narrow strategy to pursue, and an unnecessary one (Fuller and Rapoport 1984).

In addition, those who write about school quality or advocate school improvements often claim universal relationships: tightening discipline will always boost achievement, or building cooperation among school staff will always raise teachers' motivation. But clearer thinking (even speculation) is needed to identify the conditions under which such alleged indicators of higher school quality do in fact increase student performance. In addition, the literature on school quality assumes that raising standardized test scores is the universally accepted indicator of "achievement." More and more, school staff are being held accountable to increase students' vocabulary and raise their knowledge of mathematical procedures, the two biggest elements of standardized tests. Are these the exclusive or most important goals of schooling? Do parents and communities vary on the importance they place on these objectives?

Finally, the advocacy of universal models continues to constrain how we think about school quality in developing nations. For some time, research on the Third World has relied on the production-function model of improving school quality. The skeptical findings of limited school effects have significantly influenced development strategies and investments. This occurs even though the research in the United States and Western Europe obviously pertains to situations that differ markedly from schooling in the Third World. Greater efforts should be made to question self-consciously the use of any one model of school quality. And the conditions under which achievement effects are found, or not found, should be clearly specified to avoid generalizing the results to other settings. As stated before in this chapter, the bulk of empirical work in developing countries shows that an infusion of more material inputs does increase achievement—given the low baseline level of instructional resources. Yet as development groups continue to rely on the production-function metaphor of how schools work, other avenues for improving school quality remain unexplored and untraveled.

Cross-national work on school quality is also beginning to expose the assumptions that underlie thought and research in the United States and western Europe. For instance, west African schools display a high degree of hierarchical authority and uniformity in their curriculum, which stems from the centralized French system. Southern African schools, however, are more diverse and democratic, which comes in part from the British influence. Here, what defines a good form of organization varies across situations. This sensitivity to situation and cultural history is missing in most of the literature from the United States, even though different communities and parents desire different forms of socialization for their children. In addition, the symbols of school quality are often stark in developing countries: investing in chemistry labs for schools that lack books and basic materials, or constructing schools with concrete floors when no other structure in the village is similarly built. One can immediately ask,

Appendix 3.1

School Quality and Student Achievement: Review of Third World Research

(1) School Quality Indicator	(2) Expected Direction of Relationship	(3) Total Number of Analyses	(4) Number of Analyses Confirming Effect	(5) Number of Analyses Reporting No or Negative Effect
School Expenditures				
1. Expenditures per pupil	+	11	6	5
2. Total school expenditures	+	5	2	3
Specific Material Inputs				
3. Class size	−	21	5	16
4. School size	+	9	4	5
5. Instructional materials				
Texts and reading materials	+	22	14	8
Desks	+	3	3	0
6. Instructional media (radio)	+	3	3	0
7. School building quality	+	2	2	0
8. Library size and activity	+	18	15	3
9. Science laboratories	+	11	4	7
10. Nutrition and feeding programs	+	5	5	0
Teacher Quality				
11. Teacher's length of schooling				
Total years of teacher's schooling	+	25	11	14
Years of tertiary and teacher training	+	30	21	9
12. In-service teacher training	+	5	4	1
13. Teacher's length of experience	+	23	10	13

#	Variable				
14.	Teacher's verbal proficiency	+	2	2	0
15.	Teacher's salary level	+	13	4	9
16.	Teacher's social-class background	+	10	7	3
17.	School's percentage of full-time teachers	+	2	1	1
18.	Teacher's punctuality and (low) absenteeism	+	2	0	2
	Teachers Practices / Classroom Organization				
19.	Length of instructional program	+	13	11	2
20.	Homework frequency	+	7	5	2
21.	Active learning by students	+	2	0	2
22.	Teacher's expectations of pupil performance	+	3	3	0
23.	Teacher's time spent on class preparation	+	5	4	1
	School Management				
24.	Quality of principal	+	7	4	3
25.	Multiple shifts of classes each day	−	3	1	2
26.	Student boarding	+	4	3	1
27.	Student repetition of grade	+	5	1	4

Note: A total of sixty-two multivariate studies from developing countries were reviewed. Each study examined the influence of school characteristics after controlling for the influence of students' background (Fuller 1986).

What do these actions have to do with increasing student achievement? But are such actions any more symbolic than the North American principal who adopts a student-discipline policy or who buys several microcomputers—proclaiming that school quality has been significantly elevated?

REFERENCES

Anderson, C. "The Search for School Climate: A Review of the Research." *Review of Educational Research* 52: 3 (1982): 368–420.

Austin G., and Garber, H. eds. *Research on Exemplary Schools: From Theory to Practice to Policy.* New York: Academic Press, 1985.

Averch, H.; Carroll, S.; Donaldson, T.; Kiesling, H.; and Pincus, J. *How Effective Is Schooling?* Englewood Cliffs, N.J.: Educational Technology Publications, 1974.

Bangert, R.; Kulik, J.; and Kulik, C. "Individualized Systems of Instruction in Secondary Schools." *Review of Educational Research* 53: 2 (1983): 143–158.

Barr, R., and Dreeben, R. *How Schools Work.* Chicago: University of Chicago Press, 1983.

Berman, P., and McLaughlin, M. *Federal Programs Supporting Educational Change, Volume 8.* Santa Monica, Calif.: Rand, 1978.

Bridge, R.; Judd, C.; and Moock, P. *The Determinants of Educational Outcomes: The Impact of Families, Peers, Teachers and Schools.* Cambridge, Mass.: Ballinger, 1979.

Brookover, W.; Beady, C.; Flood, P.; Schweitzer, J.; and Wisenbaker, J. *School Social Systems and Student Achievement: Schools Can Make a Difference.* New York: Praeger, 1979.

Brophy, J. "Teacher Behavior and Its Effects." *Journal of Educational Psychology* 71 (1979): 733–750.

Brophy, J. "Teacher Praise: A Functional Analysis." *Review of Educational Research* 51: 1 (1981): 5–32.

Carew, J., and Lightfoot, S. *Beyond Bias: Perspectives on the Classroom.* Cambridge, Mass.: Harvard University Press, 1979.

Carter, L. "The Sustaining Effects Study of Compensatory and Elementary Education." *Educational Researcher,* September 1984.

Chavez, R. "The Use of High-Inference Measures to Study Classroom Climates." *Review of Educational Research* 54: 2 (1984): 237–261.

Coleman, J. "Methods and Results in the IEA Studies of Effects of School on Learning." *Review of Educational Research* 45: 3 (1975): 335–386.

Coleman, J.; Campbell, E.; Hobson, C.; McPartland, J.; Mood, A.; Weinfall, F.; and York, R. *Equality of Educational Opportunity.* Washington, D.C.: Department of Health, Education, and Welfare, 1966.

D'Amico, R. "Does Employment During High School Impair Academic Progress?" *Sociology of Education* 57 (1984): 152–164.

Dornbusch, S., and Scott, R. *Evaluation and the Exercise of Authority.* San Francisco: Jossey-Bass, 1975.

Dunkin, M., and Biddle, B. *The Study of Teaching.* New York: Holt, Rinehart and Winston, 1974.

Edmonds, R. "Programs of School Improvement: An Overview." *Educational Leadership* 40: 3 (1982): 4–11.

Everhart, R. *Reading, Writing, and Resistance*. Boston: Routledge and Kegal Paul, 1983.

Fisher, C.; Berliner, D.; Filby, N.; Marliave, R.; Cahen, L.; and Dishaw, M. "Teaching Behaviors, Academic Learning Time, and Student Achievement," In *Time to Learn*, edited by C. Denham and A. Lieberman, pp. 7–32. Washington, D.C.: National Institute of Education, 1980.

Fuller, B. "Raising School Quality in Developing Countries: What Investments Boost Learning?" Washington, D.C.: The World Bank, 1986.

Fuller, B., and Izu, J. "Explaining School Cohesion: What Shapes the Organizational Beliefs of Teachers?" *American Journal of Education*, in press.

Fuller, B., and Rapoport, T. "Indigenous Evaluation: Youth Programs in Israel and the United States." *Evaluation Review* 8: 1 (1984): 25–44.

Fuller, B.; Wood, K.; Rapoport, T.; and Dornbusch, S. "The Organizational Context of Individual Efficacy." *Review of Educational Research* 52: 1 (1982): 7–30.

Gage, N. *The Scientific Basis of the Art of Teaching*. New York: Teachers College Press, 1978.

Gage, N., and Berliner, D. *Educational Psychology*. Chicago: Rand McNally, 1975.

Glasman, N., and Biniaminov, I. "Input-Output Analyses of Schools." *Review of Educational Research* 51: 4 (1981): 509–539.

Glass, G., and Smith, M. *Meta-analysis of Research on the Relationship of Class Size and Achievement*. San Francisco: Far West Laboratory for Educational Research and Development, 1978.

Good, T., and Brophy, J. *Looking in Classrooms*. New York: Harper and Row, 1973.

Hallinan, M., and Smith, S. "The Effects of Classroom Racial Composition on Students' Interracial Friendliness." *Social Psychology Quarterly* 48: 1 (1985): 3–16.

Hanushek, E. "Throwing Money at Schools." *Journal of Policy Analysis and Management* 1: 1 (1981): 19–41.

Heyneman, S., and Loxley, W. "The Effect of Primary School Quality on Academic Achievement across Twenty-nine High- and Low-income Countries." *American Journal of Sociology* 88: 6 (1983): 1162–1194.

Jamison, D.; Searle, B.; Galda, K.; and Heyneman, S. "Improving Elementary Mathematics Education in Nicaragua." *Journal of Educational Psychology* 73: 4 (1981): 556–567.

Jamison, D.; Suppes, P.; and Wells, S. "The Effectiveness of Alternative Instructional Media: A Survey." *Review of Educational Research* 44: 1 (1974): 1–67.

Joyce, B., and Weil, M. *Models of Teaching* 2d ed. Englewood Cliffs, N.J.: Prentice-Hall, 1980.

Karweit, N. "Should We Lengthen the School Term?" *Educational Researcher*, June 1985, pp. 9–15.

Leithwood, K., and Montgomery, D. "The Role of the Elementary School Principal in Program Improvement." *Review of Educational Research* 52: 3 (1982): 309–339.

Levin, H. "Concepts of Economic Efficiency and Educational Production." In *Education as an Industry*, edited by J. Froomkin, D. Jamison, and R. Radner, pp. 149–191. Cambridge, Mass.: Ballinger, 1976.

Levin, H.; Glass, G.; and Meister, G. "Cost-Effectiveness of Four Educational Interventions." (Mimeographed). Stanford, Calif.: Institute for Research on Educational Finance and Governance, 1984.

Lewin, K. *The Dynamic Theory of Personality.* Translated by D. Adams and K. Tener New York: McGraw-Hill, 1936.

Marshall, H., and Weinstein, R. "Classroom Factors Affecting Students' Self-Evaluations." *Review of Educational Research* 54: 3 (1984): 301–325.

Meyer, J. "The Effects of Schooling as an Institution." *American Journal of Sociology* 83 (1977): 55–77.

Moos, R. *Evaluating Educational Environments.* San Francisco: Jossey-Bass, 1979.

Neufeld, B.; Farrar, E.; and Miles, M. "A Review of Effective Schools Research." Mimeographed. Cambridge, Mass.: Huron Institute, 1983.

Oakes, J. "Classroom Social Relationships: Exploring the Bowles and Gintis Hypothesis." *Sociology of Education* 55 (1982): 197–212.

Peaker, G. *The Plowden Children Four Years Later.* London: National Foundation for Educational Research in England and Wales, 1971.

Peterson, P.; Swing, S.; Stark, K.; and Waas, G. "Students' Cognitions and Time on Task During Mathematics Instruction." *American Educational Research Journal* 21: 3 (1984): 487–515.

Purkey, S., and Smith, M. "Effective Schools: A Review." *Elementary School Journal* 83: 4 (1983): 427–452.

Rozenholtz, S. "Effective Schools: Interpreting the Evidence." *American Journal of Education* (1985): 352–388.

Rosenholtz, S., and Rosenholtz, S. "Classroom Organization and the Perception of Ability." *Sociology of Education* 54: 2 (1981): 132–140.

Rosenshine, B. "How Time Is Spent in Elementary Classrooms." In *Time to Learn,* edited by C. Denham and A. Lieberman, pp. 107–124. Washington, D.C.: National Institute of Education, 1980.

Rosenshine, B., and Furst, J. "Current and Future Research on Teacher Performance Criteria." In *Research on Teacher Education: A Symposium,* edited by B. W. Smith. Englewood Cliffs, N. J.: Prentice-Hall, 1971.

Rowan, B. "Organizational Structure and the Institutional Environment: The Case of Public Schools." *Administrative Science Quarterly* 27 (1982): 259–279.

Rowan, B. "Shamanistic Rituals in Effective Schools." *Issues in Education* 2: 1 (1984): 76–87.

Rutter, M. "School Effects on Pupil Progress: Research Findings and Policy Implications." *Child Development* 54 (1983): 1–29.

Simmons, J., and Alexander, L. "The Determinants of School Achievement in Developing Countries: A Review of Research." *Economic Development and Cultural Change* 26: 2 (1978): 341–357.

Slavin, R. *Cooperative Learning.* New York: Longman, 1983.

Stevenson, H.; Stigler, J.; Lucker, W.; Lee, S.; Hsu, C.; and Kitamura, S. "Classroom Behavior and Achievement of Japanese, Chinese, and American Children." *Advances in Instructional Psychology,* in press.

Trickett, E., and Moos, R. "The Social Environment of Junior High and High School Classrooms." *Journal of Educational Psychology* 65 (1973): 93–102.

Walberg, H. "Improving the Productivity of America's Schools." *Educational Leadership* 41: 8 (1984): 19–30.

Walberg, H., and Shanahan, T. "High School Effects on Individual Students." *Educational Researcher* 12: 7 (1983): 4–9.

Webb, N. "Student Interaction and Learning in Small Groups." *Review of Educational Research* 52: 3 (1982): 421–445.

Weiler, H. "Legalization, Expertise, and Participation: Strategies of Compensatory Legitimization in Educational Policy." *Comparative Education Review* 27: 2 (1983): 259–277.

Withall, J. "The Development of a Technique for the Measurement of Social-Emotional Climate in Classrooms." *Journal of Experimental Education* 17 (1949): 347–361.

4

Student Achievement

Ruth B. Ekstrom, Margaret E. Goertz, and Donald R. Rock

For nearly twenty years social scientists have studied how schooling conditions can shape the cognitive, affective, and behavioral outcomes that influence student achievement.

Research during the late 1960s and the 1970s concentrated on allocating the variance in educational outcomes between institutional and individual characteristics in an effort to isolate or to estimate the degree to which school resources and facilities affect academic outcomes. Studies using this basic approach appeared in several disciplines. Sociologists concentrated on school climate or context (Alexander and Eckland 1975, 1977; Alwin and Otto 1977; Anderson 1982; Hauser 1969; Heyns 1978; Jencks et al. 1972; McDill and Rigsby 1973) and economists used input-output and production-function models (Brown and Saks 1975; Cohen and Millman 1975; Glasman and Biniaminov 1981; Hanushek 1979; Murnane 1981; Summers and Wolfe 1979). Common to both disciplines was the finding that differences among schools had only a modest impact on

The authors contributed equally and jointly to this chapter; the order of listing is alphabetical. The studies described in this chapter were conducted by Educational Testing Service under Contract No. 300–83–0247 with the National Center for Education Statistics (NCES). The opinions and findings expressed here do not necessarily reflect the position or policy of NCES and no official endorsement should be inferred.

student achievement once socioeconomic background and ability were controlled for (Bridge et al. 1979; Coleman et al. 1966; Heyns 1978; Jencks et al. 1972; Mosteller and Moynihan 1972). This position was modified somewhat in the early 1980s when James Coleman and his associates attributed the better performance of students in Catholic schools to factors related to the greater discipline and higher quality of instruction in those schools (Coleman et al. 1981; Hoffer, Greeley, and Coleman 1984).

The search for factors affecting student achievement intensified in the late 1970s when it became evident that student performance, especially as measured by nationally administered tests such as the Scholastic Aptitude Test (SAT), was declining. Although studies of this decline in SAT scores dealt with only a small portion of the high school cohort, they generated considerable concern and a number of hypotheses about the changes in high school education.

The Advisory Panel on the Scholastic Aptitude Test Score Decline concluded that the decline had occurred in two phases, and the panel gave a different explanation for each phase (College Board 1977). The explanation for the first phase of decline, which took place from 1963 to 1972, was that the SAT-taking population had undergone a drastic expansion and change. Whereas this group was once a relatively small segment of the high school population headed for elite private colleges largely in the East, it had grown to a much larger segment of the high school population seeking postsecondary education in a variety of institutions. In the second phase of the decline in scores, from 1972 to 1977, the number of students taking the SAT remained roughly constant, as did the total number of high school seniors. Factors other than the changing composition of the test-taking population were then suspected as contributing to the decline in performance. After considering approximately seventy-five hypotheses, the panel members concluded that "there is no *one* cause of the SAT score decline, at least as far as we can discern, and we suspect no single pattern of causes" (College Board 1977, p. xxx). The panel did, however, mention six possible causes: (1) proliferation of elective courses, (2) lowering of academic standards, (3) competition of television, (4) weakening of the role of the family in the educational process, (5) national tensions, and (6) diminution of students' motivation to learn.

This chapter focuses on the findings of a recent study that used two nationally representative data bases to examine the causes of test score decline (Rock et al. 1985a). The first section of this chapter addresses the questions: How did the American high school and its twelfth-grade population change between 1972 and 1980? and How were these changes related to test score decline? It concludes with a discussion of the policy implications of this study. The second section of this chapter reports briefly on a related study that identifies student behaviors and school characteristics that contribute to cognitive growth between the sophomore and senior years of high school; these findings corroborate those of the study of test score decline (Rock et al. 1985b). The chapter ends with a look at the expected contributions of forthcoming longitudinal studies to educational research and educational policy.

FACTORS AFFECTING TEST SCORE DECLINE

Two data bases compiled as part of the Longitudinal Studies Program of the National Center for Education Statistics (NCES) were used to examine the extent and causes of changes in the tested achievement of high school seniors between 1972 and 1980. The National Longitudinal Survey of the High School Class of 1972 (NLS-72) and High School and Beyond (HS&B) both included tests measuring vocabulary, reading, and mathematics as well as information about high school seniors and their schools in 1972 and in 1980.[1] This section describes changes in tested achievement in these two years and in the factors related to test score decline.

Changes in Tested Achievement

All three of the NLS-72/HS&B achievement tests showed declines between 1972 and 1980. The largest declines occurred in vocabulary and in reading. The typical senior in 1980 (a student at the fiftieth percentile in vocabulary and reading achievement) would have ranked at about the forty-first percentile among the 1972 seniors in both

---

1. The NLS-72 sample consisted of 16,683 individuals, the HS&B 1980 sample 28, of 240 individuals. In both years students were selected through a two-stage probability sample, with schools as the first-stage units and students within schools as the second-stage units. Weights were introduced for schools and for students to make the samples nationally representative. The three tests were not identical in 1972 and 1980, but a sufficient number of identical items permitted the use of Item Response Theory (IRT) for scaling of the tests. This scaling compared the pairs of tests in the two achievement areas and used this as the basis for developing a scale that would equate responses on the two tests.

vocabulary and reading. Similarly, a 1980 senior with average mathematics achievement would have been at the forty-fifth percentile among the 1972 seniors. When these changes are measured in standard deviation units, the declines were 0.22 for vocabulary, 0.21 for reading, and 0.14 for mathematics, which indicates a greater decline in verbal than in quantitative skills (see table 4.1).

Vocabulary.   Females showed a greater decline than did males on the vocabulary test. White students showed greater declines than did Black or Mexican-American students, but these racial and ethnic comparisons may be confounded by test-score floor effects. The decline for white students was relatively pervasive, cutting across socioeconomic status (SES) levels, geographic regions, curriculum type, and school type (public versus Catholic, for example).

Reading.   The decline in reading test scores was somewhat more consistent across subpopulations than was the decline in the vocabulary test scores. Declines were relatively comparable across SES, curriculum type, and school type, but white students showed a greater decline than did Black or Mexican-American students, and females showed a slightly greater decline than did males. The test score declines in reading were found primarily among students who reported doing less than five hours of homework each week.

Mathematics.   The decline in mathematics test scores was slightly larger for males than for females and larger for white students than for other racial and ethnic groups. Black students showed a small but not statistically significant increase in mathematics test scores. As with reading scores, test score declines in mathematics were found primarily among students who reported doing less than five hours of homework each week. Females and black students who reported doing more than five hours of homework per week showed significant increases in tested achievement. The largest score decline was among male students who took four or fewer semesters of mathematics and science.

The decline in the NLS and HS&B test scores paralleled in many ways the declines reported on the SAT. NLS and HS&B scores for women in the academic curriculum declined more than scores for males in this curriculum did (see table 4.1). This differential decline reversed the lead that academic women had on NLS vocabulary and

Table 4.1
NLS/HS&B Test Score Changes: 1972–1980

	Vocabulary				Reading				Mathematics			
	1972	1980	Diff.	Change in S.D. units	1972	1980	Diff.	Change in S.D. units	1972	1980	Diff.	Change in S.D. units
Sex												
Male	6.44	5.90	−0.54*	−0.14	9.83	8.95	−0.88*	−0.17	13.79	12.83	−0.96*	−0.13
Female	6.67	5.69	−0.98*	−0.26	9.95	8.96	−0.99*	−0.20	12.09	11.39	−0.70*	−0.10
Race and ethnicity												
White	7.08	6.24	−0.84*	−0.23	10.56	9.60	−0.96*	−0.20	13.95	12.98	−0.98*	−0.14
Black	3.28	3.20	−0.08	−0.03	5.94	5.56	−0.38	−0.09	6.50	6.69	0.19	0.03
Mexican-American	3.47	3.50	0.03	0.01	6.28	5.60	−0.69	−0.15	8.02	7.54	−0.48	−0.07
Curriculum												
Academic	8.29	7.62	−0.67*	−0.18	11.99	11.33	−0.66*	−0.14	16.66	16.17	−0.49	−0.08
General	5.32	4.83	−0.49*	−0.15	8.48	7.71	−0.78*	−0.16	10.41	9.89	−0.52*	−0.08
Vocational	4.70	4.15	−0.55*	−0.18	7.51	6.81	−0.70*	−0.15	8.78	8.48	−0.31	−0.05
Academic curriculum by sex												
Academic males	8.04	7.81	−0.23	−0.06	11.77	11.52	−0.25	−0.05	17.26	17.18	−0.08	−0.01
Academic females	8.56	7.56	−1.00*	−0.27	12.23	11.31	−0.92*	−0.20	16.00	15.47	−0.53*	−0.09

*Statistically Significant Decrease

Table 4.2
SAT Test Score Changes: 1972–1980

	Verbal				Mathematics			
	1972	1980	Difference	Change in S.D. units	1972	1980	Difference	Change in S.D. units
Male	454	428	−26	−0.23	505	491	−14	−0.12
Female	452	420	−32	−0.29	461	433	−28	−0.17

reading tests and increased the lead that academic men had on the NLS and HS&B mathematics tests.

SAT scores for men and women declined in a somewhat similar pattern in the same time period. As shown in table 4.2, men had a slight lead in SAT verbal scores (454 versus 452) and a large lead in SAT mathematics scores (505 versus 461) in 1972. Between 1972 and 1980 the women declined somewhat more than the men on both scales, which increased the discrepancy between men and women.

Changes in American High Schools and Their Students: 1972–1980

To determine what might contribute to test score decline, we first analyzed the changes in American high school seniors and their schools between 1972 and 1980. We found significant changes in the characteristics of high school seniors, their homes and families, the schools they attended, and their attitudes and behaviors.

Demographics. High school seniors in 1980 were more likely to be members of a minority group and from the South than were the 1972 seniors. Minorities increased from 14.2 percent of the 1972 high school seniors to 20.1 percent of the 1980 high school seniors. The largest increases were among Black and Mexican-American students. Black students increased from 8.7 percent of all seniors to 11.6 percent; Mexican-American students increased from 2.5 percent to 3.5 percent.

A larger proportion of seniors came from the South in 1980 and a smaller proportion from the Northeast. In 1972, 26.2 percent of all seniors came from the South and 26.4 percent came from the Northeast. By 1980, these figures were 30.4 percent and 22.9 percent, respectively.

Home and Family Characteristics. Between 1972 and 1980 parental occupation, parental education, and educational influences in the seniors' homes changed. For example, by 1980 the percentage of seniors' fathers with some college education had increased by six percentage points to 34 percent, and the percentage of mothers with some college education had increased by seven percentage points to 28 percent. Although there was relatively little difference in fathers' occupations in 1972 and 1980, there was a large decline in the percentage of seniors reporting their mothers' occupation as home-maker. This trend is probably a compounding of the actual increase in women's participation in paid work and a change of phrasing in the question about mother's occupation.

Mothers of the 1980 senior women had higher educational aspirations for their daughters than did the mothers of the 1972 senior women, but mothers' educational aspirations for senior men remained unchanged. In 1972, 62.4 percent of the male seniors and 51.7 percent of the female seniors reported that their mothers wanted them to obtain four or more years of college education. By 1980 these had changed to 61.9 and 58.7 percent, respectively. College aspirations for seniors in the general and vocational curriculum increased by 10 percentage points, while those for seniors in the academic curriculum increased by 3 percentage points.

Fewer study aids were found in the homes of 1980 seniors than in the homes of 1972 seniors. The average number of study aids (a place to study, reference materials, books and newspapers, and a type-writer) decreased from 3.2 in 1972 to 3.0 in 1980.

Student Behaviors and Attitudes. Between 1972 and 1980 major changes occurred in the curriculum tracks selected by the high school students as well as in the number of courses they took, the amount of homework they did, their extracurricular activities, and their educational aspirations and plans. Student attitudes and values had also changed.

More seniors were enrolled in the general or vocational curriculum in 1980 than in 1972, while fewer students were enrolled in the academic curriculum. Students in the academic curriculum decreased from 45.7 percent of all seniors in 1972 to 38.1 percent in 1980. Seniors in the general curriculum increased from 31.8 percent of all seniors in

1972 to 37.2 percent in 1980. The shift into the general curriculum was greater among males than females and occurred primarily among white students.

High school students apparently took fewer semesters of social studies, science, and foreign languages in 1980 than in 1972, but they took more semesters of mathematics. The average number of semesters taken of social studies declined from 5.2 in 1972 to 4.6 in 1980. The average number of semesters taken of science declined from 3.7 to 3.5. Students took considerably less foreign language (2.6 semesters in 1972 and 1.7 in 1980). The average number of semesters taken of mathematics increased from 3.9 in 1972 to 4.1 in 1980. However, these changes should be interpreted with caution. In 1972, information on course work was obtained from students' schools; in 1980, students supplied this information. An examination by NCES of the validity of student responses in 1980 showed that the quality of student reports on the amount of course work varied both by subject area and among subgroup populations.

Seniors reported doing less homework in 1980 than in 1972. The estimated decline was from approximately 4 3/4 hours of homework a week in 1972 to 4 1/4 hours in 1980. Students in the general curriculum and the vocational curriculum contributed most to this decline. The proportion of general and vocational seniors reporting doing less than five hours of homework a week increased from 74.3 percent in 1972 to 85.1 percent in 1980, while the proportion of academic students reporting doing this level of homework increased from 53.9 percent in 1972 to 59.3 percent in 1980.

Student participation in nonacademically oriented extracurricular activities, such as athletics, increased from 1972 to 1980, while participation in activities that could provide an opportunity for informal learning, such as subject matter clubs, declined slightly.

There was little change in the mean level of education to which students aspired. This finding, however, masks both sex differences and a considerable shift in the type of postsecondary education sought. Educational aspirations declined for males but increased for females. The percentage of seniors aspiring to four or more years of postsecondary education decreased from 50.6 percent in 1972 to 45.5 percent in 1980. The proportion of seniors aspiring to junior college or voc-tech education increased from 30.6 percent in 1972 to 38.8 percent in 1980.

Seniors' plans for their first year after high school differed somewhat from their aspirations. There was an increase, from 25.9 percent in 1972 to 29.5 percent in 1980, in students planning to work full time. Plans to enter four-year colleges rose from 32.6 percent seniors in 1972 to 35.3 percent in 1980, while plans to enter junior colleges or voc-tech programs declined from 25.6 percent to 20.3 percent.

The largest group of seniors aspired to a professional occupation at age thirty (45 percent in 1972 and 43.4 percent in 1980). There was a decline in males aspiring to a professional occupation, but females' interest in the professions remained steady.

The attitudes and values of high school seniors also changed between 1972 and 1980. Interest in correcting social and economic inequities declined, while interest in making money and in job success increased. Students became more self-confident between 1972 and 1980 but less sure of their ability to control the course of their own lives.

Schools and School Programs. Between 1972 and 1980 there were also changes in school dropout rates, the proportion of schools reporting a majority of their students in the general curriculum, and students' ratings of their schools' facilities, academic instruction, and reputation.

Schools with dropout rates of 20 percent or more grew by six percentage points, from 3.6 percent of all high schools in 1972 to 9.6 percent in 1980. Schools with a dropout rate between 10 and 19 percent increased from 13.4 to 20.4 percent.

The proportion of schools reporting that the majority of their students were enrolled in the general curriculum increased greatly. In 1972, 25.1 percent of the schools reported that more than half of their students were enrolled in the general curriculum; by 1980 this had increased to 47.4 percent. This shift in emphasis took place primarily in low and middle socioeconomic status schools. There was also a small increase in the proportion of schools reporting that the majority of their students were enrolled in the academic curriculum. This increase occurred primarily among high socioeconomic status and Catholic high schools.

Identifying the Causes of Test Score Changes

The relational analysis—designed to identify the causes of test score decline—used three methods: (1) partitioning of mean test score changes,[2] (2) analysis of covariance partitioning,[3] and (3) path analysis.[4] The mean score partitioning showed that score declines on all three tests were primarily the result of declines in subgroup means.

The analysis of covariance partitioning estimated how changes in four blocks of variables—(1) demographics, (2) home educational support, (3) student behaviors and attitudes, and (4) school characteristics—separately affected the average test score decline. The results (see figure 4.1) showed that:

1. Shifts in demographics from 1972 to 1980 were a minor factor contributing to the test score decline.
2. Changes from 1972 to 1980 in students' school-related behaviors and in school characteristics played the major roles in the score decline. This finding was consistent across all three achievement areas.
3. Students' school-related behaviors and school policies contributed equally to the vocabulary score decline.
4. School characteristics played a somewhat larger role than did students' school-related behaviors in the reading score decline.
5. Conversely, students' school-related behaviors played a slightly greater role than did school characteristics in the mathematics score decline.
6. Changes from 1972 to 1980 in home educational support were in a direction that would resist score decline. However, the magnitude of the effects of these changes were quite small compared to the changes in student behavior and in school characteristics.

Changes from 1972 to 1980 in individual student's school-related behaviors that contributed most to the score decline, in approximate order of importance, were:

1. Taking fewer semesters of foreign-language courses. This reduction was proportionately greater for females.

---

2. The mean score partitioning provides information about how much of the change is due to shifts in population and how much is due to changes within the population groups.
3. A step-down analysis of covariance was used. This permits not only determination of the influence of each block of variables independent of the other blocks but also a determination of the direction of the influence.
4. The path analysis provided an opportunity to see if race, sex, and SES groups went through a somewhat different educational process in 1980 than their counterparts in 1972.

2. Spending less time on homework. This reduction was also proportionately greater for females.
3. Taking fewer semesters of science courses.
4. Fewer students enrolling in the academic curriculum.

Changes from 1972 to 1980 in individual school characteristics
that contributed most to the score decline were, in approximate order
of importance:

1. An increase in the proportion of students rating the school as
   needing more academic emphasis.
2. A decrease in the mean amount of homework done by students.
3. A decrease in the mean number of semesters of foreign language
   courses taken by students.
4. An increase in the number of schools with high dropout rates.
5. A decrease in the mean number of laboratory courses taken by
   students.
6. A decline in students' ratings of their school's reputation in the
   community.
7. A decline in students' ratings of the quality of their academic
   instruction.
8. A decline in students' ratings of the physical condition of their
   school building.

While the score decline cut across almost all groups of individuals,
it appeared to be larger for white students and for females. Path
analysis was used to see if the educational process experienced by
these groups had changed between 1972 and 1980. In addition to race
and ethnicity, sex, and socioeconomic status, the basic model included
mother's educational aspirations for the student, private school attendance, choice of the academic curriculum, number of semesters of
language courses, number of semesters of mathematics courses,
amount of homework, and tested achievement.

Mothers' educational aspirations for their children were predicted
fairly well by the demographic explanatory variables. After controlling for SES, mothers of nonwhite students tended to have higher
educational aspirations for their children than did mothers of white
students. This difference in aspirations increased from 1972 to 1980.
Another change concerned the student's gender. In 1972 mothers had
significantly higher educational aspirations for their sons than for
their daughters, but by 1980 mothers' aspirations were essentially
independent of the children's sex.

Figure 4.1

Adjusted Mean Differences for 1972–1980 Test Scores by Selected Blocks of Explanatory Variables

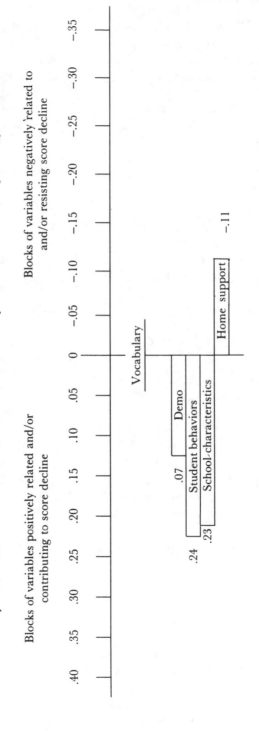

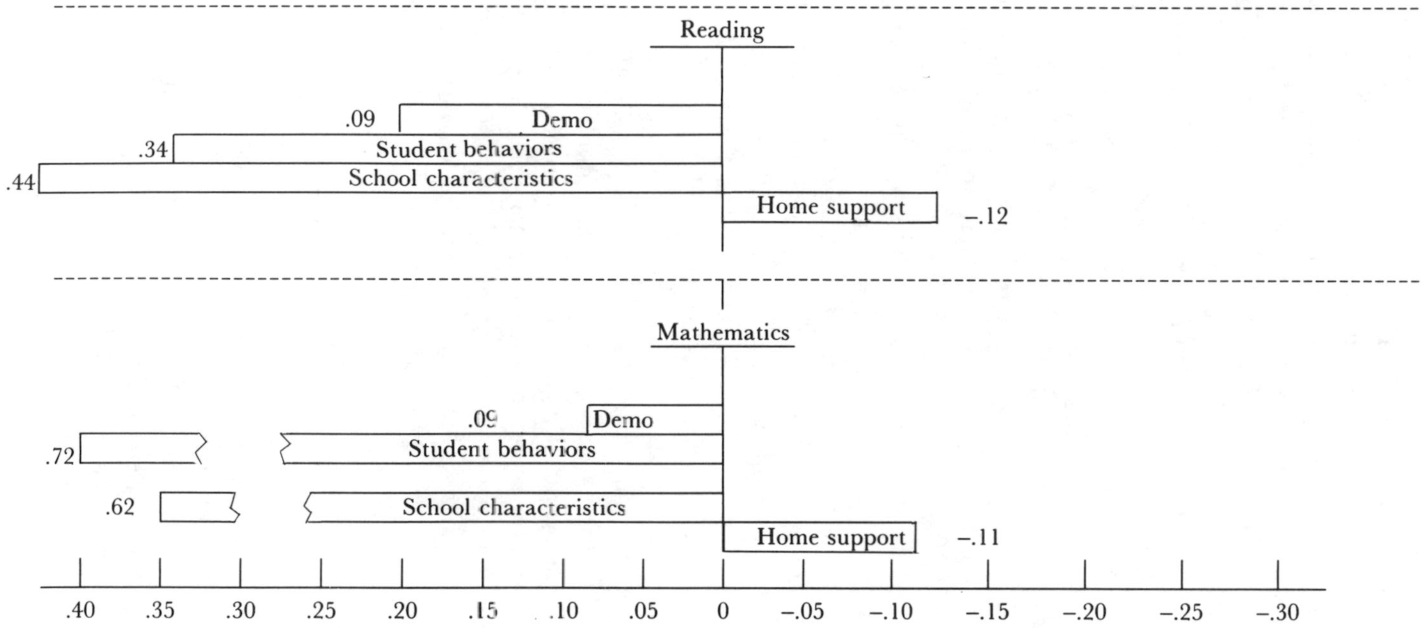

Reading

Demo .09

Student behaviors .34

School characteristics .44

Home support −.12

Mathematics

Demo .09

Student behaviors .72

School characteristics .62

Home support −.11

−.30 −.25 −.20 −.15 −.10 −.05 0 .05 .10 .15 .20 .25 .30 .35 .40

The hypothesized model was unable to predict with any accuracy whether or not a student attended a private school.

Choice of the academic curriculum by students was determined primarily by attendance at a private school, mother's educational aspirations for the student, family SES, and living in the Northeastern region of the country. A child's sex group membership was independent of enrollment in the academic curriculum in both 1972 and 1980.

The path analysis showed that females were less likely in 1980 than in 1972 to be taking foreign-language courses. The contrast between females and males indicates that, on the average, females still take more semesters of language than do males, but the difference appears to be diminishing. The path analysis also showed that both nonwhite students and females took more courses in mathematics in 1980 than in 1972.

The amount of homework done by students was only modestly explained by the model. With the exception of the contrast between females and males, the remaining variables had a weak relationship with the amount of homework students reported doing. The advantage of females over males in the amount of homework done decreased significantly from 1972 to 1980.

Inspection of the contrasts between 1972 and 1980 of the direct effects of major explanatory variables in the path analysis on test outcomes is shown in table 4.3. As can be seen, a significant reduction was found in the gap between whites and nonwhites between 1972 and 1980, when controlling for all other variables in the model. This is consistent with the reduction in other differentials between whites and nonwhites in explanatory variables such as attendance at private schools and mother's educational aspirations for the student, selection of the academic curriculum, and the number of foreign-language and science courses taken.

Mean differences in achievement scores between males and females also changed between 1972 and 1980. Changes in school behavior related to the student's sex accompanied these changes. Females showed greater test score declines than males in both reading and vocabulary, but they also showed greater declines in the amount of homework done and in the number of foreign-language courses taken. The gap between males and females in mathematics achievement grew larger between 1972 and 1980, even after controlling for the number of mathematics courses taken. While females report taking more mathematics courses, the data do not allow determina-

Table 4.3

Contrasts of the Direct Effects of Major Explanatory Variables on Test Outcomes Between 1972 and 1980

	Vocabulary		Reading		Mathematics	
	1972	1980	1972	1980	1972	1980
Race and ethnicity (white = "1", others = "0")	2.74	2.32*	3.71	3.41*	5.75	4.94*
Curriculum (academic = "1", others = "0")	1.31	1.49*	1.63	2.14*	3.07	3.54*
Mother's educational plans for child	0.91	0.63*	1.33	0.92*	1.80	1.15*
Socioeconomic status	0.80	0.70	0.59	0.71*	0.96	1.22*
Sex (female = "1", male = "0")	0.44	-0.20*	0.42	0.04*	-0.41	-0.94*
Number of related courses	0.34	0.28	0.43	0.30	1.05	0.79*
Amount of homework ("1" = 5 or more hours per week, "0" = less than 5 hours per week)	0.16	0.47*	0.20	0.68*	0.80	1.42*

*Indicates that the 1972 to 1980 comparison of direct effects differs by four pooled standard errors.

tion of the level or quality of these courses. It is possible that females are taking more lower-level mathematics courses than are males.

While the average amount of homework done decreased from 1972 to 1980, its impact on achievement increased. It would seem that those 1980 seniors who put in the time on homework were more than repaid for their efforts.

The answers to the question of whether the educational system was more or less equitable in 1980 than in 1972 were mixed. While the gap between white and nonwhite students decreased, family SES had a bigger effect on tested achievement in both reading and mathematics. Other things being equal, the gap in tested achievement between students in the academic curriculum and those in other curricula increased from 1972 to 1980 in all three achievement areas. This raises the question of whether or not students in the general and the vocational curricula received less or inferior course work in these three areas in 1980 than they did in 1972. If so, then the population shift between 1972 and 1980 from the academic to the general and vocational curricula has very serious consequences for allowing young adults to achieve their full potential.

In summary, these findings suggested that the major factor contributing to test score decline between 1972 and 1980 was a decreased academic emphasis in the educational process. The impact of this change in emphasis fell primarily on white and on upper- and middle-class students. Federal and state programs designed to strengthen basic skills in reading and mathematics appear to have prevented comparable score declines among low socioeconomic status Black students in vocabulary and reading and to have contributed to the increase in mathematics scores among this same group.

What Kinds of Policies Do These Findings Suggest?

National reports issued in 1983 and 1984 contained a wide range of recommendations designed to strengthen the educational process. They addressed the school curriculum; programs for special populations; college entrance requirements; performance standards for students; training of teachers; administrative leadership; fiscal support; and the proper role of local, state, and federal governments. Many states responded by raising high school graduation requirements and college admission standards, by requiring more testing of students, and by changing policies on the preparation and licensing of teachers. The findings of this study suggest that state policies should continue to be directed toward improving schools and toward equalizing access to educational opportunities for all students. In particular, these policies should address curriculum, course content, homework, and programs for special populations.

Curriculum. This study suggests that more course work in science, foreign languages, and mathematics contributes to higher scores on the kinds of vocabulary, reading, and mathematical skills measured by the NLS/HS&B test battery. However, policymakers must be sensitive to differences in course-taking behavior among students in different curricula. The course-taking patterns of students in the academic curriculum showed little change between 1972 and 1980. But significant numbers of students shifted into the general and vocational curricula where they took fewer new basics (English, mathematics, science, social studies, and computer science) than their academic counterparts did. Therefore, we suggest that schools increase the required number of courses in the new basics for non-academic students. These courses should not be provided at the expense of remedial work in reading and mathematics when it is needed. In addition, schools should provide more frequent opportunities for students to write and to participate in laboratory courses.

Course Content. Several recent reports have suggested that the content of textbooks and instructional materials be made more academically demanding. Since students in all curricular areas in this study were critical of the lack of academic emphasis in their course work and of the quality of their instruction, we suggest that course content and instructional methods be reviewed and upgraded, as necessary, to ensure more rigorous content.

Homework. Students in this study reported doing less homework in 1980 than in 1972, but students in the general and vocational curricula reported doing less homework and showed greater test score declines than did students in the academic program. Since data show a strong positive relationship between homework and achievement, we recommend that appropriate amounts of homework be assigned in all courses.

Programs for Special Populations. We recommend that the federal government, in cooperation with the states and with local school districts, continue to provide special programs for educationally and economically disadvantaged students, the handicapped, and language-minority students. A growing body of research findings has documented the relative improvement in achievement of Blacks and other disadvantaged students over the last decade. In this study test score declines for Black students were considerably below those of white students. This was particularly true for low SES Black students, who are the most likely beneficiaries of federal and state compensatory-education programs.

A CLOSER LOOK AT STUDENT ACHIEVEMENT

The study discussed above was constrained by several factors. First, it is cross-sectional rather than longitudinal. Because different groups of individuals and different schools are compared, it is impossible to determine in a rigorous manner the extent to which school factors contribute to individual growth over time. Second, limited information was collected on students and their schools, especially in 1972. As a consequence, the impact of factors such as school climate, after-school employment, and television watching on student achievement could not be determined. In addition, comparable data from the two years were not always available.

A second study, which used the HS&B Sophomore cohort data base, provided the opportunity for a closer look at the impact of school processes, student behaviors, and home influences on student achievement during the last two years of high school (Rock et al. 1985b). Students were tested in 1980 as sophomores and again in 1982 as seniors. This data base has several advantages:

1. Panel data provide information on the same individuals attending the same schools at two points in time.
2. The expanded sample provides better information on selected minority groups, most especially Hispanic subpopulations.
3. The expanded test battery measures achievement in science and writing as well as in vocabulary, reading, and mathematics. This test battery was the same at both points in time.
4. The expanded student and school questionnaires and the collection of high school transcripts for a large portion of the students provides a more comprehensive set of variables. In addition, comparable questions were asked of the students at both points in time.
5. Follow-up information on and testing of students who dropped out

Table 4.4
Changes in Tested Achievement Between Students' Sophomore and Senior Years: 1980–1982

Test	Mean sophomore	Mean senior	Estimated difference
Vocabulary	9.02	11.17	2.15
Reading	7.16	8.54	1.38
Mathematics	13.43	15.43	2.00
Science	9.27	10.23	0.96
Writing	8.92	10.61	1.69

of high school after their sophomore year provides an opportunity to estimate the effects of additional years of schooling on tested achievement.

This study, which focused on the determinants of growth in student achievement during the last two years of high school, found that students made significant gains in all tested areas—vocabulary, reading, mathematics, science, and writing—between their sophomore and senior years in high school. This growth in tested achievement is shown in table 4.4. These gains were observed for all racial and ethnic groups but they were greatest for students who: (1) enrolled in an academic curriculum, (2) attended a school with a strong academic emphasis and a positive school climate, and (3) took a large number of courses in the new basics. Table 4.5 shows the test score gains for major subgroups (sex, race and ethnicity, socioeconomic status, and curriculum).

Changes in Student Behaviors, Plans, Attitudes, and Values

Between their sophomore and senior years, students underwent a number of changes in their school-related behaviors, their educational and occupational plans, and their attitudes and values.

A significant number of students moved out of the general curriculum into the vocational or academic curricula during their last two years of high school. In their sophomore year 43 percent of the students who stayed in high school were enrolled in the general curriculum; by the senior year 33 percent of the students reported being in the general curriculum. The average high school student earned about 22 Carnegie Units in grades nine through twelve. The average number of units in the new basics ranged from 15.5 in the

Table 4.5

Test Score Gains from Students' Sophomore to Senior Years by Subgroups: 1980–1982

Subgroup	Vocabulary		Reading		Mathematics		Science		Writing	
	Gain	Effect size	Gain	Effect size	Gain	Effect size	Gain	Effect size	Gain	Effect size
Total	2.2*	0.4	1.4*	0.3	2.0*	0.2	1.0*	0.2	1.7*	0.3
Sex										
Male	2.0*	0.4	1.4*	0.3	2.3*	0.2	1.0*	0.2	1.6*	0.3
Female	2.3*	0.4	1.4*	0.3	1.7*	0.2	0.9*	0.2	1.7*	0.4
Race and ethnicity										
White	2.2*	0.4	1.4*	0.3	2.1*	0.2	0.9*	0.2	1.6*	0.4
Black	1.9*	0.4	1.1*	0.3	1.9*	0.2	0.9*	0.2	1.8*	0.4
Puerto Rican	2.1*	0.4	1.3	0.3	1.6	0.2	1.6*	0.3	3.0*	0.7
Mexican American	1.6*	0.3	1.3*	0.3	1.1	0.1	0.9*	0.2	1.8*	0.4
Asian American	2.3*	0.4	1.6*	0.3	2.9	0.3	1.7*	0.4	1.7*	0.4
American Indian	2.1*	0.4	1.3	0.3	1.1	0.1	0.8	0.2	1.7	0.3
Socioeconomic status										
Low	2.0*	0.4	1.3*	0.3	1.3*	0.1	0.9*	0.2	1.7*	0.4
Middle	2.2*	0.4	1.4*	0.3	1.9*	0.2	1.0*	0.2	1.7*	0.4
High	2.3*	0.5	1.5*	0.3	2.8*	0.3	0.9*	0.2	1.6*	0.4
Curriculum										
Academic	2.4*	0.5	1.6*	0.3	3.3*	0.3	1.1*	0.3	1.7*	0.4
General	2.1*	0.4	1.3*	0.3	1.4*	0.2	0.9*	0.2	1.7*	0.4
Vocational	1.9*	0.4	1.1*	0.3	0.7*	0.1	0.8*	0.2	1.7*	0.3

*Significant gains

academic curriculum to 12 in the general curriculum and 11 in the vocational curriculum. When remedial and functional-level courses (such as basic skills mathematics and functional biology), vocational mathematics and English, and ESL courses are excluded, academic students earned 13.7 units in the new basics as compared to 9.4 units for general curriculum students and 8.4 units for vocational curriculum students. Racial, ethnic, and gender differences in course taking were also found within each of the curricular areas. For example, males in the academic curriculum took 1.35 units of advanced mathematics (Algebra II, Geometry II, Trigonometry, Calculus, and so on), but females took only 1.14 units. White students in the academic curriculum took 1.32 units of advanced math, Black students took 0.73 units, and Hispanic students took 0.87 units.

The mean amount of homework done by students decreased slightly between the students' sophomore and senior years but averaged only about four hours a week at both points in time.

All types of school attendance problems (unexcused absences, tardiness, cutting classes, and suspension or probation) increased during the last two years of high school, but serious disciplinary problems decreased. Students were more likely to do paid work as seniors than as sophomores and to work more hours each week. Attitudes toward school became more positive. Students watched less television as seniors (approximately two hours a day) than as sophomores (three hours a day).

There was a downward shift in students' post-high school educational plans between the sophomore and senior years. The percentage of students planning to attend a four-year college decreased from 41 to 35 percent, while the percentage planning to enter an academic program in a two-year college rose from 6 to 10 percent. There was also a small increase in the proportion of students planning to work full-time when they completed high school. Long-term occupational aspirations of the students also changed. The percentage of students aspiring to high-level professional occupations decreased, while the proportion aspiring to lower-level professional occupations and to technical and managerial jobs increased.

The students held a more positive self-concept as seniors than they had held as sophomores, and they also showed an increased sense of control over their lives. Students placed less importance as seniors than they had as sophomores on altruistic values. Students were also less likely as seniors than they were as sophomores to hold sex-role stereotyped attitudes.

Factors Affecting Test Score Gain

Different analytic approaches as well as different units of analysis were used to identify those factors that affect achievement gains. First, path models were used to relate demographics, educational support at home, and students' behaviors in school to gains in tested achievement. A school-level analysis was directed toward answering two questions: (1) What are the school processes that explain variations in achievement gains between schools? and (2) Do members of different socioeconomic groups or different racial and ethnic groups have equal access to these school processes?

Demographics.   Growth was observed in all achievement for students of all racial and ethnic groups. White students gained relatively more than did Black and Hispanic students in vocabulary and in science. No practical differences in relative adjusted gains were found between racial and ethnic groups in reading, mathematics, and writing. Males gained relatively more than did females in mathematics and science. Females gained more than did males in writing. No practical sex differences were found in gains in vocabulary and in reading.

Home Educational Support.   Mothers' educational aspirations for their children had a positive direct impact on gains in vocabulary, mathematics, and writing, while nonschool learning opportunities (such as travel, trips to museums, and so on) had a small positive direct impact on gains in vocabulary and in science. In general, home educational support indirectly affected achievement gains by influencing students' behaviors in school, which, in turn, had direct impacts on gains.

Attitudes.   Locus of control—the belief that one's success or failure depends on one's own initiatives—was positively related to gains in vocabulary, reading, and writing.

School Characteristics and School Processes.   Several school processes and school-related behaviors of students contributed to achievement gains:

1. *The academic emphasis of the school.* Gains were greater in schools where a large percentage of students were enrolled in the academic

curriculum and in schools that offered a large number of courses in the new basics.

2. *The climate of the school.* Students showed larger achievement gains in schools that reported fewer disciplinary problems and where lack of parental interest in the school was not considered a problem.

3. *Students' ratings of their schools.* Achievement gains were greater in those schools with higher average student ratings of teachers and of instruction.

4. *Course exposure.* In each achievement area, the number of courses that a student took beyond the remedial or functional level was positively related to test score gains.

5. *Homework.* Other things being equal, students who did more homework showed greater test score gains.

6. *Curriculum.* Students enrolled in the academic curriculum showed greater gains than did students enrolled in the general curriculum, and both groups did better than students in the vocational curriculum did. This is due primarily to variations in course-taking behavior by students in the different curricula.

Policy Implications

This study of students over time supported the findings of the cross-sectional study that schools do make a difference. Curriculum choice and course-taking behavior were strongly related to test scores, tested achievement was affected by the amount of homework done by students, and the academic emphasis of a school, school climate, and the students' rating of the quality of instruction were related to student achievement. Other things being equal, these school factors had a similar impact on achievement for all groups of students, whether white or minority, male or female, enrolled in a public or in a Catholic school. However, these positive school processes are more likely to be found in a Catholic than in a public school. Finally, both studies showed that schools have been especially effective in reducing differential achievement gains in reading and in mathematics, content areas that are most sensitive to formal schooling. It appears that programs emphasizing basic skills in reading and, to a somewhat lesser extent, in mathematics have been effective in reducing the achievement gap between white and minority students and between students of different socioeconomic levels.

Unfortunately, access to those school processes that affect gains is not equal. Although access within school does not appear to favor one racial or ethnic group over another, students who attend schools with a low SES student population are exposed to a different set of educational opportunities than are students who attend school with a high SES population. Black and other minority students are nearly four times as likely to attend these low SES schools as are white students.

These findings suggest that:

1. All students should receive solid preparation in the new basics— English, mathematics, science, history and other social studies, and computer science. In addition, students entering high school at an educational disadvantage should also receive remedial services.
2. All students should have an equal opportunity to take advanced academic offerings, such as honors and Advanced Placement courses, calculus or other advanced mathematics courses, specialized science courses, and so on. These opportunities could be provided in one of three ways: (1) Curricular offerings could be enriched in all schools. (2) In large communities, magnet schools could be created to provide specialized academic programs. (3) Students could receive financial support to attend those schools that already offer advanced academic courses. The first of these approaches may not be cost-effective. The second and third approaches mean that only a limited number of students would have access to advanced academic programs. Regardless of the educational program offered, the best learning conditions and largest achievement gains are found in schools that set high expectations for their students.
3. Policies should be developed to strengthen the home educational support system, parental interest in the school and in the student's educational progress, and in providing students with a place to study and opportunities for nonschool learning experiences. Policies should also be developed to help students develop the understanding that they can influence their future through their own educational efforts.

WHAT'S AHEAD

The use of large data bases, such as those employed in this research, as a thermometer to measure the health of American education and to develop educational policy continues. Recent reports indicate that scores on the Scholastic Aptitude Tests and on the National Assessment of Educational Progress tests have begun to rise. The nine-point increase in SAT scores in 1984 was the largest since 1963, which was the year before a seventeen-year decline began. The NAEP Reading Report Card indicates that students at ages nine, thirteen, and seventeen were better readers in 1984 than in 1971.

What are the reasons for these changes? One of the most likely causes is the changes in curriculum standards that have been recently mandated by states and by local education agencies. By the end of 1984, forty-three states had raised their high school graduation standards (*Education Week* 1985) and sixteen states mandated or proposed more stringent standards for admission to state institutions of higher education (Goertz and Johnson 1985). In the latter case, these changes include high school course work requirements that exceed what is required for high school graduation.

Future research with large data bases will help us understand the consequences of these changes. The National Center for Education Statistics is planning to fund a new collection of data, to be called the National Education Longitudinal Study of 1988 (NELS:88). This work will involve obtaining base-year data from two national cohorts: (1) individuals who will be eighth graders in 1988, and (2) individuals who will be first-time postsecondary students in 1988. As has been the case with the NLS-72 and the HS&B cohorts, follow-up surveys will be conducted at regular intervals. According to NCES, the purpose of NELS:88 is to track: (1) the critical transitions experienced by young adults as they progress through high school to postsecondary education and into the world of work, and (2) the transitions experienced by individuals attending postsecondary education programs and entering (or reentering) the world of work. Follow-up surveys of the HS&B students were done in 1984, and these data are now available for analysis. They should reveal the effects that high school programs and policies of the early 1980s have had on postsecondary education and on employment. This information and that to be collected in NELS:88 will give us benchmarks for studying educational changes in the next twenty years.

REFERENCES

Alexander, K. L., and Eckland, B. K. "Contexual Effects in the High School Attainment Process." *American Sociological Review* 41 (1975): 963–980.

Alexander, K. L., and Eckland, B. K. "High School Context and College Selectivity: Institutional Constraints in Educational Stratification." *Social Forces* 56 (1977): 166–188.

Alwin, D. F., and Otto, L. B. "High School Context Effects on Aspirations." *Sociology of Education* 50 (1977): 259–272.

Anderson, C. S. "The Search for School Climate: A Review of the Research." *Review of Educational Research* 52 (1982): 368–420.

Bridge, R. G.; Judd, C. M.; and Moock, P. R. *The Determination of Educational Outcomes: The Impact of Families, Peers, Teachers, and Schools.* Cambridge, Mass.: Ballinger, 1979.

Brown, B. W., and Saks, D. H. "The Production and Distribution of Cognitive Skills Within Schools." *Journal of Political. Economy* 83 (1975): 571–593.

Cohen, E., and Millman, S. D. *Input-Output Analysis in Public Education.* Cambridge, Mass.: Ballinger, 1975.

Coleman, J. S.; Campbell, E. G.; Hobson, C. J.; McPartland, J. M.; Mood, A. M.; Weinfeld, F. D.; and York, R. L. *Equality of Educational Opportunity.* Washington, D. C.: Government Printing Office, 1966.

Coleman, J. S.; Hoffer, T.; and Kilgore, S. "Public and Private Schools: A Report to the National Center of Education Statistics by the National Opinion Research Center." University of Chicago, NORC, draft, 1981.

College Board. "On Further Examination." Report of the Advisory Panel on Scholastic Aptitude Test Score Decline. New York: College Entrance Examination Board, 1977.

Education Week. "States Launching Barrage of Initiatives, Survey Finds." February 6, 1985.

Glassman, N. S., and Biniaminov, I. "Input-Output Analyses of Schools." *Review of Educational Research* 51 (1981): 509–539.

Goertz, M., and Johnson, L. "State Policies for Admission to Higher Education." College Board Report No. 85–1. New York: College Entrance Examination Board, 1985.

Hanushek, E. A. "Conceptual and Empirical Issues in the Estimation of Educational Production Functions." *The Journal of Human Resources* 14 (1979): 351–388.

Hauser, R. M. "Schools and the Stratification Process." *American Journal of Sociology* 74 (1969): 587–611.

Heyns, B. L. *Summer Learning and the Effects of Schooling.* New York: Academic Press, 1978.

Hoffer, T.; Greeley, A. M.; and Coleman, J. S. *Achievement Growth in Public and Catholic Schools.* Mimeographed. Chicago: National Opinion Research Center, 1984.

Jencks, C. S.; Smith, M.; Acland, H.; Bane, M. J.; Cohen, D.; Gintis, H.; Heyns, B.; and Michelson, S. *Inequality: A Reassessment of the Effect of Family and Schooling in America.* New York: Basic Books, 1972.

McDill, E. L.; and Rigsby, L. C. *Structure and Process in Secondary Schools: The Academic*

Impact of Educational Climates. Baltimore, Md.: The Johns Hopkins University Press, 1973.

Mosteller, F., and Moynihan, D. P., eds. *On "Equality of Educational Opportunity": Papers Deriving from the Harvard University Faculty Seminar on the Coleman Report.* New York: Random House, 1972.

Murnane, R. J. "Evidence, Analysis and Unanswered Questions." *Harvard Educational Review* 51: 4 (1981): 483–489.

Rock, D. A.; Ekstrom, R. B.; Goertz, M. E.; Pollack, J.; and Hilton, T. L. "Factors Associated with the Decline of Test Scores of High School Seniors, 1972 to 1980." Washington, D.C.: Center for Statistics, CS 85-127, 1985. (a)

Rock, D. A.; Ekstrom, R. B.; Goertz, M. E.; and Pollack, J. "Determinants of Achievement Gain in High School." Report under review by the National Center for Education Statistics, 1985. (b)

Summers, A. A., and Wolfe, B. L. "Which School Resources Help Learning? Efficiency and Equity in Philadelphia Public Schools." (ED 139847). *IRCD Bulletin* 11 (1979): 1–15.

5

Federal and State Policy

Brenda J. Turnbull

Federal and state governments have taken many stabs at the task of reforming elementary and secondary schooling over the past twenty years. Despite the handicap of having no direct responsibility for what goes on in most classrooms, government agencies have tried to find and employ various kinds of leverage over the schools. They have identified and sought to correct a wide range of problems, notably the schools' neglect of particular types of students and shortcomings in the average measured achievement of all students. Policy initiatives in education have both followed and helped to shape professional trends in the field.

I discuss here some broad trends in educational policy since 1965, when the federal government became involved in educational reform in a major way. For convenience, I will divide this period into three chronological stages that roughly correspond to the decades of the 1960s, the 1970s, and the 1980s. In the 1960s a major policy problem was simply to establish a federal role in education, especially to improve equality of educational opportunity. That role underwent enormous elaboration and refinement in the 1970s, with effects that were felt at the state and local levels. Both the ends and the means of educational policy began to shift strikingly in the 1980s as both state and federal governments have sought new policy levers that will help them improve the quality of the schools.

My chief focus in this chapter is on federal policy, which has been the most volatile sector of policy initiatives over most of the twenty-year period, but I also discuss the state initiatives that have become more prominent on the policy scene in recent years. I discuss developments over time in the problems policymakers have recognized, the levers they have tried to use to solve these problems, and what has been learned about the effects of policy on practice.

ESTABLISHING A FEDERAL PRESENCE

The Elementary and Secondary Education Act (ESEA) of 1965, part of the Great Society legislation that swept through Congress at that time, was crafted to overcome the obstacles that had previously kept the federal government removed from what went on in schools (Bailey and Mosher 1968). Although designed to redirect resources and ultimately improve practice, the law was hedged with provisions that limited federal control over educational content. It satisfied both supporters and opponents of aid to religious schooling by offering funds to serve the students in private schools, not the schools themselves. It gave aid to segregated school systems, but the purpose was to help the low-achieving students in the poorest areas.

These compromises permitted federal funds to move into five areas of activity in education. Title I, by far the largest ESEA program in dollar terms, initially put about $1 billion into school districts for projects that would benefit the lowest-achieving students. Title II authorized funds for purchasing equipment and library resources, continuing a purpose that had been part of federal educational policy since the 1950s. Title III supported innovative local projects. Titles IV and V were efforts to build outside support structures for local schooling by establishing networks of educational research and development institutions and by strengthening state departments of education. Over the long term, then, the federal program developed in ESEA would heighten the schools' attention to underserved students and innovation and would give them better internal and external resources to draw on.

School administrators, surveyed soon after ESEA was enacted, generally believed the federal government had acceded to their wish for general aid (Bailey and Mosher 1968). They were not accustomed to the idea of receiving outside funds earmarked for the benefit of particular students. In the early years few state education agencies had the inclination to enforce compliance with this novel form of intergovernmental aid, and they were only slowly adding the staff capacity that would eventually permit them to do so (Berke and Kirst, 1972; Murphy 1973). Thus the early implementation of ESEA showed the effects of new resources on the education system but few noticeable changes in the direction of the schools.

Nevertheless, the idea of enacting special programs for special population groups began to catch on. The Bilingual Education Act was added to ESEA in 1968; it was funded at a lower level than Title I but directed funds toward the education of those students with limited English-speaking skills.

An advocacy group's report at the end of the 1960s triggered a legislative and administrative response that had lasting effects; it established the federal government as a definer and enforcer of procedures for school districts to follow. The policy embodied in Title I derived a major boost from this report, *Title I of ESEA: Is It Helping Poor Children?* (Martin and McClure 1969). The report documented local abuses such as spending the money for swimming pools, band uniforms, and air conditioners for administrators' offices.

The amendments to ESEA made in 1970 set the tone for a tougher federal role. The new law required school districts to put Title I funds into the parts of the district with the highest levels of poverty. It also introduced a new mechanism for local accountability—a requirement for advisory councils composed of parents of Title I children.

The executive branch of government, taking a more aggressive posture than before, increased its scrutiny and enforcement of local compliance. The number of Title I audits doubled in 1970. Parallel with the increased auditing, the federal program office stepped up its monitoring reviews and by the end of 1971 had visited all fifty states. At the same time, the United States Office of Education (USOE) began to seek compliance in a different way—by encouraging state and local staff to view adherence to federal goals as a professional duty. As Richard Jung and Michael Kirst (1980) describe it, USOE officials "actually invented the title of 'State Title I Coordinator' and began bombarding these mythical figures with letters and bulletins and inviting them to regional meetings where Title I regulations and program materials were discussed, modified, and disseminated" (p. 25).

During the 1970s the federal government continued and extended its use of all these approaches to increasing compliance with its programs. Legislative requirements proliferated, monitoring and en- forcement continued at relatively high levels, and federal officials encouraged their state and local counterparts to think of themselves as part of vertical networks of program managers who should act independently of the educational agencies that nominally employed them. We turn now to an examination of these policy strategies and their effects, along with an analysis of the gradual increase in states' education initiatives.

Proliferating Program Structures

The original ESEA legislation was joined by a host of other federal and state programs aimed at specific, categorical purposes. This hodge-podge of overlapping special-purpose programs reflected a series of federal and state policy initiatives that used different mechanisms to meet different goals, with no particular pattern governing the choice of mechanisms. At the most general level, the policy aim was to use the carrot of money and the stick of regulations to induce schools to serve special groups or purposes. One preferred federal strategy was to earmark funds; a variety of federal requirements were used to induce local school districts to layer these funds on top of those they would ordinarily spend for the regular school program. Another strategy was to mandate services, or at least require nondiscrimination, while partial payment for the cost of meeting the mandate was offered. Meanwhile, the states not only used these approaches but also devised their own funding formulas to direct more funds to districts, schools, or pupils with special needs. Some states also enacted service mandates or planning requirements.

I discuss here the sources of these program strategies, some of the specific forms they took, and the lessons about program implementation that were learned by the end of the decade. I begin by describing the major program for the handicapped that continues to represent one cornerstone of federal and state educational policy.

Bringing the States into Line: P. L. 94–142

Although Title I has been a model for other federal and state legislation in many respects, few other programs have gone so far in following the assumption that they provide the only special service for their target population. The federal strategy for serving another major target group, the handicapped, developed quite differently because several states had already made special provisions for this group.

Advocacy groups for handicapped children were active in both federal and state capitals in the early 1970s. Parents and professionals were concerned that the high cost of serving these children, along with a lingering social stigma, resulted in denying services altogether or providing services in segregated, inadequate settings. Legislation in some states began to require that districts identify and serve these students. In Massachusetts, for example, a 1972 law mandated that districts provide educationally effective programs for handicapped students, placing them in the regular classroom whenever possible.

Once laws like this were on the books in several states, it made little sense for the federal government to provide an add-on program like Title I to support extra services. Instead, P. L. 94–142, the Education for All Handicapped Children Act, passed in 1974, charged all states with ensuring "a free, appropriate public education" for handicapped children. The states that already had mandates of their own would simply have to make technical amendments conforming to the federal law; those that did not yet have mandates would have to enact them in order to receive funds.[1]

To a greater extent than previous legislation, P. L. 94–142 brought the states into partnership with federal educational policy. However, most states were forcibly brought on board, and there was widespread dismay over the financing arrangements that resulted from the new law. Accustomed to Title I, in which the federal government picked up the full cost of special services, state and local officials objected to the fact that federal funding under P. L. 94–142 came nowhere near meeting the cost of the mandate. This law therefore stands as a mixture of a service program and a civil rights mandate.

Building Blocks of Federal Policy in the 1970s

From the mid-1970s until the end of the decade, developments in federal educational policy consisted of refining the basic policy instruments already in place. These can be analytically divided into several groups: fiscal controls, requirements dealing with program design, oversight mechanisms, and sanctions for noncompliance. Together, they made up the federal role that state and local education agencies

---

1. New Mexico, alone among the states, has chosen to decline the federal funds available under this law. However, federal civil rights laws have compelled the state to follow procedures that are virtually identical to those required in P.L. 94-142, and so the effect of its nonparticipation is very slight.

faced—and because they remain major elements of the current federal role, they are worth outlining briefly here.

Fiscal controls begin with the eligibility criteria determining which students may receive services. P. L. 94–142 went farthest in specifying the procedures for diagnosis and consultation that would result in a student's eligibility for services, but Title I was also quite specific about ways of identifying the parts of the district with above-average poverty and, within those areas, the students with the greatest educational need. The Bilingual Education Act was amended in 1978 to include a requirement that projects test their students every two years and continue serving only those who are not yet proficient in English.

A set of other fiscal controls was designed in the belief that school districts should provide a stable base of services for all students, including those with special needs, and add special federal funds on top of this base. The controls were designed to prevent funding recipients from substituting federal aid for money they would have spent anyway. For example, Title I, the Vocational Education Act, the Bilingual Education Act, and P. L. 94–142 all required that federal funds "supplement and not supplant" the funds that a district would otherwise devote to the target group. A more far-reaching requirement, unique to Title I, was "comparability," which in effect exerted control over state and local funds by specifying that the expenditure of these funds must be equal in the schools with and without Title I services.

Probably the strongest federal policy instrument in the area of program design has been the guarantee of nondiscrimination that civil rights laws offer to racial minorities, language minorities, handicapped students, and girls. Students in these groups may not be denied benefits, excluded from program participation, or subjected to discrimination.

Another influential program-design requirement is the needs assessment mandated under P. L. 94–142, which must involve certain types of personnel and must give dissatisfied parents a right of appeal. The process is to culminate in an individualized education program (IEP) that spells out educational goals for the student and commits the school district to provide the associated resources. Other federal programs also require needs assessments, but the procedures are less elaborate.

The federal government oversees some programs directly, and in the 1970s it made an effort to enlist state departments of education in this function as well. For instance, the 1978 amendments to Title I increased the administrative funds for state agencies while requiring them to do more in reviewing applications and monitoring local program operations. State-level reviewing and monitoring of applications were also required in vocational education and the education of the handicapped.

A critical element in oversight has been the work of audit agencies at the federal and state levels. While relatively few dollars are actually paid back to Washington as a result of practices discovered through audits, the fear of audit problems (especially local headlines charging a district with "misuse of federal funds") is a powerful incentive for districts to follow federal controls strictly.

Another type of oversight that the federal government encouraged in the 1970s was scrutiny by those affected by local programs, such as parents. The parent councils that Title I required and the consultation with individual parents that P. L. 94–142 required represented federal efforts to empower parents in their dealings with the schools. In the same vein, many federal policymakers believed that by requiring evaluations of local programs they could expose program weaknesses to scrutiny and correction. Since federal and state governments do not punish districts for poor project performance, the chief hope for benefit from evaluation rested at the local level. Evaluation requirements appeared in most laws and were increasingly tightened over the course of the decade.

For all the elaborateness of the other instruments of federal influence, the instruments available for punishing or rewarding states or school districts have been surprisingly limited. The federal government has the authority to terminate funding but has seldom used it. The use of this sanction denies federal resources to the intended beneficiaries of a program—that is, a state or district that failed to serve the handicapped adequately would receive no more funds for the handicapped. Accordingly, although the threat of losing funds hangs heavy over local decision makers, actual losses are very rare.

Proliferating Requirements and Conflicting Signals

By the end of the decade it was not uncommon for school buildings to receive both federal and state funding to serve each of three special populations: low-achieving students, handicapped students, and students with limited English skills. Vocational education, heavily supported by state and federal funds, included special provisions for serving these groups as well. Nearly all school districts received special federal funds for instructional materials and equipment, and many competed successfully for federal grants (administered by states) that supported innovative projects or for special desegregation assistance that came directly from the federal level. Networks for information dissemination and technical assistance—specializing by target group, function, or both (for example, assistance in evaluating Title I programs)—sprang up with federal and state support.

Some states followed the federal lead by enacting categorical programs for students with special needs, complete with their own fiscal controls, design requirements, and compliance and enforcement mechanisms. Typically these differed in some respects from the federal initiatives. Only Wisconsin, for example, targeted its compensatory-education program according to poverty. Other states enacted such programs but aimed them at low-achieving students whatever the poverty level of their families or schools. Many states with large Hispanic populations enacted special programs for students with limited English skills, but unlike the federal program these often permitted or encouraged instruction in English as a second language rather than a bilingual approach.

Many states approached the issue of special students' needs through their formulas for school finance, which were widely reformed during the 1970s. Weights were assigned to students with each type of special need, with the result that the funds a district received from the state would be greater if it had a larger proportion of students in the target groups identified by the state. In contrast to the categorical-program approach, such funding formulas did not require that districts track the weighted funds separately or adopt particular program designs.

A school district or school participating in more than one federal program faced a huge array of requirements. Since each funding program presented local educators with a set of administrative demands and programmatic constraints, the sum total was not only a large volume of paperwork but also, in some cases, conflicting signals about educational strategies (Turnbull, Smith, and Ginsburg 1981). For example, P. L. 94–142 encouraged schools to serve handicapped students in the "least restrictive environment," namely the regular classroom, whenever possible. Similarly, the Office for Civil Rights was working to reduce the isolation of minority groups within schools. However, the fiscal controls in Title I encouraged segregation of students. The "supplement, not supplant" requirement, mandating services over and above the regular school program, resulted in the widespread use of "pull-out" instruction, or removing students from the regular classroom for instruction in special settings by special teachers. While the Title I law and regulations stated that pull-out arrangements were not required, this program design did make it easier for schools to prove that they were complying with the fiscal controls.

An issue that began to grow in importance during the 1970s was the fit between federal and state programs. Although P. L. 94–142 took account of state laws for handicapped students, it still superimposed a federal program design over the designs embodied in state laws. The other federal programs did even less to accommodate to state requirements. In fact, states that mandated remedial services for students who scored poorly on minimum-competency tests found in the mid-1970s that they faced problems in complying with the Title I fiscal controls, which were based on the assumption that schools would do nothing special for the Title I target population. These states, whose own efforts on behalf of low-achieving students theoretically should have won them some cooperation from Washington, faced the paradoxical problem that serving these students with Title I funds could pose supplanting difficulties.

Effects of the Policies of the 1970s

While most federal and state policy initiatives reflected an apparent belief that tighter regulatory control could produce predictable local results, research on program implementation has suggested that the effects are not so simple. Because of the presence of multiple local decision makers, local disagreement with an outside policy, or simply the press of other responsibilities, school districts respond in varied and sometimes disappointing ways to outside policy initiatives (Berman and McLaughlin 1978; Elmore 1980; and Farrar, DeSanctis, and Cohen 1980).

Research conducted in the 1970s showed that teachers and others at the local level have an enormous capacity for determining the actual workings of centrally conceived programs. They change the prescribed procedures in order to simplify their work and to give students the services they consider most effective; often these two rationales are mixed. For example, elementary school teachers often place limits on the number of special services for which students can be pulled out of their classrooms, although federal and state laws supposedly ensure that students have access to all special services for which they qualify. The teachers do this not only to make their own lives easier, with fewer interruptions, but also to give students more continuity of instruction within the school day.

Although implementation research brought the news that the details of program implementation were far from predictable, research also showed some major, long-term effects resulting from federal and state policy initiatives. Federal policies stimulated new actions and capacities at the state level; both federal and state policies had profound effects on the conduct of education at the local level.

State education agencies, a target of the original ESEA and many subsequent federal policies, did change in response to the federal encouragement and pressure (Moore, Goertz, and Hartle 1983). They grew in size, typically by supplementing their state-funded positions with an equal number of federally funded ones. They shifted the balance of their work, cutting back on assistance in curriculum areas while increasing their efforts in monitoring districts and helping them comply with the procedures mandated by federal programs. New chief state school officers, more interested in taking an activist stance on the behalf of special-needs groups, replaced more low-key managers in many states.

Because of this change in the capacity and character of state education agencies, federal policy had effects at the state level even when state legislatures did not choose to act in concert with federal goals. Parts of the state education agencies operated something like franchises for federal programs, although their approaches also reflected state priorities and traditions.

At the local level, despite much variation in the specifics of program implementation, several new ideas about the delivery of educational services took hold during the 1970s. (The following discussion is based on findings reported in Knapp and associates [1983].) First, the students who were intended to benefit from outside programs and mandates did receive special services, tailored in some degree to their needs, from staff who generally had special training; moreover, these services were generally concentrated rather than being spread around to all students. Second, the provision of these special services forced many schools and districts to grapple with the problem of instructional fragmentation—instruction in several settings by several different people during a single day—and to devise local solutions to it (commonly by limiting students' access to multiple programs). Third, systematic procedures for planning, needs assessment, and evaluation became far more widespread than they would have been in the absence of outside programs and mandates; although these procedures were not universally applauded, there was a general sense in districts and schools that they represented good professional practice. Finally, local staff who took the role of advocate for special-needs students gained power, often because their detailed knowledge of outside program requirements strengthened their hand in local policy debates.

What accounted for these broad-gauge effects? Several characteristics of federal and state policies seemed to make a difference (Knapp et al. 1983). One was the provision of funds, both for the obvious reason that the funds paid for special services and also because local administrators and teachers were willing to honor their side of the bargain by following the requirements that were accompanied by money. Another was that the mere fact of enacting a law served to call attention to an educational problem and to legitimize the views of local advocates for a special-needs population. Specific requirements were important, not so much because they would be scrupulously followed everywhere, but because they conveyed a message that there were boundaries around acceptable practice—for example, that earmarked funds could not be used to serve every student in a school. Finally, the existence of sanctions, whether or not they were often invoked, exerted powerful leverage on local behavior.

Another important finding emerging from implementation research at the end of the 1970s was that programs tend to settle in over time. While the introduction of a new requirement, such as the development of IEPs for handicapped students, caused consternation and problems initially, state and local staff were able to work out ways of making virtually any requirement manageable and adjusting their other routines around it. Thus, although the overall array of federal and state programs was undeniably cumbersome, most local staff insisted that they could make the whole structure work to the benefit of students.

Nevertheless, a change in overall federal policy and a backlash against the effort to prescribe educational decisions from the top down produced a change in federal policy in the 1980s. At about the same time, concerns about educational quality took hold in the states, setting the stage for new types of policy initiatives at that level. I discuss these developments next.

THE 1980s: "IN SEARCH OF EXCELLENCE"

For followers of the federal and state roles in education over the two previous decades, the policy changes of the 1980s came as a shock. Although there had been a general sense that some of the confusion associated with multiple programs and mandates needed to be sorted out, few observers would have predicted that either the federal or state governments would adopt new policy goals for education or that Washington would be so eager to take a back seat to state initiatives. Nevertheless, the quest for excellence in education, as in business, began to absorb the nation to a surprising extent.

Changes in the Federal Categorical Programs

In response to a sweeping proposal from the Reagan administration for collapsing most federal aid to education into a small number of block grants, Congress enacted the Education Consolidation and Improvement Act (ECIA), which took more modest steps toward program simplification. Chapter 1 of the act replaced the old Title I, retaining some of its overall structure but reducing its length from forty-eight pages to six. The fiscal controls were eased; requirements for parental involvement diminished dramatically; and state responsibilities were cut back. The net effect was to give districts somewhat fewer requirements to comply with and much less scrutiny of their compliance. However, old hands in federal aid at all levels of government noted that the program would still be subject to fiscal audits, and some early indications are that their attention to compliance with requirements has not lessened much (Darling-Hammond and Marks 1983).

ECIA had another part, Chapter 2, which gave districts a formula-based block grant to spend on virtually any purpose related to educational improvement. Although these grants are small, they are popular locally. They have supported the purchase of computer hardware and software along with a host of other instructional programs and purchases (Knapp and Blakely 1986). Chapter 2 signals a new federal role in education, that of providing support for locally determined purposes rather than advancing specific federal goals. Indeed, perhaps the local determination of program purposes has itself become an important federal goal.

The Reform Reports and Policy Responses

Soon after ECIA signaled at least a modest change in federal education policy, a spate of reports on the quality of the nation's schools changed the terms of policy discussion in both Washington and the state capitals. Public attention was captured by the conclusion that the schools were failing, especially in imparting advanced skills to the most talented students, but also in improving average performance across all students. Providing more and better instruction was defined as the goal. The needs of low-achieving or other special-needs students, while not disappearing from the policy landscape, were suddenly dwarfed in public importance.

The states took the most prominent role in responding to these reports for several reasons. First, they have the responsibility for educating all students—in contrast to the federal government, which has attended more selectively to special target groups. Second, the Reagan administration identified education as an area in which it would have few initiatives, both because it preferred to devolve authority to the states and in an effort to save scarce federal revenues. Third, a number of governors saw education as an issue in which they could make their mark, benefiting both their citizens and their own careers.

Often spurred on by governors, state legislatures have recently enacted many reform packages for education. These use both old and new policy instruments. Teacher certification, school accreditation, and graduation requirements, which are time-honored parts of the state role, have been vehicles for many state efforts to upgrade educational standards. Competency testing, which became prominent on the state education scene in the 1970s, has been another popular avenue for reform. In each of these areas, legislatures have demanded that students, teachers, or school buildings demonstrate higher levels of performance or suffer the consequences. Some states have also experimented with new approaches such as testing the basic skills of practicing teachers and establishing career ladders for teachers.

It is noteworthy that in these recent reforms the states virtually never use the policy instruments that the federal government employed heavily in the 1970s. The states are not creating add-on programs that necessitate fiscal controls. They are relatively unconcerned with specifying programmatic procedures such as needs assessment. Large-scale monitoring and enforcement are absent as well. The new state reforms instead tend to set standards for performance and rely on local will and knowledge to ensure that these standards are met.

In examining these reforms, it is important to remember that they arise out of a particular type of diagnosis of educational problems. Unlike the reforms popular in the 1960s and 1970s, they rest on a conviction that the overall performance of the schools is falling short, not on a special worry about particular types of students. Consequently the new reforms seek more comprehensive improvements in educational practice, and they reflect less concern about the worst-case consequences for individual students.

It is also important to point out the considerable differences among states in several respects: their political commitment to reform, the financial resources they are able (let alone willing) to commit to education, and the capacity of the state education agencies. While some of these agencies have built impressive capacity over the past twenty years, they vary greatly in the size and skills of their staffs. They also tend to reflect the nature of their mission over those years, which has been to create, monitor, and enforce regulations. Turning them into providers of technical assistance in educational practice will be no simple task, although local districts could use some outside assistance with the challenge of upgrading their practice.

While it is too early to assess the implementation or effects of state policy initiatives of the 1980s, their very existence represents a dramatic change in the policy landscape of education. The federal government has played a passive role in these initiatives, once its commission on excellence delivered its report. In addition to this change in the relative prominence of federal and state actors, there has been a real change in the terms of the conversation about educational policy. Adding special programs and tightening their design through regulation is no longer the issue; performance is.

CONCLUSIONS

Between 1965 and 1985 educational policy has evolved and changed. Once a federal role was established, which centered on improving the opportunities of special-needs groups, a decade of elaboration of that role ensued. Program requirements proliferated, professional networks spanning all levels of government came into being, and local educators did their best to make sense of the ensuing administrative tangles. Then in the 1980s both the goals and the mechanisms of policy changed, at least to some degree. Improving performance became a critical goal, and the legislative establishment of standards for teachers and students became the most talked-about mechanisms. The programs of the 1960s and 1970s still exist, however. They have reached a level of maturity and currently appear likely to remain part of local educational practice.

Research on the implementation of federal and state policies suggests that the long-term effects of outside policy on local practice are both visible and important. Although there is much variation in the local response to the details of any new policy, consistent trends can be discerned over time. The reforms of the 1960s and 1970s have left footprints such as the widespread use of specialized instruction for small groups of students and the systematic procedures often used to track students' needs and progress. More recent reforms may result in even more measurement of accomplishments and perhaps in greater creation of incentives for improvement.

REFERENCES

Bailey, S. K., and Mosher, E. K. *ESEA: The Office of Education Administers a Law.* Syracuse, N.Y.: Syracuse University Press, 1968.

Berke, J. S., and Kirst, M. W. *Federal Aid to Education: Who Benefits? Who Governs?* Lexington, Mass.: D. C. Heath, 1972.

Berman, P., and McLaughlin, M. W. *Federal Programs Supporting Educational Change, Volume 7: Factors Affecting Implementation and Continuation.* Santa Monica, Calif.: Rand Corporation, 1978.

Darling-Hammond, L., and Marks, E. L. *The New Federalism in Education: State Responses to the 1981 Education Consolidation and Improvement Act.* Santa Monica, Calif.: Rand Corporation, 1983.

Elmore, R. F. *Complexity and Control: What Legislators and Administrators Can Do About Implementing Public Policy.* Washington, D.C.: National Institute of Education, 1980.

Farrar, E.; DeSanctis, J. E., and Cohen, D. K. "The Lawn Party: The Evolution of Federal Programs in Local Settings." *Phi Delta Kappan* 62 (1980): 161–171.

Jung, R. K., and Kirst, M. W. "The Utility of a Longitudinal View of Program Implementation." *Educational Evaluation and Policy Analysis* 2 (1980): 17–36.

Knapp, M. S., and Blakely, C. *Local Operations of the Education Block Grant.* Menlo Park, Calif.: SRI International, 1986.

Knapp, M. S.; Stearns, M. S.; Turnbull, B. J.; David, J. L.; and Peterson, S. M. "Cumulative Effects at the Local Level." *Education and Urban Society* 15 (1983): 479–499.

Martin, R., and McClure, P. *Title I of ESEA: Is It Helping Poor Children?* Washington, D.C.: Washington Research Project and NAACP Legal Defense and Education Fund, Inc., 1969.

Moore, M. T.; Goertz, M. E.; and Hartle, T. W. "Interaction of Federal and State Programs." *Education and Urban Society* 16 (1983): 452–478.

Murphy, J. T. "The Education Bureaucracies Implement Novel Policy: The Politics of Title I of ESEA. In *Policy and Politics in America*, edited by A. P. Sindler. Boston: Little, Brown, 1973.

Turnbull, B. J.; Smith, M. S.; and Ginsburg, A. L. "Issues for a New Administration: The Federal Role in Education." *American Journal of Education* 89 (1981): 396–427.

PART II

Views from the Disciplines

6

On Social Psychology

Doris R. Entwisle

What do we know in 1985 about the social psychology of education that we did not know in 1965? For me this is a hard question because I am accustomed to asking opposite questions: What don't we know? What are the gaps in knowledge that we need to research? Notwithstanding, in this chapter I will take what is for me the unnatural view and sketch my impressions of how the knowledge base in developmental social psychology has increased in the past twenty years. I will focus on three major areas. In two of these areas, knowledge of cognitive development and knowledge involving the various concepts related to the development of the self, progress has been substantial. In the third area, knowledge of how to take explicit account of the social context, progress has been almost unbelievable. Cognitive development and development of the self do not proceed in a social vacuum. In fact, the more we learn about development, the clearer it becomes that even the Piagetian sequences of cognitive development can vary across social contexts. So in my view the biggest advance in the knowledge base in the past twenty years consists of the methodological and statistical tools that permit us to model individual change within a realistic social context as well as to model the dynamic interplay between individuals and the social structure.

Fortunately all three of these areas of knowledge can be integrated by taking a "life course approach" (see, for example, Riley and Foner 1968). The line of thinking underlying a life course approach is not presently well enough developed to be called a theory, but this approach calls attention to certain themes that link the three areas of research I will discuss in this chapter. One theme is the reciprocal and transactional nature of the relation between individuals and their social contexts. Teachers affect children, but children affect teachers, also. For example, by their very identity, younger sibs of bright children induce high expectations in teachers who have taught the older sibs (Seavor 1973). Another major theme of life course ideas is the continuous nature of development and the ever-present potential for change. There is less constancy in development than we had previously believed, especially between early childhood and the later stages of life (Kagan 1980).

In an ongoing study we are finding that some children will do much better during their first-grade year in school than we might predict from their initial test scores (Pallas, Alexander, Entwisle, and Cadigan 1985). In this study we use a scale that assesses children's enthusiasm and other personality characteristics, which distinguishes well between children with outstanding verbal growth and those whose performance gains are only average over a year. Children with higher scores are personally more mature. Thus we find that individuals do enhance, or diminish, their own development, even at an early stage in life. The same is true in later life. For example, Kohn's and Schooler's (1984) analyses of the effects of work on psychological characteristics demonstrate that cognitive processes continue to show plasticity throughout the life span. They have found that work conditions shape intellectual development throughout adulthood. Jobs that require employees to be self-directed and to deal with people increase the employees' intellectual flexibility. Jobs that require employees to follow others' directions and to deal with objects do not enhance the employees' flexibility.

Life course themes, which are particularly apparent in the writings of Glen Elder, Jerome Kagan, and Orville Brim, represent a profound change in the zeitgeist of social developmental psychology over the previous decade. Kagan (1980), for example, points to discontinuities in development over the life span, particularly early in life. He challenges traditional views that infancy or early childhood are periods that to a large extent forecast later stages. In the same vein Elder (1978) shows us that individuals have varying childhood experiences, which lead to correspondingly different outlooks among these individuals as adults. Emergence of life course themes is actually part of a widespread movement throughout the social sciences toward study of change.

I expect these themes will continue to be influential in the foreseeable future. In 1965 we hoped we could devise strong preschool programs that would improve children's life chances. A recent meta-analysis of the lasting outcomes of a variety of these preschool programs indicates they were probably more successful than we had previously thought (Lazar and Darlington 1982). For example, the programs prevented some children from repeating a grade later in their schooling. But in the present decade we no longer think mainly in terms of a "dose of cognitive training" or "extra practice in network English" as remedies for the dearth of socialization resources in disadvantaged homes. Nor do we think that an "extra dose of income" will necessarily bring broken families back together (Tuma and Hannan 1984) or help children from economically disadvantaged families to do well in school. Rather, we think in terms of Elder's (1974) path-breaking work, which shows that the effects of economic deprivation on children depends on their age cohort, their social-class level, the psychological climate of their family, and other contextual factors. Also, we recognize that effects of the depression continue to be visible as children of the 1930s progress through adulthood. Girls from severely deprived families married earlier and valued more strongly traditional "family values" than did girls from less deprived families. The life course approach has changed the tenor of our thinking, both in the problems we choose to think about and in how we address those problems.

I will now specifically discuss each of the three areas of knowledge in which I think substantial progress has been made over the past twenty years.

COGNITIVE DEVELOPMENT

The "central unresolved issue in cognitive development" at present is how the child himself or herself and the environment affect the child's development (Collins 1984). The Piagetians have convinced us that children are active participants in their own development, not passive recipients of adult influence. The child produces much of his or her own development, but our society aims to encourage certain kinds of development by requiring that children attend school. The life course approach impels us to determine how children's cognitive development and the social context provided by the school interact. Although some regularities in children's cognitive development certainly exist, that development still varies widely across cultures.

Returns from research on the cognitive development of school-age children, although less dramatic so far than returns from research on the cognition of infants, have exceeded the wildest dreams we had in the early sixties. At that time the textbooks on the psychology of learning discussed only a handful of experimental studies on thinking (Deese 1958). Several main theories of learning were developed by people such as Edward Tolman, Clark Hull, Kurt Lewin, and B. F. Skinner, but very little of the research on the psychology of learning had any direct relation to schooling—most of the research was conducted in a laboratory with animals. We knew that partial reinforcement worked better than 100 percent reinforcement, and a few studies even confirmed this fact with children (see Cofer and Musgrave 1963), but the matter rested there.

Contrast this with the extent of our knowledge today. The study of cognitive development, especially in school-age children, has been the focus of thousands of studies (see Fischer and Bullock [1984] for citations); this work has yielded a rich harvest. We now believe there are four times when large-scale reorganizations of children's behavior occur, and these changes signal fairly universal steps in cognitive development. The ages when these changes occur coincide with the period of school attendance—ages four to eighteen. At around age four children can deal with representations; they can relate two social categories, like teachers to students. By age six or seven they can comprehend concrete categories. For example, they can understand role interactions, such as how a husband and wife could be a principal and a teacher, respectively, in the same school. By age ten or twelve children can generalize across whole series of concrete categories. They can understand, for example, the concept of "supervisor" across a series of job settings. They are able to think in hypothetical terms: "If I were the supervisor, I would . .,. ." The fourth stage, which occurs in late adolescence, involves the ability to generate new hypotheses.

However, the consensus is that children's *performances* do not adhere strictly to stages of development. That is, at age six or seven children generally show skills and modes of thought that contrast distinctively with those they showed at age five, but these years by no means represent a time of homogeneous functioning across all children (see Collins 1984). The cognitive stage a child is in at any given age can vary widely depending on the child's environment. By the time children start school, they may already be in different developmental trajectories, depending on their differential abilities and experiences up to that time. A few studies indicate that different children and different situations may even produce different sequences of development, but this research is just beginning (see Collins 1984 for citations). While we recognize more flexibility in development, we must acknowledge that early development can set at least loose boundaries on later developmental stages. In the last twenty years we have had numerous demonstrations that the amount children learn in one school year is proportional to what they knew at the beginning of the year (see, for example, Coleman et al. 1966). In our own ongoing work it is very clear that children who had to repeat first grade knew less when they initially started school than did their promoted classmates, and they gained significantly less over their first year in school as well. Since regression effects would run in a counter direction, this failure of the repeaters to thrive in a school environment is likely even more severe than their small test gains indicate.

THE DEVELOPMENT OF THE SELF

The second major area of progress in social psychology is a result of the surge of interest in the self, called variously self-concept, self-esteem, self-image, self-awareness, or some other related name. Parenthetically, I must say that this is one of the few areas of research where sociologists and psychologists have genuinely collaborated. The research of sociologists like Morris Rosenberg (1975) and Wilbur Brookover and others (1978), for example, takes into account research by psychologists like Ruth Wylie (1979) and Stanley Coopersmith (1967), and vice versa. Unfortunately collaboration on the cognitive aspects of school learning has been rarer.

We have learned that as a child grows older his or her conception of self becomes more and more abstract (see Markus and Nurius 1984). By age eight children appreciate that the mind and body are separate and that they themselves can control their behavior. Indeed, school-age children have an elaborate system of self-knowledge. They are aware of a physical self, a social self, an academic self, and so on. They also find a general constancy of self. Development of a sense of self is important because it must precede the development of a set of personal standards. Certainly by second grade, and probably earlier, the process of self-comparison is present. First graders know who in their class can run the fastest, who can read the best, and who is better looking than they are. They can also compare their own behavior under various circumstances. For example, we asked a first-grade girl, barely six years old, "How good are you at being honest—very good, good, fairly good, fairly bad, or very bad?" She responded, "Sometimes I'm very good" (pitch rising), "sometimes I'm very bad" (pitch dropping). Self-comparison implies both a sense of self and a set of personal standards.

Studies now in progress by Jacquelynne Eccles and her colleagues at the University of Michigan as well as our own ongoing work (see Entwisle, Alexander, Pallas, and Cadigan 1985b) may tell us exactly *how* children elaborate notions about the self. These studies capitalize on the advances in modeling I will mention shortly. For example, by jointly elaborating measurement and structural models of the self, we can explore the factorial structure of self-esteem and at the same time try to understand the patterns of influence that the social context exerts on self-esteem. For first graders there may be only one clear factor representing self-esteem, but by third grade there may be two or three factors representing self-esteem. What are the antecedents of these factors? If one factor responds to teachers' expectations, the child's past academic performance, and the like, while other factors do not, we could have much more convincing evidence of the validity of a factor representing "academic self-image" than has traditionally been available for validating affective or socioemotional constructs. For the most part, the self-concept is investigated in highly artificial situations, and validity of the various indices of self continues to be problematic. But recent research has helped us to partially understand the development of self.

MODELING THE SOCIAL CONTEXT

We have made great progress in this third major area. In fact, it is startling to look back and see what we could not do in 1965. Some models, such as log linear models, were just on the horizon in 1965. For example, in 1964 Leo Goodman published a paper that explained how to isolate the three-way interaction in a 2 x 2 x 2 analysis of categoric variables. Today we routinely do analyses with any number of categories and variables, if we have sufficient data. Dudley Duncan's first paper on path analysis appeared in 1966. Now, such analyses are common in the social science literature. In 1965 even models that had been well known for a long time were not routinely used. For example, around 1965 or 1966, because we needed some examples in a course we were teaching, Arthur Stinchcombe and I surveyed the sociological literature for instances of factor analysis. We found only two. Today, factor-analysis procedures in sociology are so routine that we have the opposite problem—factor analysis often substitutes for theoretical analysis. Twenty years ago most people did not think in terms of a general linear model nor did they even understand the correspondence between regression and analysis of variance. Contrast that with the situation today—we are now into our sixth or seventh version of LISREL. We are making rapid strides in modeling discrete phenomena with time-varying rates of change (Tuma and Hannan 1984). Without high-speed computers and the sophisticated software we now take for granted, it would be gratuitous to ask penetrating questions about how development of the self and development of cognitive capacities interact across social contexts, because we would have no way to answer such complicated questions. We have come a long way indeed.

The increase in knowledge of cognitive development, development of self, and modeling of the social context are of enormous significance for understanding the social psychology of education because it enables us to ask realistic questions. We can ask serious questions about the effects of family configuration or parental socialization practices on children's educational attainment. A paper that came out recently (Alwin and Thornton 1984) describes the *relative* impact of family background on children's attainment in school at different stages in childhood. Alwin and Thornton conclude from their longitudinal data obtained from three Detroit counties that family influences on elementary students are probably greater than those same influences are on secondary students. This kind of research on the social context is essential if we are to understand the schooling process. We know parents and peers are important sources of influence on secondary students, but obviously these groups of significant others exist long before high school. It is just not sensible to assume that children's life histories before ninth grade are a complete blank.

A persistent issue, not yet resolved but better understood now than in 1966, is the confounding of home and school influences. The effects of different secondary schools on students' attainment are small (Mosteller and Moynihan 1972). But Barbara Heyns (1978) rephrased the question: Instead of asking whether some schools have greater effects on students than other schools, she asked how some schooling compares with no schooling. In her seminal study of sixth and seventh graders in Atlanta, she showed that relatively affluent children continue to gain academic competence over the summer, whereas children who are less advantaged do not gain over the summer. When school is out, middle-class children get the resources they need for their cognitive growth to continue, whereas children in less affluent circumstances do not.

In my view this is a landmark piece of research. It follows Frederick Mosteller and Daniel Moynihan's (1972) directive: "The summer loss effect for lower-class students should certainly be followed up . . . " (p. 53). Schools probably do help compensate for the dearth of socialization resources in less affluent homes and perhaps duplicate the resources in more affluent homes. So now the question is: Exactly what kinds of resources and exactly what kinds of achievement are involved? Perhaps a composite verbal measure, which is the criterion Heyns used, would respond more to summer surroundings than, say, a measure of mathematics achievement. We hope data to answer this question will be found before long.

During the past twenty years there has been no nationally based study following even one cohort of children from the time they started school to the end of their educational careers. The National Survey of Children (NCES), sponsored by the Foundation for Child Development, is the closest approximation to such a long-range study. A multicohort, nationally representative longitudinal study of children has so far carried too large a price tag—but it is a national need. Such a project could enlighten us on some of the causes of differences in children's affective or socioemotional development. An example of the payoff from this kind of research can be found in Seltzer (1982). Using two cycles of the Health Examination Survey of the NCES to examine children's psychological well-being, she shows a complete absence of association between mothers' participation in the labor force and indices of their children's psychological well-being. She also shows that children in middle childhood and in adolescence whose mothers completed more years of schooling have higher levels of psychological well-being than do children whose mothers had fewer years of education, taking into account relevant controls. I think that a large-scale study of a suitable sample, like Seltzer's study, is a faster route to strong inference than is the best of meta-analyses. Expensive large-scale studies may be cheaper in the long run than what seem like inexpensive small-scale studies. It is virtually impossible to draw inferences by piecing together findings from incommensurate small-scale grab samples where important variables like socioeconomic status cannot be controlled.

Until recently little emphasis has been placed on differences among children in their socioemotional or affective development. We have tended to focus on cognitive explanations for school achievement and to ignore the reciprocities between cognitive and affective development. But a child's self-image is itself a key outcome of schooling, and it predicts other outcomes. The distinction between self-image as outcome and self-image as mediator is often blurred or left unexamined.

Fortunately, since we can now model reciprocal relationships, we can examine feedback mechanisms. How does the achievement of children affect their self-images? How do children's self-images affect their achievement? Certainly low achievement can contribute to a child's poor self-image. But for young children beginning school, the causal flow seems to be in the direction of the self-image affecting achievement (Entwisle and Hayduk 1982; Entwisle, Alexander, Pallas, and Cadigan 1985a), whereas for secondary students the causal flow seems to be in the opposite direction (Gottfredson 1980). With the available modeling techniques, we should be able to understand some of these *structural* changes in development. The immediate future looks very exciting.

REFERENCES

Alwin, D. F., and Thornton, A. "Family Origins and the Schooling Process: Early versus Late Influence." *American Sociological Review* 49(1984): 784–802.

Brookover, W. B.; Schweitzer, J. H.; Schneider, J. M.; Beady, C. H.; Flood, P. K.; and Wisenbaker, J. M. "Elementary School Social Climate and School Achievement." *American Educational Research Journal* 15(1978): 301–318.

Cofer, C. C., and Musgrave, B. S. *Verbal Behavior and Learning.* New York: Academic Press, 1963.

Coleman, J. S.; Campbell, E. G.; Hobson, C. J.; McPartland, J.; Mood, A.; Weinfeld, F. D.; and York, R. L. *Equality of Educational Opportunity.* Washington, D.C.: U.S. Government Printing Office, 1966.

Collins, W. A. "Conclusion: The Status of Basic Research in Middle Childhood." In *Development during Middle Childhood,* edited by W. A. Collins, pp. 398–421. Washington, D.C.: National Academy Press, 1984.

Coopersmith, S. *The Antecedents of Self-Esteem.* San Francisco: Freeman, Cooper and Co., 1967.

Deese, J. *The Psychology of Learning.* New York: McGraw-Hill, 1958.

Duncan, O. D. "Path Analysis: Sociological Examples." *American Journal of Sociology* 72(1966): 1–16.

Elder, G. H. *Children of the Great Depression*. Chicago: University of Chicago Press, 1974.

Elder, G. H. "Family History and the Life Course." In *Transitions*, edited by T. K. Hareven, pp. 17–64. New York: Academic Press, 1978.

Entwisle, D. R.; Alexander, K. A.; Pallas, A.; and Cadigan, D. "Determinants of the Academic Self-Image." Final report, Grant Foundation, grant no. 83079682, 1985. (a)

Entwisle, D. R.; Alexander, K. A.; Pallas, A.; and Cadigan, D. "Educational Attainment over First Grade." Final report, Grant Foundation, grant no. 83079682, 1985. (b)

Entwisle, D. R., and Hayduk, L. A. *Early Schooling*. Baltimore: Johns Hopkins Press, 1982.

Fischer, K. W., and Bullock, D. "Cognitive Development in School-Age Children: Conclusions and New Directions." In *Development during Middle Childhood*, edited by W. A. Collins, pp. 70–146. Washington, D.C.: National Academy Press, 1984.

Goodman, L. A. "Simple Methods of Analyzing Three-Factor Interaction in Contingency Tables." *Journal of American Statistical Association* 59 (1964) 319–352.

Gottfredson, D. C. "Personality and Persistence in Education: A Longitudinal Study." Paper presented at the annual meeting of the American Psychological Association, 1980.

Heyns, B. *Summer Learning and the Effects of Schooling*. New York: Academic Press, 1978.

Kagan, J. "Perspectives on Continuity." In *Constancy and Change in Human Development*, edited by O. G. Brim and J. Kagan, pp. 26–74. Cambridge: Harvard University Press, 1980.

Kohn, M. L., and Schooler, C. *Work and Personality*. Norwood, N.J.: Ablex, 1984.

Lazar, I., and Darlington, R. "Lasting Effects of Early Education." *Monograph of the Society for Research in Child Development*. Serial no. 195, vol. 47, nos. 2–3, 1982.

Markus, H. J., and Nurius, P. S. "Self-Understanding and Self-Regulation in Middle Childhood." In *Development during Middle Childhood*, edited by W. A. Collins, pp. 147–183, Washington, D.C.: National Academy Press, 1984.

Mosteller, F., and Moynihan, D. P., eds. *On Equality of Educational Opportunity*. New York: Vintage Books, 1972.

Pallas, A.; Alexander, K. L.; Entwisle, D. R.; and Cadigan, D. "Children Whose End-of-Year CAT Scores Are Exceptionally High." Final report, Grant Foundation, grant no. 83079682, 1985.

Riley, M. W., and Foner, A. *Aging and Society*. New York: Russell Sage, 1968.

Rosenberg, M. "The Dissonant Context and the Adolescent Self-Concept." In *Adolescence in the Life Cycle: Psychological Change and Social Context*, edited by S. Dragastin and G. H. Elder, pp. 97–116. Washington, D.C.: Hemisphere Publications, 1975.

Seavor, W. B. "Effects of Naturally Induced Teacher Expectancies." *Journal of Personality and Social Psychology* 28(1973): 333–342.

Seltzer, J. A. "Family Characteristics and Children's Psychological Well-being." Working paper 81–18. Center for Demography and Ecology, University of Wisconsin, Madison, 1982.

Tuma, N. B., and Hannan, M. T. *Social Dynamics*. New York: Academic Press, 1984.

Wylie, R. C. *The Self-Concept*. Lincoln: University of Nebraska Press, 1979.

7

On the Sociology of the Classroom

Elizabeth G. Cohen

More than ten years have passed since I last surveyed work on the sociology of the classroom (Cohen 1972). My recent review of the literature from 1972 to 1984 has brought me a sense of both cumulation and discovery. Clearly, we have moved away dramatically from the older model we inherited from the educational psychologists, a model that looked at teachers' behavior, teaching style, and classroom climate. Using correlational techniques, we tried to leap from these variables over to learning. We have moved away from this simple kind of input-output study to a detailed conceptualization and study of structure and processes inside the classroom.

In exploring the complexities of the social system of the classroom, the sociology of education has come into its own. By our use of concepts like authority, task and evaluation structure, and status order, we have placed a social system inside the "black box" of the classroom. Furthermore, we have carried out research that has related the operation of some of these concepts to each other and to organizational and contextual factors. Finally, we have begun to develop propositions about the conditions under which we will find learning as an outcome of the operation of this social system.

After I briefly sketch earlier reviews of the literature, I will organize what we have learned according to the following key concepts and their interrelationships: effects of technology or task structure, effects of the evaluation system, and antecedents and consequences of the status order. Then, I will examine findings on learning outcomes that are conditioned on the operation of the classroom social system. Finally, I will conclude with some comments on the implications of this knowledge for current methods of classroom instruction.

I have selected to review only the research that tells us something about the key concepts that have been of special interest to sociologists. I have looked especially carefully at literature that provides clues about how these concepts relate to each other and to learning.

I have omitted that part of the time-on-task literature that is not inherently sociological. Also omitted are those rich observational and descriptive studies, so popular in the last few years, that tell us a story about classrooms at given times and places without attention to theory. Finally, I have omitted policy research on classrooms, such as the effects of desegregation on the relationships between black and white students.

EARLY REVIEWS OF THE LITERATURE

In 1972 I documented the change in focus from teachers' behavior and students' learning to a new interest in the patterns of student participation (Cohen 1972). I argued in that paper that it was necessary to make the relationship between teachers' activities and students' learning conditional on the social system in the classroom. The social system included the operation of status orders that had the power to affect participation and, indirectly, learning. Status in the classroom had multiple bases in societal status characteristics, sociometric status, and achievement status.

At that time the analysis of the teacher as a bureaucratic authority was emerging as a rich direction for future research, one that had scarcely begun at the time I wrote the review. Finally, I put in a plea for the use of multiple theoretical frameworks for studying the different dimensions of classrooms. I argued that fundamentally different phenomena were at work in the classroom. I thought it necessary to understand the operation of these phenomena with different explanatory theories. To quote this argument more precisely: "The would-be theorist must isolate the phenomenon in the classroom he wants to explain through analysis and preliminary study. Then he must consider the other dimensions as *conditions* under which his propositions about learning hold, become modified or fail to hold." (p. 450).

Six years later, Sarane Boocock's (1978) review of the social organization of the classroom proposed what some of those theoretical frameworks might be. She used sociological theory to link organizational differences in the classroom to differences in students' attitude, behavior, and achievement. For her, a key concept was *technology*, which refers to the set of materials, procedures, and knowledge that the organization uses to carry on its work (Hickson, Pugh, and Pheysey 1969). In school classrooms, the technology is primarily the instructional methods and materials used by teachers. This classic sociological concept has proved invaluable in studies of the classroom, but it is difficult to explain to readers who automatically think of machines whenever they hear the word *technology*. Boocock also described research on variation in classroom reward structure and research on peer status and peer groups as reference groups.

EFFECTS OF CHANGING THE TECHNOLOGY OR TASK STRUCTURE

The years from 1970 to approximately 1980 were years of profound innovation in the elementary classroom and to a lesser extent in the secondary school. This was the heyday of individualized instruction, which called for many different tasks to be carried on simultaneously, and of open classrooms, wherein students were allowed to choose which of the many tasks they would do. In the typically eclectic fashion of the American teacher, these innovations were carried out to different extents and in different combinations in different classrooms.

Instead of every child doing the same task, which is the rule in conventional classrooms, different children were doing different tasks. Instead of the teacher having total control of what was going on in the classroom, some teachers delegated authority to individual students. Instead of children working individually, they were working interdependently. To sociologists this was a grand natural experiment in which they could study what would happen if the technology or task structure of the classroom were radically changed.

Technology and Work Arrangements

In 1973 in the Bay Area of California, individualization was becoming increasingly popular in elementary schools. This meant that in any one classroom an observer might find up to six or seven sets of reading materials in simultaneous use. Relatively common was the use of flexible small groups to which children were assigned and reassigned according to their mastery of particular reading skills (Cohen, Deal, Meyer, and Scott 1979). At that moment in the history of educational innovation, a team of sociologists and educational researchers with a strong background in practice came together in the Environment for Teaching Program at Stanford University to study the organization of schools. Team members were in conflict over whether or not anything but the simplest technology might be found in elementary classrooms. Those members of the team who were the closest to the practice of teaching insisted that something important was happening out there; in the classic language of the organizational theorist, a more complex technology was operating.

As it turned out, they were right and the organizational sociologists on the team were wrong. Furthermore, what was happening in classrooms provided support for a central hypotehsis of what was then current in organizational theory: Complex technologies generate more complex organizational structures.

In a longitudinal study of elementary schools, which took place between 1973 and 1975, Terrence Deal, John Meyer, Richard Scott, and I predicted that the proportion of teachers in a school who were engaged in collaborative relationships, as well as a measure of how closely they worked together, would rise in response to increased complexity in the teaching of reading in the early grades (Cohen, Deal, Meyer, and Scott 1979). Regression analysis showed that, holding constant the level of teaming in 1973, the complexity of the technology as measured by the variety of reading materials and groupings used was a significant predictor of the work arrangements reported in 1975. There was no evidence of a causal flow in the other direction, that is, work arrangements had no effect on technology; nor was there any evidence that the presence or absence of teams was related to systematic policies of the district.

Using the 1975 body of data, two dissertations on innovative classrooms were able to use a related proposition from organizational sociology: If the complexity of the task generates uncertainty and requires nonroutine decision making, then lateral relations between workers can serve as a source of problem solving and processing of information as well as coordination (March and Simon 1958; Perrow 1972; Galbraith 1973.) Joanne Intili (1977) was particularly interested in studying the impact on the work arrangements of teachers of carrying out individualized instruction that fit the ideal version envisioned by the developers of these new methods. She reasoned that the kind of uncertainty generated by having to diagnose and prescribe individualized reading activity would demand a high degree of reciprocal interdependence from the staff, that is, they would have to relate to each other continuously over a period of time. The body of data collected by the Environment for Teaching Program showed a strong correlation between reciprocal interdependence among the staff and a nonroutine, highly differentiated technology such as individualized instruction.

Susan Robbins (1977) used yet a different indicator of nonroutine, complex instruction to test the same proposition. She was interested in open classrooms, defined as those where children were given a high level of choice. She argued that within those classrooms the use of a system of individual systematic conferencing was a nonroutine technology characterized by considerable uncertainty. She was able to show that a complex feedback/management system in "high-choice" classrooms was associated with greater interdependence of teachers working with other teachers, aides, and specialists. Furthermore, high-choice classrooms that employed systematic individual conferences had higher levels of task engagement than those that did not use such a system.

Utility of Organizational Theory.   At the same time that application of organizational theory to the classroom was producing these rich results, it was gradually becoming clear that, above the level of the classroom, the same propositions did not apply. Classic organizational theory that relates technology to authority structures and work arrangements has turned out, on the whole, to be a poor fit to schools. Because of what is called "loose coupling" in the organization of schools, very weak relationships exist between the ways that schools are administered and the nature of the instruction. John Meyer and Brian Rowan (1983) have argued that schools should be seen not as technical organizations but as institutional organizations, where close oversight of instruction would not be expected—indeed, it would be avoided.

Technology and Classroom Authority

At the classroom level, however, we have continued to find many uses for organizational theory. For example, viewing the teacher's authority in relationship to the complexity of the technology has led to many useful results. If the teacher is seen as a supervisor with thirty workers who must function under crowded conditions, there are several propositions concerning the delegation of authority. As technology becomes more complex and uncertain, authority should move from routine bureaucratic supervision to delegation to the workers. If this does not take place, the organization will be less effective than if there is a "match" between the type of supervision and the complexity of the technology (Perrow 1972).

One such complex instructional setting is used with "Finding Out/Descubrimiento," an instructional approach that requires multiple learning centers, with different learning tasks operating simultaneously at each center. In evaluating the consistency of implementation from classroom to classroom, we found considerable variability in the number of learning centers in simultaneous operation (Cohen and Intili 1981). Some teachers had simplified the technology by operating only three learning centers with each adult (a teacher, an aide, and a parent volunteer) directly supervising a center. Clearly, some teachers were unable or unwilling to delegate authority, that is, to "let go" and to allow the children to solve problems for themselves. Analysis of these data showed that the proper implementation of the curriculum depended strongly on the extent to which the teacher delegated authority. Delegation of authority was measured by the number of children under direct supervision of adults—the fewer the children under direct supervision, the more authority had been delegated. If teachers were unable to delegate authority, multiple learning centers failed to operate, and children did not have the experience of talking and working together. Talking and working together was a prescribed behavior for the development of thinking skills, which was a goal of the activities (Cohen and Intili 1982). Furthermore, those classrooms with the greatest learning gains were precisely those where teachers were successful in delegating authority so that more children could talk and work together at multiple learning centers.

Steven H. Rosenholtz (1981), in studying this same curriculum in comparison to the regular mathematics classes taught by the same teacher, used the presence of lateral relations among the workers (or in this case the frequency with which students talked and worked together) as an index of delegated authority. The more complex was the technology, in terms of grouping and materials, the more lateral relations were observed between the students. Furthermore, student engagement was related to the frequency of lateral relations. Direct supervision by the teacher was related to engagement only under conditions of low complexity of grouping and materials. This latter finding is of particular interest because it is often assumed today that one should use large-group instruction, since direct supervision is the only way to maximize time on task. Quite the contrary is the case: When authority is delegated, it is quite possible to obtain very high levels of engagement through lateral peer relations.

I would argue that much of the failure of open classrooms and individualization was due to misunderstanding of the difference between delegated authority and laissez-faire. Teachers were given no particular advice about how to maintain control in a classroom where authority had to be delegated to students. Either they began to simplify the innovations to the point where they could use direct supervision, or they essentially lost control of the classroom by trying to be everywhere at once as a direct supervisor over differentiated instruction, or they thought that having an open classroom meant that a teacher *should* give up his or her control of the classroom. The last two possibilities were obviously accompanied by a dramatic loss in effectiveness through frequent disengagement of students.

Much can be gained from delegating authority in classrooms. I have developed a method of training teachers to delegate authority with the use of cooperative learning groups that has turned out to be both effective and extremely practical for teachers (Cohen and DeAvila 1983). With this method I use simple organizational concepts of how a teacher can delegate authority and yet maintain control through children's internalization of norms of how to behave in cooperative groups (Cohen, Intili, and Robbins 1979; Cohen, forthcoming).

Impact on Students of Innovations in Task Structure

One unanticipated consequence of the recent era of innovation was a change in the informal world of student relations. Sociological researchers studying classrooms where changes had been made in task structure have consistently found that the informal organization of the classroom is closely related to the formal task structure. In particular, the state of sociometric relations among schoolchildren that had been accepted as generally true since the 1940s was found to change markedly when task structures were changed.

A remarkable number of independent studies all attest to one powerful generalization: Increased opportunities for children to interact with one another while they do tasks in the classroom will increase friendliness (Hallinan 1976; Epstein and Karweit 1983; Bossert 1979; Sussman 1973; Slavin 1983). These studies have used open classrooms; grouping for instruction; or cooperative, interdependent task groups as indicators of increased opportunities to interact.

Beyond this generalization, there are a number of theoretical questions on the nature of this process. Is it the interaction itself that produces the friendliness? Is it the fact that in some settings such as open classrooms students may choose the classmates with whom they wish to interact and to work? Or is it the interdependent nature of the interaction that brings about these changes in social relations?

To begin to answer these questions it is necessary to synthesize rather different kinds of literature. Some of the studies were designed to test whether or not a particular innovation would produce increased friendliness; researcher-developers wanted to prescribe the techniques for settings in which social acceptance was particularly desirable (Slavin 1983). Other studies simply evaluated the effects of innovations (Sussman 1973; Epstein and Karweit 1983). Still a third kind of study was carried out by basic researchers interested in friendship or theories concerning task activity structures (Hallinan 1976; Bossert 1979).

Open Versus Traditional Classrooms.   Sociologists were not slow to see what a remarkable opportunity the open classroom provided to study the impact of a radical change in task structure on friendship and other informal relations among students. Typically, open classrooms were compared to traditional classrooms. The definition of open classrooms used in this research reveals that this innovation changed three variables at once: (1) it increased opportunities for interaction; (2) it gave students considerable choice of whom they would work with as well as what they would work on; and (3) it was marked by interdependent peer relationships.

Maureen Hallinan (1976) classified elementary classrooms as open, semi-open, or traditional according to the extent to which the classrooms were teacher centered or child centered. Important in this classification was whether or not students were free to move about and to make decisions concerning academic activities. In open classrooms she found a sociometric pattern quite different from that claimed as "universal" for elementary children in earlier sociometric literature. Instead of the familiar classroom pattern of an unequal number of choices of which a great many are given to the stars and few or none are given to the isolates, she found a less hierarchical distribution of choices and fewer social isolates and sociometric leaders. Furthermore, asymmetric dyads (where friendship choices were unreciprocated) and intransitive triads (where all three children did not choose each other) occurred less frequently in the open classroom than in the traditional classrooms and were resolved more quickly over time into balanced states.

Joyce Epstein and Nancy Karweit (1983) compared high- and low-participatory secondary school classes, and their results were very similar. In high-participatory classes students were given more frequent opportunities to walk around, to talk with others, to choose seats and activities, and to work in small groups. She too found less hierarchical structure in the friendship choices for high-participatory classes, where fewer students were isolated and more students were selected. More of the students' friendship choices were reciprocated. She also found evidence that in the high-participatory classes friends were selected from a wider set of contacts.

Steven Bossert's conceptualization of task activity involves the size of the work group, the number of different tasks in simultaneous operation (the division of labor), the degree to which pupils choose tasks, and the extent to which students work together (Bossert 1979, p. 10). Bossert makes a theoretical contribution by abstracting these separate dimensions and by connecting the research on effects of changed task activity to research on the relationship between task activity and intragroup relations found in work settings. Those classrooms with multiple tasks, a high degree of pupil choice, and increased interdependence are called "high on multitask activities." Using this distinction, James Rothenberg (1982) found that classrooms with a higher percentage of multitask activities as compared to classrooms with a lower percentage of these activities had stronger associations between sociometric choices and actual peer interaction. Classrooms with a high proportion of recitation and common worksheet assignments have clear sociometric stars who interact with only a small group of peers—mostly from their own high-performing reading group. The peer relations in classrooms with a high proportion of multitask activities were more positive and less marked by cleavages and static status hierarchies.

Bossert's original study of four classrooms also suggests powerful connections between task activity and the importance of academic ranking as a basis for friendship choices. In those classrooms dominated by recitation and seatwork, friendship groups tended to be closely aligned with academic standing. In non-recitation-dominated classrooms, relative achievement level did not affect peer associations because task performance was less visible than in the recitation-dominated classrooms. Each student's performance was largely independent of others' performances and was noncomparable (p. 91). Bossert's analysis suggests that task structure affects the way pupils evaluate each other. This is an important theoretical proposition, which I will discuss later in this chapter in the section on evaluation.

An unpublished case study of open classrooms revealed that the effects on informal social relationships of intensive peer interaction when choice of work group and work activity is left up to the student may not be entirely benign. L. Sussman (1973), after intensive observations of two schools with open classrooms (grades one through three), confirmed that it was indeed the case that open classrooms had a much higher rate of peer interaction and a much lower rate of interaction between the students and the teacher than did traditional classrooms. However, she also observed that as peer groups invaded central learning activities they became a major factor in the dynamics of the activities. The peer groups (or some of their members) chose activities collectively; the peer group thus became the task group. Peer groups demanded conformity to their norms and tended to set output norms for how much work they would complete. Larger and more enduring peer groups had obvious leaders and a hierarchy of influence and prestige within the group. The open classrooms may have had fewer isolates, but the life of the isolate was an unhappy one; they were actively rejected and were sometimes the object of verbal and physical aggression.

Sussman's case study in connection with the other studies of open classrooms has powerful theoretical implications. Social psychology has previously documented the status structures and norms of informal group relations. Under conditions in which the actors are permitted to choose coworkers and tasks, these informal norms and status arrangements appear to be a good deal stronger than are the official norms and work arrangements of the school. Of course, it has often been noted that informal social relations play some part in formal classroom behaviors. However, in this study the balance of power shifted markedly toward informal social relations as the more influential in governing behavior.

Instructional Groups and Interaction

The elements of abundant opportunity for unsupervised interaction and student choice of activity and work group are inextricably entangled in this research on open classrooms. It was not until five years later that these two elements were disentangled by Maureen Hallinan and Nancy Tuma (1978), who studied the effects of membership in relatively traditional reading groups. In some classrooms children had the opportunity to choose their reading group. Here is variation that is far less extreme. Reading groups were evidently supervised directly by the reading teacher, although a stable reading-group assignment gave fairly extensive opportunities for peer interaction.

The percentage of reading time spent in groups predicted stability and change in friendships in more cases than any other characteristic examined. These data provided strong and consistent evidence that small-group interaction (even under supervised conditions and independent of how groups were formed) fosters formation and stability of close friendships within the classroom. The percentage of class time spent in groups formed by students' choice was associated with an increase in friendly relations but did not affect close friendships.

Cooperative Groups and Interaction

The use of cooperative groups for instruction in the various versions of this technique, as described by Robert Slavin (1983), Shlomo Sharan (1980), and David and Roger Johnson (1975), is markedly different from the peer groups observed by Sussman in open classrooms. Each one of these methods involves careful preparation of the students for the cooperative experience in which they learn special norms for behavior in cooperative settings. Developers of cooperative learning techniques do not allow informal peer-group norms to govern relationships, but they substitute a new kind of behavior suitable to the changed task structure. As Slavin (1983) puts it, "It is not enough to simply tell students to cooperate. A program based on cooperation among students must be 'engineered,' both to solve the problems inherent in cooperation and to adapt cooperative activities to the needs and limitations of the typical classroom" (p. 23).

Generally, research on cooperative groups finds increased friendliness and acceptance in treated as opposed to untreated classrooms. In a detailed review of the effects of cooperative learning on the probability of increasing cross-racial friendship choices, Slavin (1983) finds consistently favorable results for the methods of "Student Teams and Academic Divisions (STAD)" and "Teams-Games-Tournaments" as well as for the methods advocated by the Johnsons. In an earlier review Sharan (1980) concurs in this evaluation, although he points out that the gains are modest and cooperative group methods differ in effectiveness.

The various cooperative techniques differ greatly in their reward structure, in interdependence of goals and means, and according to whether or not the product is collective or individual. I would argue that the critical features of the task structure that lead to increased friendliness are the opportunities for interaction and task interdependence in which the participants are specifically trained to behave in a cooperative manner.

I take this position because there is some evidence that if the students are not specifically trained how to behave in a cooperative setting, the results of relatively unsupervised interaction in groups composed by the teacher may not be friendly. In a unique classroom experiment in which Joan Bloom and George Schuncke (1979) devised a curriculum on cooperation, students experienced various collective activities designed specifically to teach them the utility and value of cooperation. They were not taught how to behave in this setting, but were simply exposed to experiences where they learned that cooperative modes were more effective in many situations than were individualistic modes. In one version of the curriculum the students were constantly recomposed into new groups for the activities. In the other version they maintained stable group membership. The main predictions for this study were borne out in that both groups of students who had been exposed to the curriculum on cooperation showed a marked preference for cooperative as opposed to competitive rules on a criterion task. Nevertheless, the students who were in stable groups showed less cohesive and less friendly behavior during their criterion task than did the controls who had not been exposed to the curriculum. Clearly, some of the groups with stable membership experienced conflict and had been given no way to resolve their difficulties.

Another cooperative classroom experiment that did not show consistent gains in liking of each other was that of Russell Weigel, Patricia Wiser, and Stuart Cook's (1975). Their experiment too had not trained for cooperation.

In review, it appears that increased opportunity for interaction is a necessary precondition for increasing friendliness and changing sociometric patterns from those reported in earlier literature. Beyond this, interaction may produce changes in informal relations between students by at least three different processes: (1) Friendliness may be broadened and intensified by allowing the students to make their own choices for work groups and by allowing informal group norms to govern formal work groups; (2) friendliness may be increased by extended opportunities for interaction under direct supervision of the teacher, as in reading groups; and (3) friendliness and cross-ethnic acceptance may be increased by interaction in interdependent task groups that are governed by special behavioral norms for cooperation.

Task Structure and Its Impact on Preferred Modes of Activity

An interesting effect of changing task structure so that individuals must work together to achieve their goals is that the individuals come to prefer cooperative over individualistic modes of activity. Early experimental and theoretical work by Paul Breer and Edwin Locke (1965) provides a theoretical base for this outcome. The experiment by Bloom and Schuncke described in the previous section provides support for the notion that classroom experience with cooperative modes will produce a distinct preference for that method of working.

In a large-scale field experiment that contrasted Slavin's STAD method and Sharan's Group Investigation method of cooperative learning with traditional classrooms, Sharan and colleagues (1984) found that either of the two cooperative learning techniques produced significantly more cooperative behaviors and fewer competitive behaviors on a criterion task than did traditional classroom task structure. The behavior of the students was measured in a cooperative task in which participants worked under instructions that encouraged them to work together. Cooperative behavior included helping others, offering help, responding positively to requests for help, and evidence of coordination and collaboration. Competitive behaviors included interfering with others' work, negative responses to requests for help, rejecting requests to coordinate efforts, and the like. For those pupils who had studied with the Group Investigation methods, 85 percent of the behaviors recorded were cooperative; 72 percent of the behaviors for pupils who had experienced the STAD method were cooperative; and 55 percent of the behaviors for pupils from traditional classrooms were cooperative. Sharan states, "Unmediated interaction structured by a cooperative task and sustained by appropriate norms during classroom learning fosters markedly improved relations among children from the same or diverse cultural backgrounds" (Sharan et al., 1984, p. 95).

Analysis of cross-ethnic helping within Israeli groups (Middle-Eastern or Western Jews) showed that the Group Investigation method was superior to the other two methods in producing two-way cooperative behaviors between the ethnic groups (Sharan et al. 1984, p. 97). This difference was interpreted as stemming from the one-way peer-tutoring relationships in STAD where Western Jews assisted Middle Eastern Jews, while the Group Investigation method used a division of labor where everyone's contribution was important to the final product.

EVALUATION PROCESSES IN THE CLASSROOM

In many ways evaluation may be seen as the jugular of the classroom social system. The way the teacher evaluates students and the way that students come to evaluate themselves and others have powerful consequences for students. The status order of the classroom is rooted in these evaluation processes. Furthermore, the individual's expectations for competence, sense of his or her own intellectual ability, and participation in collective tasks in the classroom, and even the effort the individual exerts toward accomplishing classroom goals, have been shown to be associated with features of classroom evaluation. An understanding of these connections has developed mostly in the last ten years.

Evaluation and Effort

Evaluation by teachers can be examined analogously to evaluation by any organizational authority. A promising line of work is to apply Sanford Dornbusch and Richard Scott's (1975) theory of evaluation and authority to the classroom setting. Gary Natriello and Dornbusch (1984) have recently published a volume in which they apply (and adapt) this theory to the relationship between evaluation and student effort, and they also report results from a lengthy research program.

One of the basic propositions of the theory is that organizational participants (in this case, students) will exert effort to the extent that they perceive the evaluations made by their supervisors are soundly based. Participants will also exert effort to the extent that they see that evaluations are important. Examples of an unsoundly based evaluation system in a classroom would be the perception by students that poor performance will not result in poor grades or that good performance will not result in good grades. Another example would be the perception that a student can pass the course if he or she merely attends the class.

Ruben Espinosa (1975) found that lack of student effort in school-work was related to the perception that the evaluation system was not soundly based. Natriello and Dornbusch (1984) report that the relationship of students' perceptions of soundly based evaluation to their effort in school has not been consistently sustained in the research. They conclude that although students do not see school evaluation systems as very soundly based, they still consider evaluations they receive and associated tasks to be important. Furthermore, they still tend to devote effort to those tasks considered important whether or not they perceive evaluation as soundly based (p. 139).

In testing the relationship between soundly based evaluation and student effort in college classes, Judith Gonzales (1982) included in her measure of perceptions of soundly based evaluations an item on the detail and specificity of the feedback received from instructors on written work. She also used simultaneous controls of self-assessment of competence and the importance of graduation. With these two variables controlled, she found a positive association between soundly based evaluation and student effort. The effect was particularly strong for students who perceived that they had average academic competence. Those with perceptions of high competence tended to exert more effort regardless of their perceptions of the evaluation system.

Using other propositions from the theory of evaluation and authority, Natriello and Scott (1981) related disengagement of high school students to incompatibility in the evaluation system. Measures of disengagement included being willing to settle for less than an optimum grade as well as negative activities such as vandalism. Incompatible evaluations are those that are contradictory, uncontrollable, unpredictable, and unattainable (whenever students are faced with inappropriately high standards). Natriello conducted interviews with sixty-five high school students; reports of incompatibilities in the academic evaluation system were frequent. Students who reported that they were subjected to incompatible academic evaluation systems were also more likely to report being disengaged than were students who reported being subjected to compatible evaluation systems.

Effects of Teachers' Evaluative Behavior

The specific ways in which a teacher lets students know how they are doing and what kind of a person they are have effects on student effort, on the students' attributions of the cause of their grades , and on the students' evaluations of their own competence. In their studies of student perception, Natriello and Dornbusch (1984) consistently found that more frequent teacher praise, greater friendliness and warmth, and more frequent and challenging academic, evaluative behavior from teachers were all positively associated with student effort. These teaching behaviors were more strongly associated with students' subjective perceptions of their effort than they were with students' reports of behavior concerning academic effort and engagement. The measure of academic evaluative behavior included the perceived difficulty of the work, the frequency with which students were encouraged to ask questions, and the frequency with which the teacher tried to figure out what work would be just right for individual students. Especially provocative are the findings that low-achieving students reported praise and perceptions of teacher friendliness and warmth but not challenging academic evaluative behavior. Teachers appear to employ friendliness and warmth to motivate effort among low-achieving students, but they do not employ challenging standards (p. 141).

The specificity and academic nature of teachers' evaluative behavior are predictors not only of effort but of perceptions that students have of themselves and of their control over the evaluations they receive. Ditza Oren (1980) examined in great detail the evaluation techniques of teachers in twenty-one classrooms of three racially integrated schools. She found that teachers' evaluations were often eclectic. Rather than conforming to either a pure version of a noncompetitive model where comparative grading was de-emphasized or to a more traditional competitive model where grading was emphasized, some teachers combined frequent use of grading with frequent conferences with individuals in which they informed the students how well they were doing and in which areas they needed improvement. Oren created a detailed thirteen-item index, which she named "varied and specific feedback." High-scoring classrooms had a mix of marking and grading with individual communication. In contrast, classrooms with a lower value on the feedback index focused on numbered scores and on letter grades without individual conferences. In still a third type of classroom, she found little feedback of any kind.

Oren found that fewer children made external attributions about the causes of good or poor grades in classrooms with varied and specific feedback. The variance of the distribution of attribution scores in these classrooms was smaller than in classrooms with other evaluation systems. Using this data set and Oren's index of feedback, Maria Macias-Sanchez (1982) found that minority students had higher academic performance expectations in classrooms where they experienced varied and specific feedback. The dependent variables in these two studies are ordinarily seen as more or less permanent features of individual personality. What is most interesting about these findings is that charateristics such as academic self-concept and attributions can vary as a function of the evaluation system of the classroom; thus they appear to have situational origins.

Ability as a Consequence of Task and Evaluation Structure

Susan Rosenholtz and Carl Simpson (1984) have developed a theory of ability formation; intellectual ability is a social construct central to American culture. It is primarily in the elementary school that children come to understand that human ability can be seen as a single dimension on which people can be ranked from high to low. What is critical for this review is their argument that students' ideas about ability are powerfully shaped by processes of social comparison that take place both within classroom tasks and by teacher evaluations.

Rosenholtz and Simpson provide evidence in support of their theory by examining the way children's evaluations of their own and others' ability vary according to key features of the classroom. The consensual nature of this social construct is illustrated by data showing the high level of agreement between peers and between peers and teachers on ranking of reading ability or academic ability (Rosenholtz and Wilson 1980; Simpson 1981).

In their view, social-comparison processes are most powerfully shaped by what they call the "dimensionality" of classroom organization. Unidimensional organization of instruction establishes conditions that facilitate "ability formation." In unidimensional classrooms, daily activities tend to be organized around comparison, and they tend to imply a single underlying dimension of comparison. When instruction and student performances imply few different performance dimensions, students' perception of ability should become one-dimensional.

In practice, unidimensional classrooms have academic task structures that are undifferentiated, and in these classrooms all students work on similar tasks or with a narrow range of materials and methods. For example, classes that require reading as a prerequisite for successful performance of most tasks and classes with a high reliance on paper-and-pencil tasks would classify as unidimensional.

This task structure facilitates social comparison; students can easily tell how well they are doing in comparison to others. A second feature of unidimensional classrooms is a low level of student autonomy. This cuts down on the variety of tasks and prevents students from using their own evaluations of performance. A third feature of unidimensional classrooms is the use of whole-class instruction or clear-cut ability groups. A final feature is the emphasis on grading as a means of conveying clear-cut unidimensional evaluation by teachers.

The multidimensional classroom, in contrast, has varied materials and methods, a higher degree of student autonomy, more individual tasks, varying grouping patterns, and less reliance on grading. Studies that have contrasted these two types of classrooms have found that students' self-reported ability levels have a greater variance in unidimensional classrooms (Rosenholtz and Rosenholtz 1981; Simpson 1981). In contrast, in multidimensional classrooms fewer children will define themselves as "below average," thus restricting the distribution of self-evaluations. Students' reports of their peers' ability levels are also more dispersed and more consensual (as measured by a coefficient of concordance) in unidimensional classes, and perceptions of individual ability are much more closely related to ratings by teachers and peers.

In their extensive review of the literature on children's conceptions of their own ability, Rosenholtz and Simpson (1984) cite evidence to support their position that the frequently observed tendency for young children to have unrealistically high academic expectations is due to the early grade school teachers' pattern of rewarding effort rather than objective performance. Thus, the basis of the teachers' evaluation and the nature of social-comparison processes of peers are fundamental to the formation of the construct of ability.

ANTECEDENTS AND CONSEQUENCES OF STATUS

Status characteristics are social rankings in which it is generally believed it is better to be in the high state than the low state. The process by which status characteristics come to affect interaction and influence is described by expectation states theory (Berger, Cohen, and Zelditch 1966, 1972).

Race and ethnicity are examples of diffuse status characteristics that have been shown to affect the behavior of schoolchildren as they interact while doing collective tasks. When a status characteristic is diffuse, general expectations for competence and incompetence are attached to the characteristic. For example, when a racial status characteristic becomes salient in the situation, the prestige and power order of the small group working on a collective task comes to reflect the broader social-status ranking of the races in a kind of self-fulfilling prophecy. White children turn out to be more active and influential than black children. (For a full description of this process, see Berger, Rosenholtz, and Zelditch 1980.) Researchers in the United States, in Canada, and in Israel have repeatedly shown through the use of a standardized game task that race and ethnicity can act as a status characteristic, and thus high-status students are more active and influential than low-status students (Cohen 1982).

This status-organizing process is related to expectations of competence that actors in collective task groups have of themselves and one another. It bears no relationship to feelings of friendliness. Thus the use of cooperative interracial groups in desegregated classrooms can confirm racist stereotypes related to the lesser competence of black and brown students and, simultaneously, generate increased feelings of friendliness between the races.

Other status characteristics at work in the classroom can have an impact on students' interactions as they do collective tasks. The most powerful are academic status characteristics. These are closely related to the construct of intellectual ability that Rosenholtz and Simpson discuss. When students see themselves and are seen by classmates as having more and less academic ability or reading ability than others have, those who are seen as having more ability will be more active and influential than those who are seen as having less ability (Hoffman and Cohen 1972; Rosenholtz 1984; Tammivaara 1982). Presumably when students strongly agree on the ranking of classmates according to reading ability or academic ability in the classroom, the status characteristic will more powerfully affect interaction in a smaller group. This particular proposition has yet to be tested.

Sex operates as a status characteristic in mixed-sex groups of adolescents and adults (Lockheed and Hall 1976), particularly when the task is gender neutral or male oriented (Lockheed 1985). However, when Marlaine Lockheed, A. M. Harris, and W. P. Nemcef (1983) composed mixed-sex groups of fourth and fifth graders and had them play the standardized game task, there were no differences in behavior related to sex. Girls were, however, perceived as less competent and less leaderlike than boys. Just why sex becomes a status characteristic as students move toward adolescence but does not reliably appear as a status characteristic with younger children is an intriguing mystery that has not yet been solved.

Although sex is not a status characteristic in the early elementary years, it is a powerful basis for the organization of social behavior in the school. In a review of research, Lockheed states that studies show that most friendships are within-sex; on a sociometric instrument, schoolchildren will choose to work or sit with classmates of the same sex, not with classmates of the opposite sex; observed interaction in the classroom shows that students have many more interactions with the same sex than with the opposite sex (Lockheed 1985). Lockheed cautions against overreliance on sociometric instruments as measures of sex segregation, because interaction between the sexes is far greater than what would be expected from the preferences stated on questionnaires.

Treating Status Characteristics in Ongoing Classrooms

The classroom is a multicharacteristic situation. Students vary on three different types of status characteristics: social, academic, and peer. Social status characteristics are those ascribed characteristics brought into the classroom from the outside society (race, ethnicity, and sex). Academic status characteristics are created and maintained in the classroom setting. Peer status characteristics are created in the informal relationships among students. Very few studies have specifically tested the operation of peer status on behavior; one of those studies is Murray Webster and James Driskell's (1980) work on attractiveness as a status characteristic.

Expectation states theory has been used to create various interventions that modify the operation of status characteristics. These interventions have been successful in laboratory and in controlled classroom settings (Cohen 1982). In 1972, Marlaine Lockheed, Mark Lohman, and I ran an experimental summer school in which we were able to produce and maintain equal status relations between black and white students over a six-week period (Cohen, Lockheed, and Lohman 1976.) However, this summer school employed no conventional academic tasks. Susan Rosenholtz (1985) was able to modify the effects of reading ability on peer relations with an experimental one-week curriculum featuring the use of multiple intellectual abilities. Her aim was to produce in each child a mixed set of expectations for competence on the three different abilities featured in the curriculum rather than a uniformly high or low set of competence expectations based on reading ability.

Despite these successes, the classroom is one of the most difficult places to produce lasting equal-status behavior because of the strong relevance of academic ranking as a status characteristic. Given what we know about the effects of the unidimensionality of the classroom on the formation of conceptions of ability, unless these features of the classroom are permanently changed, a new academic status characteristic is likely to be re-created as soon as the old one is modified.

The complexity of the classroom requires that one have a considerable knowledge of the various factors that can affect the operation of status characteristics before one can successfully modify the effects of status in a particular organizational context in a way that will persist. In the last few years we have made considerable progress in understanding what some of these factors might be.

Evidence for Centrality of Academic Status. Evidence shows that teachers respond more to children's academic status than to their race or ethnicity. In an extremely large sample of students from integrated sixth- and eighth-grade classrooms (Mercer, Iadicola, and Moore 1980), teachers' expectations for each student were measured by questions on how much schooling they expected students to complete and the kind of occupation teachers expected students would attain. The strongest single predictor of teachers' ratings was students' scores on a test of word knowledge. Ethnic group was not an important predictor of teachers' ratings, although students' socioeconomic status did make a statistically reliable contribution to teacher evaluation in all but one of the analyses. Similarly, a study of fifth graders by Marlaine Lockheed and W. R. Morgan (1979) suggests that teachers' expectations are primarily based on students' prior achievement. In studying children's and teachers' expectations in early elementary grades, Doris Entwisle and Leslie Hayduk (1982) found that the children's achievement rather than other factors such as race and sex affect teachers' evaluations and expectations. Finally, an analysis by Aage Sorensen and Maureen Hallinan (1984) found no direct individual-level effect of race on the assignment of individuals to ability groups after achievement was controlled.

Several studies have shown the power of academic status to determine peer status. In a study of the effects of sex, race, and achievement on children's friendships, Tuma and Hallinan (1979) showed that children's being of the same race did not significantly influence change in friendship choices once their achievement was controlled. The greater was the difference in achievement between two children, the less stable was a choice of a child as a best friend. Moreover, a choice of a child as a nonfriend was significantly more stable as the difference in achievement became greater. Thus, academic status was evidently a determinant of peer status, while race was not. In desegregated schools, Norman Miller (1980) has shown that the popularity or acceptance of black children is produced by their academic achievement rather than their academic achievement being produced by their social acceptance, as had been claimed by the early students of desegregated classrooms.

Academic status is also one of the most reliable predictors of rate of participation in class and rate of initiation toward the teacher (Brophy and Good 1974). In Greta Morine-Dershimer's (1983) analysis of reading lessons in six elementary classrooms, being a boy or a high achiever and being seen as an attentive model student by the teacher were all independent predictors of frequency of participation in discussion, while ethnicity was not a predictor of participation.

Simultaneous Operation of Multiple Status Characteristics. When multiple status characteristics are operating, people tend to combine the expectations from different status characteristics; thus if a person is high on one characteristic and low on another and his partner is likewise high on one characteristic and low on the other, the result may be equal status behavior. If a person is high on two status characteristics, he or she should be more influential than if he or she were high on only one status characteristic (Humphreys and Berger 1981).

The operation of inconsistent status characteristics can be seen in those classrooms where peer status is not positively associated with academic status. In the classrooms studied by Rosenholtz and Simpson (1984), academic and peer status were always highly positively associated. Under these conditions, the impact of the task and evaluation structure of the classroom on the status system could easily be measured by calculating the degree of agreement on ranking of academic ability.

When Bruce Wilson (1979) tried to carry out a similar analysis on twenty-one fifth- and sixth-grade racially integrated and extremely academically diverse classrooms, he found a lower level of agreement on ability ranking than in previous studies and little consistent relationship between the task and evaluation structure and agreement on ability ranking. In these classrooms, academic status and measures of social influence were often unrelated or even negatively related.

The simplest interpretation of what is happening under these special conditions is that in those schools where black teachers and students occupy powerful social positions, blacks often have high peer status. The operation of this alternative status characteristic affects the ratings on academic ability in that those who are seen as socially powerful are credited with higher academic status by some classmates than by others. This leads to the greater dissensus on the ability rankings found by Wilson.

When groups that varied according to race and perceived reading ability were composed from these same desegregated, academically heterogeneous classrooms and were given the standard game task used to test status characteristics, the results were also very puzzling. When a black student who was seen as low in reading ability but high in social power was combined with a white student who was seen as high in reading ability but low in social power, the result was a pattern of equal status behavior. Only when a black student who ranked equally low in reading ability and social power was combined with a white student who was perceived as having good reading ability did the expected pattern of white dominance clearly emerge (Cohen 1982). Regression analysis showed that both the academic status characteristic and perceived social influence were influencing participation.

Particularly in schools where blacks are numerous in the student body (and on the faculty) but are of lower social class than the whites, the higher peer status of black students can combine with their lower academic and racial status. The net effect can be equal status behavior in interracial groups (Cohen 1984). This interpretation is supported by the work of Peter Iadicola (1979), who found that in schools with higher proportions of minority students and faculty and with multicultural curricula, Anglos were much less dominant over minority students in collective task situations. Expectation states theory would describe this effect as the result of (1) referent actors in the environment who have the same status as some of the participants in the collective task displaying high competence, and (2) the tendency of actors to combine information about competence from different status characteristics (Humphreys and Berger 1981). (For a thorough discussion of this effect see Cohen 1982.)

LEARNING OUTCOMES AND THE SOCIAL SYSTEM OF THE CLASSROOM

I have deliberately omitted mention of learning measures until this point because I first wanted to describe what is known about the operation of the social system. Educational researchers have consistently tried to short-circuit the complexities of the classroom by doing research in which they have correlated the presence or absence of an educational technique such as open classroom or cooperative learning groups with test score gains. This type of research does not conceptualize exactly what these techniques do to the task structure, to the evaluation system, or to the operation of status characteristics, nor does it measure implementation in the classroom. As a result, the research has quite consistently turned up no difference or inconsistent differences in comparing experimental classes with the innovation to control classrooms.

The recent research I have reviewed has multiple consequences for learning outcomes. In the first place, task structure affects interaction, which can, under certain conditions, affect learning outcomes. Second, evaluation systems affect effort and engagement—two variables with a well-documented relationship to learning outcomes (Berliner et al. 1978). Third, task and evaluation structure have been shown to affect the operation of the status system in the classroom. Status, in turn, affects participation, which predicts learning gains under certain circumstances. This network of interrelationships is shown in figure 7.1.

Figure 7.1
Social System of the Classroom and Learning Outcomes

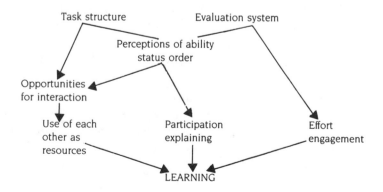

Task Structure and Learning Outcomes

David Johnson and associates (1981) conducted a meta-analysis in which they concluded that cooperative learning, in general, yielded superior academic achievement compared to traditional, whole-class, or individualistic instruction. However, as Sharan points out, this finding did not consider pupils' ethnic background or the level or kind of cognitive functioning involved, whether it be skill learning or more conceptually sophisticated subjects, nor did it specify which particular cooperative methods were employed. Sharan concludes that a better characterization of the literature is the more conservative statement that cooperative learning methods, in general, are not likely to yield achievement results inferior to traditional direct instruction.

Noreen Webb's review (1982) makes a major step forward by focusing on the interaction processes themselves and their relationship to learning rather than on the particular innovation that changed the task structure from that of traditional classrooms to small-group learning. She concludes that giving help and receiving help are positively related to learning gains, while off-task behavior and passive behavior are negatively related to achievement. Thus, she directs attention to particular behaviors like "explaining" as conducive to learning. She provides evidence that students may benefit from the use of other persons in the group as resources in completing the task. Her review also proposes that when learning tasks are conceptual, groups provide critical opportunities for cognitive restructuring.

Webb's review suggests at least three basic factors that will affect whether or not the experience of interdependent task structure will increase the learning of a given individual. They are: (1) the activity rate of that individual within the group; (2) whether or not individuals are able to use the group as a resource to understand the task; and (3) the relationship between the behaviors students practice in the group and the criterion measure for learning. The first two points are obvious, but the third is not well understood. An excellent example of this third point is the finding of Sharan and associates (1984) that in teaching English in Israel, cooperative group treatments showed superior gain scores in only one respect—listening comprehension. He relates this finding to basic research on how languages are learned; discourse in the group gave children opportunities for practice in comprehending language that are quite unavailable in the drill and recitation of the whole-class method.

Too often, sociologists and psychologists neglect to examine the character of the curriculum materials employed in studies that relate task structure to learning outcomes. Given the right kind of challenging group task, the rate of talking and working together can be a predictor of conceptual learning. The task must provide the necessary learning experiences for the grasp of concepts. Using detailed observation of children working at learning centers during "Finding Out/ Descubrimiento," a bilingual program designed to improve thinking skills, Cohen and Intili (1981) found that the rate of talking and working together was related to gains in conceptual measures. These conceptual measures included CTBS (California Test of Basic Skills) Concepts and Applications and a criterion-referenced test of thinking skills. In a second set of data taken on thirteen classrooms in 1982–83, the percentage of children talking and manipulating the materials was correlated with average gains of the whole class on mathematics concepts and applications ($r = 0.72$). We argue that this relationship is a product partly of the intrinsically interesting, carefully engineered curriculum materials and partly a product of the fact that in this approach, children are allowed to use each other as resources to gain access to the materials, to use trial and error, and to make mistakes on their own. Allowing children to solve problems for themselves is related to conceptual gains in comparison to methods where the teacher closely monitors the learner's response.

Cecilia Navarrete (1985) took videotapes of second graders interacting in groups during the "Finding Out/Descubrimiento" program and found that much of the interaction was related to figuring out how to do the tasks from reading the activity cards. The extent to which individuals sought assistance, received it, and returned to their tasks was significantly related to gains in reading. This finding suggests that the very process of decoding the instructions on activity cards and worksheets with the help of peers can lead to improvement in reading skills.

Black students made consistently better achievement gains than did white students in Slavin's (1983) cooperative group approach that involved peer tutoring. Since in his classrooms blacks were initially lower achievers, this may be a product of their receiving critical assistance in reading and thus understanding the material to be learned. Since the material was not highly conceptual in nature, the higher achievers received no particular benefit (or disadvantage) from helping the lower achievers. They did not require assistance in reading and understanding the material.

A cooperative context along with training in rational argumentation is the preferred setting for constructive controversy between students (Johnson and Johnson 1979). In a review of research the Johnsons found that when students engage in constructive controversy, a number of highly desirable cognitive outcomes such as creativity and better student problem solving are more likely to occur.

Ability Grouping and Learning: A Renewed Interest

There is a renewed interest in instructional grouping among both sociologists and psychologists working in education. Peterson, Wilkinson, and Hallinan have recently edited a volume of papers entitled *The Social Context of Instruction: Group Organization and Group Processes* (1984). Contemporary work is more theoretically oriented and tends to involve detailed observations of what goes on inside groups.

By conceptualizing ability grouping as a response to organizational and management constraints faced by the elementary school teacher, sociologists have been able to show that ability grouping is not exactly what people think it is: a systematic attempt to produce groups with homogeneous ability. Hallinan and Sorensen (1983) find that the number and size of ability groups remain about the same regardless of the ability distribution in the classroom. Ability groups increase variance in achievement only if they are homogeneous in ability (which they often are not). Factors that affect student assignment to ability groups include organizational needs and constraints within a classroom, student management, and student discipline (Barr and Dreeben 1983).

In her overall summary of the volume on instructional grouping (Peterson, Wilkinson, and Hallinan 1984), Hallinan (1984) concludes that both tracking and ability grouping depress growth in academic achievement for students in low-ability groups (p. 232). One of the major reasons is not the grouping per se but the fact that the kind of teaching and learning experience in low groups is different from that in high groups. To quote Hallinan's summary:

Empirical evidence demonstrates that different modes of instruction are used in different tracks and ability groups. In low tracks and ability groups teachers present material at a slower pace than in higher level groups (Barr 1975; Barr and Dreeben 1983). More time is spent off-task for administrative and disciplinary reasons (Eder 1981; Evertson 1982; Persell 1977). . . . In general students in low tracks and ability groups are given fewer and poorer opportunities to learn than their peers in higher level groups. [P. 231]

It is important to note that neither teachers' expectations nor even teachers' attention and feedback account for low achievement in low-ability groups (Weinstein 1976). The researcher must pay attention to materials, to pacing, and to the creation of different learning environments that results from composing groups of children who may present difficult management problems (Eder 1981; Felmlee and Eder 1983).

Status and Learning

Status occupies a pivotal position in the classroom social system. Academic status characteristics are shaped by the task and evaluation structure; status characteristics, in turn, are a determinant of learning under some conditions. (See figure 7.1.) The scope conditions of expectation states theory state that status will be a determinant of participation when a collective task is performed by a mixed status group. Most classroom tasks are not collective. Nevertheless, status appears to affect participation under classroom conditions where these scope conditions are relaxed. Effects of status can be seen in differential probabilities of student initiation toward the teacher, in participation in reading lessons, and in informal social relations.

Under some conditions, increased participation is instrumental in learning. In the reading lessons studied by Morine-Dershimer (1983), teachers only called on children who volunteered. Given that higher status children participated more frequently under these conditions, it is not surprising that status had an important impact on gains in reading achievement.

I have studied the impact of status during "Finding Out/Descubrimiento," the program previously described in this chapter. In the 1979 data set, when mixed status groups worked at learning centers on activities using mathematics and science concepts, the children were not really engaged in a collective task, although they were permitted and encouraged to help each other. Status was measured by the frequency with which children were chosen as good in mathematics and science and the frequency with which they were chosen as friends. The frequency of choice was translated into quintile scores for each classroom. Because people are known to combine status information, the scores on academic and peer status were added for each individual. A path analysis revealed that status was a determinant of the rate at which the children talked and worked together. Holding constant the pretest scores on achievement, the rate of task-related interaction was, in turn, a predictor of gains on a criterion-referenced science test (Cohen 1984). In subsequent analysis, working with a measure of mathematical concepts and applications, I have been able to document two separate effects of status: one direct path from the status characteristic to posttest score and a second path to posttest score mediated by talking and working together.

Noreen Webb and Cathy Kenderski (1984) found somewhat similar results in an analysis of interaction in cooperative learning groups of junior high school mathematics classes. Ability scores *relative to other members in the group* predicted both giving explanations and achievement gains. Absolute ability as measured by test scores did not predict these dependent variables. The effect of relative ability strongly suggests that it was a specific status characteristic based on mathematics ability that was the determinant of interaction and achievement in Webb's study.

CONCLUSION

To talk about the classroom as a social system, we must interconnect the concepts and findings presented in this chapter. I think about them in this way: Task structure or technology comes onto center stage along with the evaluation system. These are two concepts almost totally neglected in psychological research on classrooms. Task and evaluation structure have important consequences for the use of authority by the teacher and for the way teachers and aides or teaching teams work together. Second, task and evaluation structure partly determine the status system in the classroom, especially the operation of academic status. Third, the task structure also determines the interaction pattern in the classroom and thus has an indirect influence on informal social relations among students. The joint operation of task, evaluation, and status has many effects on behavior that are relevant to learning: participation, effort, the possibility of using peers as resources, the opportunity to discover concepts for oneself, and the benefits of explaining things to others. If interdependent task groups are used, the level of interaction and learning will be related to the individual's status in the group.

If We Knew Then What We Know Now

Innovations such as learning centers, open classrooms, and individualization changed something at the heart of the classroom social system—its task structure. This change toward a more differentiated technology and a more uncertain technology had some very serious consequences for teachers. It meant that teachers were going to need some help in changing from routine bureaucratic supervision to delegated authority. It meant that teachers were going to need support in solving problems with the uncertain technology, support in learning how to work with aides, help with learning to work with teaching team members. Because no one gave the teachers the help they needed, these innovations often degenerated into forms capable of direct supervision. For example, the marvelous science activity materials developed in the sixties are today found sitting in dusty closets. Despite the excellent National Science Foundation institutes on the teaching of science, teachers could not manage the complexity that these activities created for classroom supervision.

It was not until the most recent developments of cooperative learning techniques that developers gave teachers practical assistance in retraining students with new norms for behaviors that are necessary if students are to function without direct supervision by the teacher. This is the only practical way to delegate authority to children, but many teachers who struggled with open classrooms were left to try to discover this rather elementary sociological principle for themselves.

I think it was a mistake to introduce radical changes in the classroom without creating the support and training teachers require to manage such complexity. Now we might be able to design a workable support system for the changes teachers would have to make, but with the exception of those educators interested in cooperative learning, nobody wants our services.

Today's Practice in Light of What We Know

If yesterday's mistakes give us cause for regret, today's practices may be an even more serious cause for concern. Look at today's return to large-batch processing, ability grouping, and constant testing. The return to direct instruction was inspired partly by the almost complete reliance on seatwork that followed the degeneration of individualized instruction. In a study of over one thousand classrooms across this country, John Goodlad (1984) found that three categories of activity marked by passivity—written work, listening, and preparing for assignments—dominate in the likelihood of their occurring at any given time at all three levels of schooling. All three activities are almost exclusively set and monitored by teachers (p. 95).

Demographic shifts and new waves of immigration have produced extraordinarily heterogeneous classrooms because of differences in language proficiency and academic skills. In order to deal with this complex mix of student problems, more complex instruction is obviously needed. Instead, what is widely recommended is nothing other than the unidimensional classroom that Rosenholtz and Simpson described.

If heterogeneous classrooms use only large groups, ability groups (Goodlad 1984, p. 141), and seatwork, then the result will be an agreed-upon ranking according to ability, in which the more academically advanced, more middle-class children will be the "smarts" and the lower status children and newcomers to the country will be the "dumbs." Because of the operation of a strong academic status characteristic, low-ranking individuals will be unlikely to speak up and get the help they need. Their classmates will be unavailable to them as intellectual resources. They are likely to be relegated to the low-ability groups where, the researchers have concluded, they will have an inferior educational experience. If they are struggling with the English language, they will not understand much of what the teacher says to them; furthermore, this task structure gives them no chance to learn language in the way children readily learn it, that is, by talking with each other. As a sociologist, I could not have devised a more fiendishly perfect system within the classroom with which to reproduce the status order of the outside society. I believe that we as researchers have some responsibility to sensitize developers and educators who are disseminating techniques such as direct instruction to stop and think about the consequences of the new orthodoxies.

A Note to the Researcher

I do not mean to imply that the research is complete. On the contrary, my experience with trying to apply status treatments to ongoing classrooms has given me too much humility for that. We have much to learn about how contextual effects modify status systems and behavior. We are only beginning to sense the basis for peer status in different settings and to understand how peer status interacts with academic status. We are still struggling with the application of interventions designed to change status and interaction, which might give students equal opportunities for interaction in ongoing classrooms.

Given what we do know, I wish we could declare a moratorium on research that compares classrooms according to the techniques they are supposedly using and looks only at achievement outcomes. We now know too much to permit that kind of research; it is unlikely to advance our understanding. We are ready to make a more theoretical argument about why we would expect learning to occur under specified task and evaluation structures and as a result of certain behaviors and processes. That argument should take advantage of the theory and research that has already been developed. The researcher must then find out to what extent the classrooms exhibit the desired task and evaluation structures and to what extent learning is related to the prescribed behaviors and social processes. The argument may turn out to be wholly or partly wrong; but at least we will continue to learn more about the sociology of the classroom.

REFERENCES

Barr, R. "How Children Are Taught to Read: Grouping and Pacing." *School Review* 83 (1975): 479–498.

Barr, R., and Dreeben, R. *How Schools Work*. Chicago: University Press, 1983.

Berger, J.; Cohen, B. P.; and Zelditch, M., Jr. "Status Characteristics and Expectation States." In *Sociological Theories in Progress*. Vol. 1. Edited by J. Berger, M. Zelditch, Jr., and B. Anderson. Boston: Houghton Mifflin, 1966.

Berger, J.; Cohen, B. P.; and Zelditch, M., Jr. "Status Characteristics and Social Interaction." *American Sociological Review* 37 (1972): 241–255.

Berger, J.; Rosenholtz, S. J.; and Zelditch, M., Jr. "Status Organizing Processes." *Annual Review of Sociology* 6 (1980): 479–508.

Berliner, D.; Fisher, C.; Filby, N.; Marliave, R.; Cahen, L.; Dishaw, M.; and Moore, J. *Beginning Teacher Evaluation Study—Teaching Behaviors, Academic Learning Time and Student Achievement: Final Report of Phase II-B*. San Francisco: Far West Laboratory, 1978.

Bloom, J., and Schuncke, G. "The Effect of a Cooperative Curriculum Experience on Choice of Task Organization." *Journal of Experimental Education* 48 (1979): 84–90.

Boocock, S. S. "The Social Organization of the Classroom." *Annual Review of Sociology* 4 (1978): 1–28.

Bossert, S. T. *Tasks and Social Relationships in Classrooms*. New York: Cambridge University Press, 1979.

Breer, P., and Locke, E. A. *Task Experience as a Source of Attitude*. Homewood, Ill.: Dorsey Press, 1965.

Brophy, J. E., and Good, T. L. *Teacher-Student Relationships: Causes and Consequences*. New York: Holt, Rinehart and Winston, 1974.

Cohen, E. G. "Sociology and the Classroom: Setting the Conditions for Teacher-Student Interaction." *Review of Educational Research* 42 (1972): 9–24.

Cohen, E. G. "Expectation States and Interracial Interaction in School Settings. *Annual Review of Sociology* 8 (1982): 209–235.

Cohen, E. G. "Talking and Working Together: Status, Interaction, and Learning."

In *The Social Context of Instruction: Group Organization and Group Processes*, edited by P. L. Peterson, L. C. Wilkinson, and M. Hallinan. San Diego: Academic Press, 1984.

Cohen, E. G. "The Desegregated School: Problems in Status Power and Interethnic Climate." In *Desegregation: Groups in Contact: Psychology of Desegregation*, edited by N. Miller and M. B. Brewer. Academic Press, 1984.

Cohen, E. G. *Designing Groupwork for the Classroom.* New York: Teachers College Press, forthcoming.

Cohen, E. G.; Deal, T. E.; Meyer, J. W.; and Scott, W. R. "Technology and Teaming in the Elementary School." *Sociology of Education* 52 (1979): 20–33.

Cohen, E. G., and DeAvila, E. "Learning to Think in Math and Science: Improving Local Education for Minority Children." *Final Report to the Johnson Foundation.* Stanford University, School of Education, 1983.

Cohen, E. G., and Intili, J. K. "Interdependence and Management in Bilingual Classrooms. *Final Report*, NIE Grant. Stanford: Center for Educational Research, Stanford University, 1981 and 1982.

Cohen, E. G.; Intili, J. K.; and Robbins, S. "Task and Authority: A Sociological View of Classroom Management. In *The National Society for the Study of Education: Seventy-Eighth Yearbook*, edited by D. Duke, 1979, Part II, 116–143.

Cohen, E. G.; Lockheed, M. E.; and Lohman, M. R. "The Center for Interracial Cooperation: A Field Experiment. *Sociology of Education* 49 (1976): 47–58.

Dornbusch, S. M., and Scott, W. R. *Evaluation and Exercise of Authority.* San Francisco: Jossey-Bass, 1975.

Eder, D. "Ability Grouping as a Self-fulfilling Prophecy: A Micro-Analysis of Teacher-Student Interaction." *Sociology of Education* 54 (1981): 151–162.

Entwisle, D. E., and Hayduk, L. A. *Early Schooling: Cognitive and Effective Outcomes.* Baltimore, The Johns Hopkins University Press, 1982.

Epstein, J. L., and Karweit, N. *Friends in School: Patterns of Selection and Influence in Secondary Schools.* New York: Academic Press, 1983.

Espinosa, R. W. "The Impact of Evaluation Processes upon Student Effort in Ethnic Groups which Vary in Academic Preparation." Ph.D. dissertation, Stanford University, 1975.

Evertson, C. "Differences in Instructional Activities in Average- and Low-achieving Junior High English and Math Classes." *Elementary School Journal* 82 (1982): 329–350.

Felmlee, D., and Eder, D. "Contextual Effects in the Classroom: The Impact of Ability Groups on Student Attention." *Sociology of Education* 56 (1983): 77–87.

Galbraith, J. *Designing Complex Organizations.* Reading, Mass.: Addison-Wesley, 1973.

Gonzales, J. "Instructor Evaluations and Academic Effort: The Chicano in College." Ph.D. dissertation, Stanford University, 1982.

Goodlad, J. I. *A Place Called School: Prospects for the Future.* New York: McGraw-Hill, 1984.

Hallinan, M. "Friendship Patterns in Open and Traditional Classrooms." *Sociology of Education* 49 (1976): 254–265.

Hallinan, M. T. "Summary and Implications." In *The Social Context of Instruction: Group Organization and Group Processes*, edited by P. L. Peterson, L. C. Wilkinson, and M. Hallinan. San Diego: Academic Press, 1984.

Hallinan, M. T., and Sorensen, A. B. "The Formation and Stability of Instructional Groups." *American Sociological Review* 1983, pp. 838–851.

Hallinan, M. T., and Tuma, N. B. "Classroom Effects on Change in Children's Friendships." *Sociology of Education* 51 (1978): 270–282.

Hickson, D. J.; Pugh, D. S.; and Pheysey, D. C. "Operations and Technology and Organization Structure: An Empirical Reappraisal." *Administrative Science Quarterly* 14 (1969): 378–397.

Hoffman, D., and Cohen, E. G. "An Exploratory Study to Determine the Effects of Generalized Performance Expectations upon Activity and Influence of Students Engaged in a Group Simulation Game." Paper presented at the annual meeting of the American Educational Research Association, Chicago, 1972.

Humphreys, P., and Berger, J. "Theoretical Consequences of the Status Characteristics Formulation." *American Journal of Sociology* 86 (1981): 953–983.

Iadicola, P. "Schooling and Social Power: A Presentation of a Weberian conflict model." Ph.D. dissertation, University of California at Riverside, 1979.

Intili, J. K.: "Structural Conditions in the School that Facilitate Reflective Decision-Making." Ph.D. dissertation, Stanford University, 1977.

Johnson, D. W., and Johnson, R. T. *Learning Together and Alone.* Englewood Cliffs, N. J.: Prentice-Hall, 1975.

Johnson, D. W., and Johnson, R. T. "Conflict in the Classroom: Controversy and Learning. *Review of Educational Research* 49 (1979): 51–70.

Johnson, D. W.; Maruyama, G.; Johnson, R. T.; Nelson, D.; and Skon, L. "Effects of Cooperative, Competitive and Individualistic Goal Structures on Achievement." *Psychological Bulletin* 89 (1981): 47–62.

Lockheed, M. E. "Some Determinants and Consequences of Sex Segregation in the Classroom." In *Gender Influences in Classroom Interaction*, edited by L. Cherry Wilkinson and C. Marrett. San Diego, Calif.: Academic Press, 1985.

Lockheed, M. E., and Hall, K. "Conceptualizing Sex as a Status Characteristic: Applications to Leadership Training Strategies." *Journal of Social Issues* 32 (1976): 111–124.

Lockheed, M. E.; Harris, A. M.; and Nemcef, W. P. "Sex and Social Influence: Does Sex Function as a Status Characteristics in Mixed-Sex Groups of Children? *Journal of Educational Psychology* 75 (1983): 877–886.

Lockheed, M. E., and Morgan, W. R. *A Causal Model of Teachers' Expectations in Elementary Classrooms.* Research Report 79–12. Princeton, N.J.: Educational Testing Service, 1979.

Macias-Sanchez, M. "Instructional Organization and Academic Self-concept." Ph.D. dissertation, Stanford University, 1982.

March, J. G., and Simon, H. A. *Organizations.* New York: Wiley, 1958.

Mercer, J. R.; Iadicola, P.; and Moore, H. "Building Effective Multiethnic Schools: Evolving Models and Paradigms." In *School Desegregation: Past, Present and Future*, edited by W. G. Stephan and J. R. Feagin, pp. 281–307. New York: Plenum Press, 1980.

Meyer, J. W. and Rowan, B. "The Structure of Educational Organizations." In *Organizational Environments: Ritual and Rationality*, edited by J. W. Meyer and W. R. Scott. Beverly Hills, Calif.: Sage Publications, 1983.

Miller, N. "Making School Desegregation Work. "In *School Desegregation: Past, Present and Future*, edited by W. G. Stephan and J. R. Feagin, pp. 309–342. New York: Plenum Press, 1980.

Morine-Dershimer, G. "Instructional Strategy and the 'Creation' of Classroom Status." *American Educational Research Journal* 20 (1983): 645–661.

Natriello, G., and Dornbusch, S. M. *Teacher Evaluative Standards and Student Effort*. New York: Longman, 1984.

Natriello, G., and Scott, P. "Secondary School Evaluation Systems and Student Disengagement." Paper presented at the annual meeting of the American Educational Research Association, Los Angeles, 1981.

Navarrete, C. "Problem-Resolution in Small-Group Interaction: A Bilingual Classroom Study." Ph.D. dissertation, Stanford University, 1985.

Oren, D. R. "Classroom Structure and Attributions: The Effects of Structural Characteristics on Attributional Tendencies." Unpublished Ph.D. dissertation, Stanford University, 1980.

Perrow, C. *Complex Organizations: A Critical Essay*. Glenview, Ill.: Scott-Foresman, 1972.

Persell, C. *Education and Inequality: The Roots and Results of Stratification in America's Schools*. New York: The Free Press, 1977.

Peterson, P. L.; Wilkinson, L. C.; and Hallinan, M., eds. *The Social Context of Instruction: Group Organization and Group Processes*. San Diego, Calif.: Academic Press, 1984.

Robbins, S. H. "An Exploration of Student Choice in the Elementary School Classroom: Implications for Implementation." Ph.D. dissertation, Stanford University, 1977.

Rosenholtz, S. H. "Effect of Task Arrangements and Management Systems on Task Engagement of Low-Achieving Students." Ph.D. dissertation, Stanford University, 1981.

Rosenholtz, S. J. "Treating Problems of Academic Status." In *Status, Rewards, and Influence*, edited by J. Berger and M. Zelditch. San Francisco: Jossey-Bass, 1985.

Rosenholtz, S., and Rosenholtz, S. H. "Classroom Organization and the Perception of Ability." *Sociology of Education* 54 (1981): 132–140.

Rosenholtz, S. J., and Simpson, C. "The Formation of Ability Conceptions: Developmental Trend or Social Construction?" *Review of Educational Research* 54 (1984): 31–63.

Rosenholtz, S. J., and Wilson, B. "The Effects of Classroom Structure on Shared Perceptions of Ability." *American Educational Research Journal* 17 (1980): 175–182.

Rothenberg, J. "Peer Relations and Activity Structures in Elementary School Classrooms." Ph.D. dissertation, University of Michigan, 1982.

Sharan, S. "Cooperative Learning in Small Groups: Recent Methods and Effects on Achievement, Attitudes and Ethnic Relations." *Review of Educational Research* 50 (1980): 241–271.

Sharan, S.; Kussell, P.; Hertz-Lazarowitz, R.; Bejerano, Y.; Raviv, S.; and Sharan, Y. *Cooperative Learning in the Classroom: Research in Desegregated Schools*. Hillsdale, N.J.: Lawrence Erlbaum Associates: 1984.

Simpson, C. "Classroom Structure and the Organization of Ability." *Sociology of Education* 54 (1981): 120–132.

Slavin, R. E. *Cooperative Learning*. New York: Longman, 1983.

Sorensen, A. B., and Hallinan, M. "Effects of Race on Assignment to Ability Groups." In *The Social Context of Instruction: Group Organization and Group Processes*, edited by P. L. Peterson, L. C. Wilkinson, and M. Hallinan. San Diego, Calif.: Academic Press, 1984.

Sussman, L. "The Functioning of Peer Groups in Open Classrooms." Unpublished manuscript, Tufts University, 1973.

Tammivaara, J. "The Effects of Task Structure on Beliefs about Competence and Participation in Small Groups." *Sociology of Education* 55 (1982): 212–222.

Tuma, N. B., and Hallinan, M. T. "The Effects of Sex, Race, and Achievement on Schoolchildren's Friendships." *Social Forces* 57 (1979): 1265–1284.

Webb, N. M. "Interaction and Learning in Small Groups." *Review of Educational Research* 52 (1982): 421–445.

Webb, N., and Kenderski, C. M. "Student Interaction and Learning in Small-group and Whole-class Settings." In *The Social Context of Instruction: Group Organization and Group Processes*, edited by P. L. Peterson, L. C. Wilkinson, and M. Hallinan. San Diego, Calif.: Academic Press, 1984.

Webster, M., Jr., and Driskell, J. E., Jr. "Attractiveness and Status." Paper presented at the annual meeting of the American Sociological Association, 1980.

Weigel, R. H.; Wiser, P. L.; and Cook, S. W. "Impact of Cooperative Learning Experiences on Cross-ethnic Relations and Attitudes." *Journal of Social Issues* 31 (1975): 219–245.

Weinstein, R. S. "Reading Group Membership in First Grade: Teacher Behaviors and Pupil Experience Over Time." *Journal of Educational Psychology* 68(1976): 103–116.

Wilson, B. L. "Classroom Instructional Features and Conceptions of Academic Ability." Ph.D. dissertation, Stanford University, 1979.

8

On Anthropology

Frederick D. Erickson and Gary J. Bekker

INTRODUCTION

During the last twenty years the anthropology of education has emerged from being a theme in general anthropology to become a field of study in its own right with its own literature base, professional organization, journal, and place in university curricula. Thus, a review of the last twenty years encompasses much of the history of educational anthropology.

This chapter concerns the content or findings of educational anthropology rather than the issues of method and philosophy of science. Frederick Erickson treats both of these matters extensively in his chapter entitled "Qualitative Research on Teaching" in the forthcoming *Handbook of Research on Teaching* (1986a). There he argues that "the primary significance of interpretive approaches to research on teaching concerns issues of content . . . interpretive methods do not dictate content; rather interests in interpretive content lead one to search for methods that will be appropriate for study of that content" (p. 120). In this chapter major assertions of educational anthropologists are discussed in an analytic framework that groups together sets of main ideas. This is not an attempt at an exhaustive literature review; rather, references to exemplary publications illustrate a few major themes.

OVERVIEW OF THE HISTORY OF EDUCATIONAL ANTHROPOLOGY

A survey of the formation of educational anthropology as a field of study serves as a framework for discussing the field's specific contributions to our understanding of schooling in America. This survey focuses on the major themes around which research and reporting has been organized during the last twenty years.

The first monograph-length educational ethnography was Margaret Mead's *Coming of Age in Samoa*, published in 1928. Despite the current controversy surrounding her work (see, for example, Freeman 1983), Mead's contributions were significant because they focused attention on the study of childrearing.

After World War II, ethnographers began to focus directly on issues of formal education. Although concerned still with the influence of childrearing on personality formation in early childhood, they turned their attention to the impact of such socialization on children's behavior in schools. Early work in the field, particularly the initial work of George Spindler (1955a, 1955b, 1963, 1974a, 1974b) and Solon Kimball (1956a, 1956b, 1965, 1974; Kimball and McClellan 1962), was substantially influenced by the work of Mead. The "hidden curriculum" of unintended learning received special emphasis in this work, and it is exemplified in its extreme form by Jules Henry (1965). During this period the work of anthropologically trained ethnographers was paralleled in part by that of qualitative sociologists. An important study of professional socialization of young adults was conducted by Everett Hughes and his students (Becker, Geer, Hughes, and Strauss 1961).

In 1968 the anthropology of education received stimulus as a professional concern with the formation of the Council on Anthropology and Education, part of the American Anthropological Association. The council provided an organizational focus and a forum for discussion for a discipline that was previously an area of interest but was not a recognized field of study. The council's journal, *Anthropology and Education Quarterly*, grew from a newsletter to a full journal in only a few years.

The creation of the National Institute of Education (NIE) in the early 1970s did not contribute to educational anthropology per se. However, because key NIE personnel encouraged the submission and funding of ethnographic research projects, the Institute enabled educational anthropologists to contribute in unprecedented numbers to our understanding of American schools.

Much of the work that can be classified as educational anthropology has shared a concern for differences among cultures and the implications of such differences for learning. Educational anthropologists have disagreed about the nature of these cultural differences and the roles that they play in explaining school problems in modern Western societies. Interest in differences can be traced from Mead's chapter entitled "Our Educational Problems in the Light of Samoan Contrasts" (1928) to the very latest work that examines schools as arenas of active conflict between competing interests in society.

The literature that has appeared since the publication of Mead's work can be categorized chronologically into three sets. The first set of studies examined the hidden curriculum of childrearing and personality formation outside the schools. The second set examined hidden curriculum issues inside the schools in relation to family and community communication patterns. The third set looked at the generation of differences in the form of oppositional culture between students and staff within schools and the impact such activity has on life outside the schools. Thus, the literature of the anthropology of education paralleled the development of the field itself; it began with studies of early childhood socialization outside the schools, moved to a consideration about the differences between what happens inside the schools and the outside cultural patterns (especially community patterns of communication), and has now shifted attention to the issues inside schools that influence what happens outside schools. In a sense the field has rotated 180 degrees in the last twenty years, from concern with teaching and learning inside schools to interest in the political and economic influence that students' school experiences may have on society and on the lives of adults.

CONTRIBUTIONS OF EDUCATIONAL ANTHROPOLOGY TO OUR UNDERSTANDING OF SCHOOLING IN THE UNITED STATES

Building on the work of Mead, early studies of childrearing used personality psychology as an analytic tool for understanding child development across cultures. Beatrice Whiting (1963) and John Whiting (1941; Whiting and Whiting 1975) produced the most extensive of the cross-cultural studies of childrearing. The Whitings documented empirically two assertions about differences between traditional societies (which are nonindustrial and, for the most part, nonliterate) and modern societies and the implications of these differences for problems in schools. The first assertion was that children who were socialized in traditional societies tended to be less competitive and to have a greater sense of social responsibility than did their counterparts in modern societies. The second assertion was that families in traditional societies tended to have more children than did families in modern societies. Both assertions had been made previously, but only at the level of conjecture and casual observation; the Whitings, however, developed a large cross-cultural data base. They found that in traditional societies, with their large families and cooperative rather than competitive values, children contributed labor to their family's economic base and freed adults for doing other work by caring for their younger siblings. Children reared in traditional societies, it appeared, behave more altruistically and responsibly toward both peers and adults than do children raised in small families in which the children do not contribute to their family's economic base. The heightened concern for others that is inculcated by traditional societies appears maladaptive when children enter Western schools as they are usually organized. Teachers in such schools expect children to call attention to themselves and to respond as individuals when answering direct questions. Competition rather than cooperation, and calling attention to oneself and being judged as an individual rather than as a member of a group, tend to characterize interaction designed to foster motivation in modern Western schools. The Whitings contributed to our understanding of childhood socialization and schooling by finding empirical evidence that differences between traditional and modern societies in family organization and socialization practices have consequences for children's behavior, attitudes and personality development, and, indirectly, achievement as measured by schools.

There may be similar culture differences across social classes, with upper-middle-class children being more individualistic, seeking the limelight of attention and the rewards for individual achievement that schools provide. In contrast, the personality disposition of working-class children in modern societies may be more sharing, less competitive, and less desirous of certain kinds of attention than the disposition of middle-class children. This could result in working-class children displaying fewer of the behaviors that teachers interpret as indicators of ability. Hence, the ability and motivation of working-class children might be systematically underestimated by classroom teachers. The topic of culture difference across social classes is an important one, and it is a topic that has not yet been addressed adequately by the social sciences.

Cognitive psychology provided another avenue for early studies of childrearing and the relationship of childrearing to school experiences. At this time Michael Cole was beginning to examine the contextual embedding of intelligence. Even in his early work in Liberia (Gay and Cole 1967; Cole, Gay, Glick, and Sharp 1971), he started to find that what were construed by test and measurement specialists as general learning competencies were in fact capacities for performance in specific tasks. From this perspective, task domains such as sorting leaves have no necessary relationship to the task domains of sorting triangles and squares in standard psychological tests. This led Cole to begin criticizing various notions commonly accepted by standard learning psychology, such as transfer of training and transfer of learning (Scribner and Cole 1981).

The early studies of childrearing and Cole's related work used cross-cultural work to illumine difficulties in accepted notions about children and about what ought to happen in schools. We can date these early studies from 1963 (see Whiting 1963) until about 1971 (see Cole, Gay, Glick, and Sharp 1971). Paralleling much of this early work and extending beyond it came studies that looked at schools and schooling in relation to homes and home life, the communities within which the schools resided, and the wider societal context of the school. It is important to stress that the work here differed from the earlier cultural-deficit theories that claimed that domestic minority life ways provided inadequate cognitive and emotional stimulation to children during early childhood. The anthropological work criticized that of the cultural deficit researchers, many of whom were educational psychologists (for example, Hess and Shipman 1965). A slogan emerged: "Difference is not necessarily deficit." While the anthropological work stressed cultural relativism and was, in that sense, a bit more intellectually sophisticated than the well-intended but often ethnocentric views of the cultural-deficit researchers, the anthropologists had their own problems with limited vision. These problems involved an implicit or explicit theory of culture as static, as a relatively fixed body of tradition transmitted from generation to generation. An additional difficulty was the implicit assumption (derived by analogy from interference theory in studies of learning a second language) that culture difference necessarily made for difficulties between children and teachers in schools, or, at least, *usually* made for such difficulties.

STUDIES OF SCHOOL COMMUNITIES AND OF CULTURE DIFFERENCES BETWEEN HOME AND SCHOOL

Two sets of major studies can be distinguished during the late 1960s and early 1970s. The first set used participant observational field work to discover strong patterns of stable local meanings and stable social relationships in school communities. The second set studied "invisible cultural differences" between school and community by examining face-to-face interaction in classrooms and homes.

The first set of studies illuminated some of the reasons schools do not change and why attempts at school reform from the cosmopolitan center out to the local periphery did not seem to work. These studies used classic community ethnography to frame the school in the community and the classroom in the school. They found that classrooms did not operate independently of other influences.

In terms of specific literature, two series of case studies, one edited by George Spindler for Holt, Rinehart, and Winston, and the other by Solon Kimball for Teachers' College Press, have special importance. In addition to Spindler's own studies of the stability of schooling patterns in German villages (1973, 1974b), several other publications are illustrative examples of ethnographic work. These include Jacquetta Hill Burnett's (1969) examination of a small rural midwestern town, which recalled earlier community studies; Harry Wolcott's *The Man in the Principal's Office* (1973) and *Teachers Versus Technocrats* (1977); and Elizabeth Eddy's study on the socialization of teachers, titled *Becoming a Teacher* (1969). John Ogbu's *The Next Generation* (1974) examined the relationship of American black children's willingness to work hard in school to the labor market. Of special importance for an understanding of later studies in educational anthropology is Ogbu's assertion that black students, whom he identified as a castelike minority, perceive that in the social order a job ceiling exists that represents a barrier, excluding them from occupations with higher social status and income. He examined the negative influence of these perceived barriers on the morale of black students. Ogbu has extended this argument in cross-cultural survey research on minority group status and school achievement (for example, Ogbu 1978).

Another impetus for anthropological research in education came from the National Institute of Education, which in the early 1970s funded a series of case studies of rural and urban schools (Datta 1982; Fetterman 1982; Firestone 1980; Firestone and Herriott 1984; Herriott 1982; Herriott and Firestone 1982, 1984). Many of these were attempts to use participant observation work to monitor the implementation of planned change. The studies discovered barriers to implementation at various local levels, such as political interests within school district staffs. Central planners do not see these barriers because of the distance between themselves and the local scene; they do not ordinarily take the barriers into account in planning large-scale change. Thus the chief contribution of this work was to uncover and to document some of these barriers, which, although often highly visible to people on the local level, remain hidden from central policymakers three or more steps removed from local classrooms. Even on a small scale, the studies uncovered local-level barriers hidden from school district central offices. In short, people at the core may not understand what is happening at the periphery.

One theory that emerged from these studies sheds light on some of the reasons schools on the local level seem to resist changes mandated by planners working from central offices. This theory describes spheres of influence across differing levels of social organization. In this conception the planners are seen as sitting at the center of a set of concentric circles. The full set of these rings represents a loosely coupled system, not a tightly coupled one such as is found in a manufacturing corporation with its clearly stipulated managerial roles and systems of accountability. In school systems, mandates flow from the federal level to the state level, from the state to the school district, then to the building, and finally to the classroom. The ethnographic studies of the implementation of planned change found empirical evidence that American classroom teachers have considerable on-site policymaking autonomy as *street-level bureaucrats*. Therefore, they could neglect or even resist implementation of schemes planned centrally and diffusing out from the center to the periphery. The literature on this theory took an interesting position on the importance of local meaning in understanding local resistance to centralized planning and centralized attempts at implementing change in schools. In general these studies took a holistic, ecological view of schooling. By examining communities as their unit of analysis, these studies portrayed classrooms as one segment within wider social bodies.

The NIE studies focused attention on teaching and learning in the classroom by asking two key questions: "What is happening here, specifically?" and "What do these happenings mean to the people engaged in them?" Local meanings and specific local interests and tugs of war are uncovered by research questions emerging from these two fundamental questions of ethnographic research designs. Again, interest centered on why at the local-classroom level and then at the school-district level nothing seemed to change in spite of curricular reforms and various federal financial incentives for reform.

Other studies paralleled those sponsored by the NIE. In studies on planned variation of the sort developed in the 1970s and based on Campbell and Stanley's (1966) and Cook and Campbell's (1979) work, a crucial question became not "What were the effects of the treatment?" (which had been and is a standard question asked by Campbell for educational research and for other types of applied research), but rather "What was the treatment?" Did what actually happened resemble what the developers of the policy set forth originally? This was a fundamentally different question from that posed in usual studies of school effects. In case studies of science education, funded by the National Science Foundation, Robert Stake and John Easley (1978) found that just because a curriculum statement or school catalog included "Biology" as a course, one could not assume that certain kinds of concepts were being taught. For example, Easley found that the more closely he examined elementary school mathematics instruction, the more he began to conceptualize it as moral discipline rather than as intellectual discipline. The goal in the class was to get right answers and to act in an orderly manner by following the rules because such actions were portrayed as morally virtuous. The younger girls followed rules well and, as a result, received high grades. However, years later, when they encountered real mathematical reasoning or at least reasoning of a more complicated sort, their grades plummeted. Easley suggests that the more complicated forms of mathematical reasoning involve rewards for certain kinds of daring and not for orderly following of the rules. But the girls had been socialized away from daring by early mathematics instruction. For our purposes, the point to observe is that researchers were looking at the specifics of what was happening by asking, "What are people doing here?" Such questions yield answers very different from those that can be posed by a printed curriculum guide prepared at the district or state level.

The previous section discussed analyses of stable cultural patterns through the lens of institutional studies. This work saw culture not simply as artifacts or value patterns or even as language systems, but also as including more subtle background assumptions about etiquette and the value of social relationships. These phenomena are much harder to perceive in daily life than are the gross organizational patterns that had intrigued the students of childrearing or the researchers of local relationships and meanings (which is the first of the two sets of interests discussed previously in this chapter). Another way of looking at these patterns of stable cultural meaning and social relationship came from very close observation of face-to-face interaction inside classrooms. This research, influenced by work pioneered by John Gumperz and Dell Hymes (1972) in sociolinguistics and the ethnography of communication and also influenced by Cole's work on cross-cultural psychology, produced a set of studies of what can be called "invisible cultural difference." A book edited by Courtney Cazden, Dell Hymes, and Vera John, titled *Functions of Language in the Classroom* (1972), proved influential in setting forth many of the key ideas of this set of studies. In the introduction, Hymes discusses the importance of studying the subtle cultural differences between home and school in expectations of the appropriateness of ways of speaking. This notion of culturally conventional expectations for ways of speaking included not only dialect features of language but also expectations for how others use speech in framing topic, humor, irony, politeness, and initiative, as well as expectations of appropriateness of nonverbal behavior. One of the papers, written by Paul Byers and Happy Byers (1972), showed nonverbal patterns of gazing and the timing of interaction between white teachers and black preschool children resulted in black children receiving far fewer turns at speaking in small groups than white children did. This was a small but intriguing study done by slow-motion analysis of film.

Susan Philips, a student of Hymes, conducted one of the most extensive participant observational studies in educational anthropology (Philips 1982). She studied a Native American community in Oregon and found large differences in speech etiquette and discourse patterns between children's Native American homes and their classrooms with white Anglo teachers. Philips asserted that home etiquette and discourse patterns were characterized by an indirectness of social control, by a reluctance for making oneself conspicuous by displaying either superior knowledge of how to do something or ignorance. Philips claimed that these children, who were expected not to call attention to themselves at home, were expected to display knowledge publicly in their classrooms, especially when questioned directly by the teacher. Philips argued that the discourse patterns operated on an invisible level, that is, the white and Native American speakers whom she studied were not consciously aware of their discourse behavior nor did they ordinarily articulate what such behavior meant for them. This view understands culture not simply as artifacts or as value patterns or even as language systems, but as subtle background assumptions about etiquette and the values placed on particular forms of social relationship.

Other studies reported findings similar to those of Philips. In studying Native Americans in Northern Ontario, Erickson and Gerald Mohatt (1982) replicated part of Philips's study, with similar findings. Carol Barnhardt (1982) found similar patterns in central Alaska. There appears to be solid evidence that Native Americans from many different tribal backgrounds share assumptions about the exercise of social control in discourse that are radically different from those held by people with western European backgrounds. Of significance to educational anthropology, these studies found that differences in discourse patterns between Native American children and Anglo teachers contribute to difficulties in classroom lessons. If the conclusions of these studies are valid, then many of the learning difficulties that Native American children and other cultural minority students have experienced in American schools can be attributed at least in part to cultural differences between them and their teachers.

Parallel conclusions have been made in research on other inter-ethnic situations, such as Jeffrey Schultz, Susan Florio, and Frederick Erickson's (1982) study of a working-class Italian-American community. Shirely Heath (1982) found similar problems in a southern community of working-class blacks and whites. Kathryn Au and her associates (Au 1980; Au and Jordan 1980; Au and Mason 1981) found the same problems among native Hawaiian children. Au's work is especially intriguing because it shows that children learn more, as measured by standardized tests, when patterns of conversation and lesson discourse are altered in reading lessons to be more congruent with conversational patterns the children use in community life outside school.

The work reported thus far can lead to an optimistic conclusion that if only cultural patterns of daily classroom life could be changed in the direction of children's home culture, all students in the early grades would have equal opportunities to learn in classrooms. Such a conclusion, however, seems naively hopeful. The work reviewed here did document empirically ways in which culture differences, especially differences in communication style, can be involved in the production of miscommunication between teachers and students. But culture difference is not the only source of difficulty and miscommunication in schools. Indeed, culture difference can be seen as both cause and effect in situations of social conflict. We now turn to the last set of studies, those that focus on processes of conflict in schools and in society.

CULTURE DIFFERENCE AND SCHOOL FAILURE AS POLITICAL PROCESS

This final set of studies focuses on schools as crucial sites for the reproduction of social inequality, or to put it even more strongly, for the creation of inequality. All the studies in this set take into account resistance theory (Willis 1977; Giroux 1983). Resistance theory offers an explanation for what happens in schools that differs from that offered by the previous structural-functional theory in anthropology and from individually centered psychological theory. Resistance theory asserts that when children's school achievement appears to be low, it may have something to do with their withholding of effort and, indeed, of learning in situations of recurrent conflict with teachers. School failure is thus seen as an achievement jointly accomplished by students and teachers.

Three subcategories can be discerned within the wider body of studies of social reproduction in the light of resistance theory. The first can be called *resistance theory* proper. The second can be called *collusion theory*. The third lacks a specific title, but is characterized by concerns for resistance and for manifest curriculum or subject matter.

The earlier anthropological studies of school communities and of differences between home and school focused on stable sociocultural patterns. Researchers attributed the learning problems of ethnically different students, particularly minority students, to miscommunication between the students and their teachers. Sources of miscommunication were identified in differing cultural patterns, which were increasingly seen as residing in differing communicative patterns in face-to-face interaction. Researchers whose work derives from resistance theory agree that conflicting cultural patterns do make a difference in children's school experience. However, they find the notion of differing but stable sociocultural patterns inadequate as an explanation for children's failure in school. They reject what they regard as an idealized, homeostatic view of sociocultural patterns for a view that understands these same patterns as fluid and emerging. This recent work by anthropologists has been influenced by the so-called new sociology of education in Britain, by ethnomethodology of Harold Garfinkel (1967) and Aaron Cicourel (1986), and by the social-constructivist psychology of Lev Vygotsky and his current American disciples (Vygotsky 1978; Wertsch 1985).

On the level of the individual classroom, basic work in light of resistance theory asserts that not only do culture differences cause trouble in schools but also *the trouble increases the culture differences.* Some of this has to do with the creation of invidious distinctions, or at least with institutionalized emphasis being placed on such distinctions among groups of children. Teachers do not simply make such invidious distinctions deliberately when marking tests or assigning grades. Rather, they make them without conscious thought as they make assessments of children's motivation and intelligence, for example, as the children talk to the teacher and as the teacher observes the children playing.

Additional informal assessments enter into teachers' judgments of the ways children complete assigned work. James Collins and Sarah Michaels (1980) and Michaels and Collins (1984) showed that even outside the classroom lessons, children's social identities in school are constructed in how they speak and listen. During sharing time, for example, the ways of speaking they use to relate about events in their homes influence teachers' informal judgments about their intelligence. These judgments influence the placement of children in ranked reading groups. Placement in reading groups can have substantial implications for further learning because, as Elizabeth Cohen and others have shown (Cohen 1980, pp. 261-262; Rosenholtz and Cohen 1983; Rosenholtz and Wilson 1980), it influences dramatically the remainder of a child's school career. Thus, *culture difference can make a difference* for children's learning in school. It is not that culture difference is irrelevant to the school careers and institutional biographies of minority children. The point is that it seems a fallacy to assert that culture difference simply causes failure in school in an automatic or uniform manner (as some scholars, including Heath [1982], seem to claim), because minority children are socialized at home in ways of speaking that they persist in using in school, as if they were on "automatic pilot." These ways of speaking, so the argument goes, invariably get students into trouble with the teacher. But the role of culture difference in school failure can be seen differently. Culture difference can be seen as operating probabilistically in specific situations, becoming implicated in the production of children's failure in school in certain circumstances through the unexamined and routine patterns of assessment and teacher-student conflict that can often arise in classrooms but do not necessarily arise in every case.

Thus culture difference can be thought of as a risk factor in the school experience of students and teachers; it need not cause trouble, but it usually provides opportunities for trouble. Those opportunities can serve as resources for escalating conflict that might already exist for other reasons, such as conflict between social classes, genders, or races.

The work of Collins and Michaels can be seen as a transitional stage between work that looks for differences among stable cultural patterns, as exemplified by Heath (1982), and work that views such patterns as fluid and looks for struggle and conflict in individual classrooms and in schools. Such work focuses on the production, not merely the operation, of inequality in schools. For example, Erickson and Shultz (1982) examined ethnically and racially differing working-class junior college students in interviews with counselors. They found that culture differences could account for much of the difference in the way in which the counseling conversations progressed. However, what Erickson and Shultz called "performed social identity" and "co-membership" (attributes that persons have in common) helped in some conversations to establish rapport between persons with differing class and ethnic backgrounds and with differing patterns of communication style. Sometimes culture difference seemed to be a source of conflict and miscommunication, but sometimes it was not.

Other studies are relevant to this point. Sylvia Scribner (1984) and Evelyn Jacob (forthcoming) have examined literacy in situations where people actually use reading and writing, rather than in classrooms only. Jacob found that workers in a Baltimore milk plant showed fluidity in the social construction of their thinking. How they read work tickets and how they actually used reading and writing on the job differed greatly from the standard idealized models of literacy and conceptions of the differences between literate and illiterate people. Culture differences did not prevent workers from acquiring literacy skills; in fact, they *were* literate, although not in the sense of having mastered canonical, "school-like" literacy practices. Thus their literacy skills were likely to go unrecognized by the standardized tests used to assess those skills. This suggests that the "social fact" of low levels of literacy skills in work places (and in high schools) may be as much the result of contradictory standards and means of assessment as they are of the actual illiteracy of large numbers of workers and students so assessed. This line of research suggests that "literacy," like other aspects of cultural knowledge, may be better conceived of as the result of formal and informal assessment practices or situations of social conflict, rather than as entities that actually exist within individuals.

Other researchers have found in classroom situations patterns of action (and of judgment by which meaning is assigned to action) that may, on the surface, appear static across time but that are, in fact, fluid and changeable. Donald Dorr-Bremme (1982) studied conversations during classroom sharing time in a kindergarten/first-grade room. Each year in that classroom the first graders leave, new kindergartners enter, and last year's kindergartners become first graders. Dorr-Bremme studied the classroom for two successive years and found that the norms for discourse changed from year to year. A few new children present and a few old ones absent made a substantial difference in the local ecology of social relations in the room. What appeared at first glance as stable sets of classroom norms were reorganized abruptly.

In a thesis on the conversation of black children in integrated first-grade classrooms, Jon Piestrup (1973) found that if the teacher negatively sanctioned the use of black dialect, by the end of the year working-class black children in the class spoke a broader form of the dialect than they did in classrooms in which the teacher did not negatively sanction such speech. This happened in both sets of classrooms regardless of whether the teacher was black or white. The point to be emphasized is that in the classrooms in which the black or white teacher did not negatively sanction black dialect, the black children's language by the end of the year more closely approached standard English. This recalls William Labov's study of Martha's Vineyard inhabitants (Labov 1963), whose dialect broadened across a generation, becoming increasingly more different from the speech style of the growing numbers of summer tourists.

In the studies by Piestrup and Labov we see culture difference in situations of conflict, in which speech style has become a political symbol. Cultural style is not simply a neutral attribute of persons by which the social indentities of individuals can be dispassionately compared and contrasted. Rather, culture difference becomes an occasion or resource for social evaluation that is highly charged culturally. It has become a medium for the display of opposition, and pairs of oppositional cultures become more and more different across time, in a process that Gregory Bateson described as complementary schizmogenesis (Bateson 1975, pp. 107–127). Features of oppositional culture become symbolic resources for conflict; otherwise, why would it be an outrage for an Englishman to spit on the Irish flag (it is only a piece of cloth, after all), or why would it be a punishable offense for a young black man in an urban American high school to wear his leather coat in the school hallway, or why does it annoy the teacher that a particular child in the bottom reading group opens her book to the wrong page day after day?

The Piestrup study foreshadows later work by Ray McDermott (1974, 1977; McDermott and Gospodinoff 1979; McDermott and Goldman 1983; McDermott and Tylbor 1983) and by the sociologist Hugh Mehan (1976, 1978, 1979, 1980, 1982a, 1982b). McDermott and Mehan take a pessimistic view of life in schools. They do so with a theory of the mutual construction of disability in everyday life. If a teacher can influence a child to talk more nonstandard English within a year or a principal can suspend an adolescent for wearing a leather coat, some kind of interactional process of evaluation is happening in which judgments of social identity change in negative directions. If students are talking and dressing in such ways, then perhaps the problem is not just a matter of cultural patterns that do not fit. Rather it would seem that struggle is going on—struggle that is mutually constructed by teachers and students, who, as conflict escalates over time and their forbearance for one another runs out, become locked in regressive social relationships to which all parties in the local social system contribute, as in pathological interaction systems in families. McDermott and Henry Tylbor (1983) use the term *collusion* when describing this cycle of progressively intense conflict. We can see schools as places where individuals collude in definitions of other and of self. The definitions can be negative or positive, and they can be seen as locally produced, at least in part.

A final observation of what the anthropology of education has taught us about schooling in America has less to do with what it has accomplished than with what it can and ought to discover next. In an overview of much of the literature of anthropology in education a few years ago, Erickson (1982) emphasized the fact that the literature had much to say about hidden curriculum but that it had very little to say about manifest curriculum, especially about deliberate instruction in cognitive skills. In his own field notes, written in the years before 1981, Erickson found few references to arithmetic or reading. Published studies discussed turn taking between speakers but almost nothing was said about the subject matter content of the turns at talk that were being taken. Very recent work in the anthropology of education is attempting to bring together the study of the hidden and the manifest curriculum. Researchers are attempting to show how the social identity of students becomes constructed in mathematics, reading, social studies, and playground (Finnan 1982). These are attempts to make visible the transparency of activities by which students and teachers collude in mutually affirming or nonaffirming ways in classroom talk as the students reveal that they know an answer or do not know it, or as they try for an answer or avoid trying for it. This work also examines how teachers and students together find the answers, jointly making sense and nonsense of subject matter content (Campbell 1986). With all the current interest in the role of "higher order reasoning" in pedagogy, it seems appropriate that some anthropologists of education are turning their attention to academic subject matter as it is deliberately taught. (See the additional discussion in Erickson 1986b.)

To conclude, in the last twenty years educational anthropologists have turned from looking at childrearing practices outside schools, to looking at cultural differences as explanations of school failure, to examining the depressing ways in which schools create symbolic interactional resources for the production of social inequality. Some of the most recent work in the field is trying to consider the classroom not only as an arena for social struggle but as a place where the manifest curriculum is crucially constitutive of that struggle.

REFERENCES

Au, K. H. "Participation Structures in a Reading Lesson with Hawaiian Children: Analysis of a Culturally Appropriate Instructional Event." *Anthropology and Education Quarterly* 11 (1980): 91–115.

Au, K. H., and Jordan, C. "Teaching Reading to Hawaiian Children: Finding a Culturally Appropriate Solution." In *Culture and the Bilingual Classroom*, edited by H. Trueba, G. P. Guthrie, and K. H. Au, pp. 139–152. Rowley, Mass.: Newbury House, 1980.

Au, K. H., and Mason, J. "Social Organizational Factors in Learning to Read: The Balance of Rights Hypothesis." *Reading Research Quarterly* 17: 1 (1981): 115–152.

Barnhardt, C. "Tuning In: Athabaskan Teachers and Athabaskan Students." In *Cross-Cultural Issues in Alaskan Education*, edited by R. Barnhardt. Vol. 2. Fairbanks: Center for Cross-Cultural Studies, University of Alaska, 1982.

Bateson, G. *Steps to An Ecology of Mind*. New York: Ballantine, 1975.

Becker, H. S.; Geer, B.; Hughes, E. C.; and Strauss, A. L. *Boys in White*: *Student Culture in Medical School*. Chicago: University of Chicago Press, 1961.

Burnett, J. H. "Ceremony, Rites, and Economy in the Student System of an American High School." *Human Organization* 28 (1969): 1–10.

Byers, P., and Byers, H. "Non-Verbal Communication and the Education of Children." In *Functions of Language in the Classroom*, edited by C. B. Cazden, V. P.

John, and D. Hymes, pp. 3–31. New York: Teachers College Press, 1972.

Campbell, D. R. "Developing Mathematical Literacy in a Bilingual Classroom." In *The Social Context of Method*, edited by J. Cook Gumperz. London: Cambridge University Press, 1986.

Campbell, D. T., and Stanley, J. C. *Experimental and Quasi-Experimental Designs for Research.* Chicago: Rand-McNally, 1966.

Cazden, C.; Hymes, D.; and John, V., eds. *Functions of Language in the Classroom.* New York: Teachers College Press, 1972.

Cicourel, A. V. *The Social Organization of Juvenile Justice.* New York: John Wiley, 1968.

Cohen, E. "Design and Redesign of the Desegregated School: Problems of Status, Power, and Conflict." In *School Desegregation: Past, Present and Future*, edited by W. G. Stephan and J. R. Feagin. New York: Plenum Press, 1980.

Cole, M.; Gay, J.; and Sharp, D. *The Cultural Context of Learning and Thinking.* New York: Basic Books, 1971.

Collins, J., and Michaels, S. "The Importance of Conversational Discourse Strategies in the Acquisition of Literacy." In *Proceedings of the Sixth Annual Meeting of the Berkeley Linguistics Society*, pp. 143–156. Berkeley, Calif.: Berkeley Linguistics Society, 1980.

Cook, T. D., and Campbell, D. T. *Quasi-Experimentation: Design and Analysis Issues for Field Settings.* Chicago: McNally, 1979.

Datta, L. "Strange Bedfellows: The Politics of Qualitative Methods." *American Scientist* 26:1 (1982): 133–144.

Dorr-Bremme, D. *Behaving and Making Sense: Creating Social Organization in the Classroom.* (Unpublished doctoral dissertation) Harvard University, 1982.

Eddy, E. M. *Becoming a Teacher: The Passage to Professional Status.* New York: Teachers College Press, 1969.

Erickson, F. "Taught Cognitive Learning in its Immediate Environments: A Neglected Topic in the Anthropology of Education." *Anthropology and Education Quarterly* 13:2 (1982): 149–180.

Erickson, F. "Qualitative Research on Teaching." In *Handbook of Research on Teaching*, edited by M. C. Wittrock, 3rd. ed. New York: Macmillan, 1986. (a)

Erickson, F. "Tasks in Times: Objects of Study in a Natural History of Teaching." In *1986 Yearbook of the Association for Supervision and Curriculum Development*, edited by K. K. Zumwalt. Washington, D.C.: Association for Supervision and Curriculum Development, 1986. (b)

Erickson, F., and Mohatt, G. "The Cultural Organization of Participation Structures in Two Classrooms of Indian Students." In *Doing the Ethnography of Schooling: Educational Anthropology in Action*, edited by G. Spindler, pp. 132–174. New York: Holt, Rinehart and Winston, 1982.

Erickson, F., and Shultz, J. *The Counselor as Gatekeeper: Social Interaction in Interviews.* New York: Academic Press, 1982.

Fetterman, D. M. "Ethnography in Educational Research: The Dynamics of Diffusion." *Educational Researcher* 11: 3 (1982): 17–22, 29.

Finnan, C. R. "The Ethnography of Children's Spontaneous Play." In *Doing the Ethnography of School: Educational Anthropology in Action*, edited by G. Spindler, pp. 356–380. New York: Holt, Rinehart and Winston, 1982.

Firestone, W. A. *Great Expectations for Small Schools: The Limitations of Federal Projects.* New York: Praeger, 1980.

Design and Implementation Issues." In *Ethnography in Educational Evaluation,* edited by D. M. Fetterman, pp. 63–88. Beverly Hills, Calif.: Sage Publications, 1984.

Freeman, D. *Margaret Mead and Samoa: The Making and Unmaking of an Anthropological Myth.* Cambridge, Mass.: Harvard University Press, 1983.

Garfinkel, H. *Studies in Ethnomethodology.* Englewood Cliffs, N.J.: Prentice-Hall, 1967.

Gay, J., and Cole, M. *The New Mathematics and Old Culture: A Study of Learning among the Kpelle of Liberia.* New York: Holt, Rinehart and Winston, 1967.

Giroux, H. A. "Theories of Reproduction and Resistance in the New Sociology of Education: A Critical Analysis." *Harvard Educational Review* 53 (1983): 257–293.

Gumperz, J. J., and Hymes, D. *Direction in Sociolinguistics: The Ethnography of Speaking.* New York: Holt, 1972.

Heath, S. B. *Ways with Words: Language, Life and Work in Communities and Classrooms.* Cambridge, Eng.: Cambridge University Press, 1982.

Henry, Jules. *Culture Against Man.* New York: Random House, 1965.

Herriott, R. E. "Tensions in Research Design and Implementation: The Rural Experimental Schools Study." *American Behavioral Scientist* 26: 2 (1982): 23–44.

Herriott, R. E., and Firestone, W. A. *Multisite Qualitative Policy Research in Education: A Study of Recent Federal Experience.* Authors Final Report No. NIE–400–80–0019, 1982.

Herriott, R. E., and Firestone, W. A. "Multisite Qualitative Policy Research: Some Design and Implementation Issues." In *Ethnography in Educational Evaluation,* edited by D. M. Fetterman, pp. 63–88. Beverly Hills, Calif.: Sage Publications, 1984.

Hess, R., and Shipman, V. "Early Experience and the Socialization of Cognitive Modes in Children." *Child Development* 34 (1965): 869–886.

Jacob, E. "Literacy Tools: Reading and Writing of Entry-level Production Workers." In *Becoming a Worker,* edited by C. Bosman and J. Reisman. Norwood, N.J.: Ablex, forthcoming.

Kimball, S. T. "Anthropology and Education." *Educational Leadership* 13 (1956): 480–483. (a)

Kimball, S. T. "The Role of Education in Community Development." *Teachers College Record* 57 (1956): 386–391. (b)

Kimball, S. T. "The Transmission of Culture." *Educational Horizons* 43 (1965): 161–186.

Kimball, S. T. *Culture and the Educative Process: An Anthropological Perspective.* New York: Teachers College Press, 1974.

Kimball, S. T., and McClellan, J. E., Jr. *Education and the New America.* New York: Random House, 1962.

Labov, W. "The Social Motivation of a Sound Change." *Word* 19 (1963): 273–309. (Also published in W. Labov, *Sociolinguistic Patterns.* Philadelphia: University of Pennsylvania Press, 1973, pp. 1–42.)

McDermott, R. P. "Achieving School Failure: An Anthropological Approach to Literacy and Social Stratification." In *Education and Culture Process,* edited by G. D. Spindler. New York: Holt, Rinehart and Winston, 1974.

McDermott, R. P. "The Ethnography of Speaking and Reading." In *Linguistics,* edited by R. Shuy. Newark, Del.: International Reading Association, 1977.

McDermott, R. P., and Goldman, S. "Teaching in Multicultural Settings." In *Multicultural Education*, edited by L. Van der Berg, S. de Rijcke, and L. Zuck, pp. 145–164. Dordrecht, The Netherlands: Faris Publications, 1983.

McDermott, R. P., and Gospodinoff, K. "Social Contexts for Ethnic Borders and School Failure: A'Communicative Analysis." In *Nonverbal Behavior*, edited by A. Wolfgang. London: Academic Press, 1979.

McDermott, R. P., and Tylbor, H. "On the Necessity of Collusion in Conversation." *Text* 3: 3 (1983): 277–297.

Mead, M. *Coming of Age in Samoa: A Psychological Study of Primitive Youth for Western Civilization*. New York: Morrow, 1928.

Mehan, H. "Assessing Children's School Performance." *Recent Sociology* 5 (1976): 240–264.

Mehan, H. "Structuring School Structure." *Harvard Educational Review* 48 (1978): 32–64.

Mehan, H. *Learning Lessons: Social Organization in the Classroom*. Cambridge, Mass.: Harvard University Press, 1979.

Mehan, H. "The Competent Student." *Anthropology and Education Quarterly* 11:3 (1980): 131–152.

Mehan, H. "The Role of Language and the Language of Role in Institutional Decision Making." *Language in Society* 12 (1982): 187–211. (a).

Mehan, H. "The Structure of Classroom Events and Their Consequences for Student Performance." In *Children In and Out of School*, edited by P. Gilmore and A. Glatthorn, pp. 59–87. Washington, D.C.: Center for Applied Linguistics, 1982. (b)

Michaels, S., and Collins, J. "Oral Discourse Styles: Classroom Interaction and the Acquisition of Literacy." In *Coherence in Spoken and Written Discourse*, edited by D. Tannen, pp. 219–244. Norwood, N.J.: Ablex, 1984.

Ogbu, J. U. *The Next Generation: An Ethnography of Education in an Urban Neighborhood*. New York: Academic Press, 1974.

Ogbu, J. U. *Minority Education and Caste: The American System in Cross-Cultural Perspective*. New York: Academic Press, 1978.

Philips, S. U. *The Invisible Culture: Communication in Classroom and Community on the Warm Springs Indian Reservation*. New York: Longman Press, 1982.

Piestrup A. *Black Dialect Interference and Accommodation of Reading Instruction in First Grade*. (Monograph No. 4). Berkeley, Calif.: Language-Behavior Research Laboratory, 1973.

Rosenholtz, S. J., and Cohen, E. G. "Back to Basics and the Desegregated School." *The Elementary School Journal* 83: 5 (1983). Chicago: University of Chicago Press.

Rosenholtz, S. J., and Wilson, B. "The Effect of Classroom Structure on Shared Perception of Ability." *American Educational Research Journal* 17 (1980): 75–82.

Scribner, S. "Studying Working Intelligence." In *Everyday Cognition: Its Development in Social Context*, edited by B. Rogoff and J. Lave, pp. 9–40. Cambridge, Mass.: Harvard University Press., 1984.

Scribner, S., and Cole, M. *The Psychology of Literacy*. Cambridge, Mass.: Harvard University Press, 1981.

Schultz, J.; Florio, S.; and Erickson, F. "Where's the Floor: Aspects of the Cultural Organization of Social Relationships in Communication at Home and at School" in P. Gilmore and A. Glatthorn (eds.), *Children In and Out of School*, pp. 88–123. Washington, D.C.: Center for Applied Linguistics, 1982.

Spindler, G. D. "Education in a Transforming American Culture." *Harvard Educational Review* 25 (1955): 145–156. (a).

Spindler, G. D. *Education and Anthropology*. Palo Alto, Calif.: Stanford University Press, 1955. (b)

Spindler, G. D. *Education and Culture: Anthropological Approaches*. New York: Holt, Rinehart and Winston, 1963.

Spindler, G. D., ed. *Burgbach: Urbanization and Identity in a German Village*. New York: Holt, Rinehart and Winston, 1973.

Spindler, G. D. "Beth Anne—A Case Study of Culturally Defined Adjustment and Teacher Perceptions." In *Education and Cultural Process: Toward an Anthropology of Education*, edited by G. D. Spindler, pp. 139–153. New York: Holt, Rinehart and Winston, 1974. (a)

Spindler, G. D. "Schooling in Schonhausen: A Study in Cultural Transmission and Instrumental Adaptation in an Urbanizing German Village." In *Education and Cultural Process: Toward an Anthropology of Education*, edited by G. D. Spindler, pp. 230–271. New York: Holt, Rinehart and Winston, 1974. (b)

Stake, R. E., and Easley, J. A., eds. *Case Studies in Science Education*. 2 Vols. Prepared for the National Science Foundation. Washington, D.C.: U.S. Government Printing Office. (ERIC Document Reproduction Service No. ED 166 058 and ED 166 059), 1978.

Vygotsky, L. S. *Mind in Society: The Development of Higher Psychological Processes*. M. Cole, V. J. Steiner, S. Scribner and E. Souberman (eds.). Cambridge, Mass.: Harvard University Press, 1978.

Wertsch, J. V. *Vygotsky and the Social Formation of Mind*. Cambridge, Mass.: Harvard University Press, 1985.

Whiting, B. B., ed. *Six Cultures: Studies of Child Rearing*. New York: Wiley, 1963.

Whiting, B. B., and Whiting, J. W. M. *Children of Six Cultures: A Psycho-Cultural Analysis.* Cambridge, Mass.: Harvard University Press, 1975.

Whiting, J. W. M. *Becoming a Kwoma: Teaching and Learning in a New Guinea Tribe*. New Haven: Yale University Press, 1941.

Willis, P. E. *Learning to Labour: How Working Class Kids Get Working Class Jobs*. Farnborough, Eng.: Saxon House, 1977.

Wolcott, H. F. *The Man in the Principal's Office: An Ethnography*. New York: Holt, Rinehart and Winston, 1973.

Wolcott, H. F. *Teachers Versus Technocrats: An Educational Innovation in Anthropological Perspective*. Eugene, Oregon: Center for Educational Policy and Management, University of Oregon, 1977.

9

On Organizational Studies

Charles E. Bidwell

Having been asked to take a long view of the past and prospects of organizational studies in education, I could not resist. After all, I thought, there has been an increasingly large and interesting literature in which organizational theory and our understanding of school organizations have developed in mutual sympathy. Sitting down to prepare my remarks, however, was sobering. The literature on school organizations is in fact sparse. To realize this was especially sobering to me because I teach and write in the field, but as I reflected on my own courses I saw that in them I present a general theoretical literature that has little to do directly with schools. I then apply this literature to schools, school districts, colleges, and universities. Although I use the applications to criticize and add to the theories, the dominant intellectual flow is from theory to application.

The theoretical literature on organizations has developed in response in part to the Pittsburgh call some thirty years ago for a general theory of administration (for example, Litchfield 1956; Thompson 1956), in part to a concern for the analysis of the firm (from March and Simon 1958, through Cyert and March 1963, to Williamson 1975), and in part to an interest in governmental decision making (for example, Allison 1971; Crecine 1969; Levy, Meltsner, and Wildavsky 1974).

There is certainly the occasional important study of schools as organizations. Willard Waller's (1932) was such a work. More recently, Dan Lortie's (1975) treatise on schoolteaching has a strong organizational resonance, and we have Ann Swidler's (1979) case studies of the triangular relationship between organizational control, professionalism, and market demand.

Now and again an original theoretical contribution to the organizational literature has its roots in an effort to understand the organizational workings of schools. One thinks especially of Karl Weick (1975) on loose coupling, John Meyer and Brian Rowan (1977) on the mythic elements of organizational practice, and James G. March and Johan Olsen (1976) on ambiguity and choice in organizational decision making.

Even so, the study of educational organizations has been a relatively minor applied area in the broader field of organizational studies. I find three prime reasons for this state of affairs. First, in contemporary Western societies, business and government have greater institutional centrality than education has; the interests of investigators and research sponsors tend toward the institutional center of a society.

Second, there is the post–World War II social-scientific preoccupation with problems of national development in the Third World and social stratification and equity in the West. American sociological research in education up to World War II used Durkheimian ideas to build a social organizational conceptualization of schools (especially Waller 1932, but see also the work by W. Lloyd Warner and his colleagues, culminating in Warner, Havighurst, and Loeb 1944). This research was especially concerned with tensions between the technological aspects of instruction; the recalcitrance of students; and consequences for coordination, control, and the maintenance of organizational legitimacy. This agenda has a very contemporary sound. However, with the domestic and international political aftermath of the War, macrosocial concerns took center stage not only in the sociology but also in the economics and politics of education. (For good examples of this line of work see Halsey, Floud, and Anderson 1961.)

Third, consider the problems of special theories of different organizations. In organizational studies, one might argue, two special theories have realized a premature claim to generality. One is concerned with economic organizations (for example, Coase 1937; Cyert and March 1963; Williamson 1975) and the other with governmental organizations (for example, Allison 1971; Blau 1970; Crecine 1969;

Levy, Meltsner, and Wildavsky 1974). The prematurity of this claim comes from the absence of good cross-organizational evidence. The altruistic social scientists ready to provide such evidence have not come forward.

Moreover, building special theories runs against the generalizing scientific grain, and it is not clear how best to approach a special theory of one or another kind of organization. It is by no means certain that the everyday categories of organizations make analytical sense. In what sense is it useful to theorize separately about profit and nonprofit organizations or about firms and schools?

Fruitful theorizing comes from metaphorical thinking that involves the capacity to cut through empirical complexity to identify or invent a small number of fundamental constructs on which to ground an account of observed events. One thinks, for example, of Emile Durkheim's (1961) notion of schools as little societies, Willard Waller's (1932) decision to make power a dominant element of his analysis of schools, or Karl Weick's (1976) argument that a key to understanding school organizations can be found in Herbert Simon's (1962) view of the architecture of complexity.

We return, then, to the effort toward a general theory. In this vein, I think that there is an excellent chance now for studies of school organization to move toward the center of theoretical advance in organizational studies. This opportunity comes from a confluence of two lines of conceptual development—one in organizational theory, the other in the social-organizational study of instruction. If I am right and the work is pursued, we will know more than before about organizations generally, about the ways in which educational organizations are shaped and changed, and about the ways in which their structural form may affect what is taught and learned. In the remainder of this chapter I shall outline schematically what I think is the principal direction of organizational theorizing, trace its parallels in extant work on educational organizations, and conclude with some remarks on the future.

THE DEVELOPMENT OF ORGANIZATIONAL THEORY

The story of organizational theory is the story of efforts, only partly realized, to build on and surpass Weberian (Weber 1947) closed-system theories of organization. These efforts have somewhat opened the closed-system theories of organizations to further analysis.

Closed Systems

When an organization is analyzed as a closed system, it is treated as if it were a machine, in essentially the same way the Newtonians treated the physical world. To account for the existence of the system, one assumes a prime mover (such as an entrepreneur or monarch) whose action, though unanalyzed, gives the organization its mandate, sets its goals, endows it with resources, and may design its structure. The prime mover is the one link between the organization and its environment. By assuming a prime mover, closed-system structuralists can take as given the work that an organization does and the resources that it consumes. By appealing to the action of a prime mover, they seek to explain persistence and change of organizational form. The underlying processes thereby remain unanalyzed. To explain existing differences in the form of organizations, these theorists are restricted necessarily to relationships among an organization's structural, demographic, and material properties.

The structural and demographic properties have received more of the structuralists' attention—perhaps because so many of the structuralists are sociologists. In their view, if organizations look morphologically different from one another or if their form changes, the explanation will be found in varying degrees of compatibility between attributes of the organizational machine—such structural attributes as the intensity of the division of labor and such demographic attributes as the size of subunits. Here the action of the prime mover is often implicit—it could be, for example, an unseen hand that adjusts certain structural attributes of the organizational machine to fit other such attributes or to fit the requirements of the number or the kinds of members.

The most interesting closed-system, Weberian work is found in the writings of Blau and his students on structural covariation in organizations (Blau 1970; Hall, Haas, and Johnson 1967; Klatzky 1970; Meyer 1972) and Derek Pugh and his collaborators on the dimensions of organizational structure (Pugh et al. 1963, 1968, 1969), and in Amatai Etzioni's (1961) depiction of organizational form as a solution to the problem of members' compliance. These Weberian structuralists have sought explanations of varying organizational form among interrelations of structural attributes themselves and among the structuring effects of the size and composition of an organization's membership.

Structural theories are theories of comparative statics rather than of organizational dynamics. Moreover, their closed-system character excessively narrows the range of explanation. It was realization of these two limitations that fostered approaches in which an organization's structure is treated as environmentally stimulated and constrained.

Control and Open Systems

These newer approaches—most notably the behavioral theory of the firm, sociotechnical and contingency theories, and political-economic analyses of organizational decision making—have helped us think of organizations as systematically related to actors and events in their environments and as something other than solely rational constructions. Nevertheless, as dynamic theories they have notable weaknesses that arise especially from their retention (in varying measure) of certain assumptions initially made by the closed-system structuralists: (1) that organizations are strongly bounded, (2) that stability is essential within this boundary, and (3) that organizational form is primarily a consequence of managerial decisions.

As a result, these approaches have treated organizations not as open systems but as control systems (Boulding 1968). Control systems have two chief components: operators and regulators. The operator is the machine (like the furnace, pipes, and radiators in a heating system or the production subunit of an organization). The regulator (like the thermostat or the organizational decision maker) receives information about the state of the system's environment (for example, the temperature of the air or the demand for an organization's products). It responds by altering the operator's level of activity or, if necessary, rebuilding the operator to a new design, so that its output satisfies the predetermined target criterion. Entropy is not assumed to pertain. The regulator sets a level of structural complexity sufficient to attain the target, given the inputs that the environment provides. That is, control systems can be both stable and complex to the degree that the regulator's target and information about the environment require complexity.

The control-system approach to organizations considers the maintenance of strong boundaries—and, hence, of stability, order, and differentiation—as the sole set of processes connecting an organization's environment and the formation of its structure. Management thus comes to center stage as the agent that maintains organizational equilibrium in the face of nonrandom shocks from "outside." By contrast, a truly open-system theory would assume that stability, order, and differentiation are problematic for organizations. It would treat their boundaries as highly permeable and shifting, so that structure can be affected by inputs to locations throughout the organization.

The very openness of an open system means that in the absence of environmental input, the system will tend toward entropy. In the presence of such input, the system acquires just that degree of structural variety and instability that this input requires. In this fundamental sense, an organization's environment becomes part of the organizational system.

Nevertheless, control-system theories have considerably advanced our understanding of organizations. This advance inheres in the notion of the environment as a more or less continuous source of influence on organizational form and activity and in the possibility of dynamic analysis.

Control-system theories of organizations have proceeded in two rather different directions. One centers on the behavior of individuals in organizations and has had its most creative statement in the behavioral theory of the firm. The other, in the closely related sociotechnical and contingency varieties, tries to show how the structure of organizations responds to the technologies that are used in these organizations and to the inscrutability or variability of their environments.

At this point I should stress that I believe technology is properly considered as one of the inputs that an organization receives from its environment. This input occurs in the form of knowledge, tools, and procedures. Hence such an input is a function of the technological level and composition of an organization's environment and of the ways in which technology is distributed therein.

The Behavioral Theory of the Firm. The behavioral theory of the firm (Cyert and March 1963) is a theory of the organizational regulator, which is an unusual regulator because it not only may alter the activity levels or structure of the operator but also may set its own goals. The regulator here, of course, is the set of organizational decision makers, and the principal focus of the behavioral theory of the firm is on the ways in which a firm's regulatory activities are limited by imperfect information and conflicting preferences, so that organizational regulation inexorably departs from rational problem solving toward persuasion and bargaining.

In one stroke, the behavioral theory of the firm presented a dynamic theory, moved to an explicit control-system perspective, opened the possibility of a political analysis of organizational control, and thus showed the impossibility of explaining organizational dynamics without taking into account how organizations receive, process, and adapt to information.

Nevertheless, the behavioral theory of the firm is not a theory of organizational structuring. That it is not imposes two important limitations on this theory. First, it does not link cumulatively to the structural analyses of the Weberians. Second, it affords only a narrow glimpse of the organizational system. The regulator is analyzed as a system of individual actors. How this regulator acts on the organizational operator, with what effects and under what conditions, and how attributes of the operator may affect the action or attributes of the regulator go unexplained.

Sociotechnical and Contingency Theories. By contrast, sociotechnical and contingency theories try to explain structural variation among organizations. Each is a partly developed control-system approach, centering, on the one hand, on the technological determination of organizational structure and, on the other, on the environmental stimulation of the decision making that modifies organizational form. Although Joan Woodward (1965, 1970) was the pioneer of sociotechnical theory, Charles Perrow (1970) provides the most satisfactory sociotechnical formulation. His effort has a nascent dynamic character. It is an effort to show how technology itself emerges out of variation in key properties of raw materials and knowledge about work—that is, how it arises in the environment and how this developing technology affects an emerging production organization. Thus, both technological and structural variables are environmentally situated and are problematic rather than given.

Further sources of structural variation among organizations are found in the exigencies of production activities. That is, the division of administrative labor arises as a solution to problems of coordinating both an organization's internal production activities and its external relationships.

However, for the most part the underlying processes remain within a strong organizational boundary. There are only two inputs from the environment—raw material and knowledge about how the product can be made. These inputs are treated as fixed rather than variable. Moreover, Perrow has told us little about the ways in which structuring comes about. Structural evolution is represented clearly by only certain of its antecedents. Thus, as is true of the behavioral theory of the firm, we have a partial depiction of the organization as a dynamic system.

Although contingency theorists (a theoretical strain named by Lawrence and Lorsch 1967) assume constant exchange between the organization and the environment, in fact this interaction occurs only through the action of a managerial regulator that tailors organizational structure to environmental requirements. Moreover, this regulatory process is even less well analyzed by contingency theorists than it is by sociotechnical theorists.

Thompson's Synthesis. Despite the foregoing limitations, sociotechnical and contingency theories are important, at the least, because they, along with the work on functional bases of organizational structure by Alfred Chandler (1962) and Talcott Parsons (1960), provided key material for James Thompson's (1967) theoretical synthesis. Thompson maintained a control-system frame within which the regulatory function was specific to managerial decision making. Nonetheless, he envisioned a broadly adaptive regulatory process in which decision making leads to organizational action to alter both environmental and organizational structure and composition.

Adaptation here is more than a reactive response. Top managers seek a favorable environmental situation that will provide a sufficient and predictable flow of resources. Thus, top management is an organizational regulator engaged positively with both the organizational machine and its surroundings.

However, Thompson narrowed the definition of an organizational environment to exclude technology and its sources. In contrast to Perrow's dynamic view of technology and its structuring consequences, Thompson collapsed the distinction between technology and the division of production labor so that technology could not serve as a significant analytical component of environmental effect on organizational structure.

Instead, the structuring effects of adaptation were seen to occur only at the organization's boundary and not in its division of production labor—its "technical core." The division of production labor, to be sure, is strongly constrained by technological requirements, and the principal task of management—the prime regulatory task—is to maintain the stability of the core by either altering the nontechnological environment or establishing "boundary-spanning" roles or units (like purchasing or personnel management) that can fit inputs to technology and its corresponding production organization.[1]

Although Thompson provided the rudiments of a dynamic theory by regarding technology as a fixed constraint on production organization, he took too narrow a view of the connection between the organization and the environment and the processes by which organizations are shaped and act in their environments.

Political Economy Theories. In its more recent forms, behaviorally oriented theory has considered the possibility that regulation may be a pervasive process in organizations rather than a process limited to the managerial subunit. However, because these later theories view regulation as a summative function of individual behavior, the explanation remains unsatisfactory. This limitation can be seen clearly in theories of the "political economy" of organizations.

This line of theory has had its most systematic statement in the work of Peter Abell and his colleagues (Abell 1975). Here technology and the distribution of preferences and power among an organization's members are the two principal sources of variation in organizational form and activities. Technology, or, more precisely, the division of production labor, affects actors' control of tasks. By virtue of such task characteristics as predictability, this control in turn affects their power. This power distribution, in conjunction with the actors' preferences, influences the outcomes of decisions and thus affects organizational structure.

Although we are not told very much about the way in which these structural effects come about, Abell and his coworkers have made two contributions. First, they have explicitly introduced the concept of power into the analysis of organizational regulation. Second, like Perrow, they have corrected the managerial bias that pervades so much theorizing about organizational structure and activity by extending the regulator to incorporate all individual actors in the organization and their interpersonal ties.

By thus apparently collapsing the organizational regulator and operator (the internal polity and the division of production labor), Abell and his associates encourage us to envision widespread sources

---

1. Essentially the same control-system perspective will be found in Coase (1937) and Williamson (1975), although the problem to which the managerial or entrepreneurial regulator responds is different—the problem of transaction costs and the enactment of hierarchy to allow deliberate coordination to replace market coordination.

of structural change within an organization. Coupled with the notion of an open boundary, this possibility suggests an equally pervasive environmental influence on organizational structuring. Nevertheless, Abell's analysis stops short of open-system theory. By virtue of his behavioral persuasion, he deals with only one aspect of structural emergence and change—the development of interpersonal relationships among an organization's members.

Moreover, on close inspection one sees that Abell has maintained a strong analytical distinction between regulatory and operational structures in organizations. Although he and his collaborators tell us in detail how the operator (the production organization) affects the regulator (the internal organizational polity), they only assert effects of the regulator on the operator.

Because they do not show how the operator is regulated, they give us a curious control-system theory, and the organizational system that they describe is badly asymmetric. Moreover, its ties to its environment appear almost entirely as sources of varying political power within the organization proper. The triadic structure of control, production, and environment, constituting an open organizational system, remains only partly depicted. In fact, it is somewhat distorted when viewed through the lens of political economy.

THE DEVELOPMENT OF STUDIES OF EDUCATIONAL ORGANIZATIONS

The path followed by studies of educational organizations parallels the broader course of organizational studies. They have moved from an interest in building a theory of educational administration to efforts to understand how educational organizations are related to their environments, both local and nonlocal.

Theories of Administration

As I have suggested, although sociological treatments of education have always had a strong organizational resonance, it was the post–World War II movement toward general administrative theory, articulated in the 1956 papers by Edward Litchfield and by James Thompson, that provided the chief impetus to the emergence of education as a distinct subfield of organizational theory and research.

That same period saw the establishment of the *Educational Administration Quarterly* and the Kellogg Foundation's funding of centers for educational administrative studies at several research universities. Through these centers, it was thought, the soon-to-develop general administrative theory could be specified as a theory of educational administration.

Although this effort defined educational organizations more forcefully than before as objects worth social scientific attention, it met the same fate as the movement toward a general administrative theory. The approach taken in this literature was essentially that of the behavioral theory of the firm, in which the behavior of educational administrators was the prime object of analysis. (For an overview of much of this literature, see Getzels, Lipham, and Campbell 1968.)

This literature displays the same narrow focus and inattention to the organizational system that one finds in the parent theory. Environment is essentially absent from the analysis except as it is represented by information inputs to administrators. Moreover, one finds in this literature no consideration of the form or constituent activities of the division of production labor in schools, their consequences for the form or constituent activities of the administrative division of labor, or the ways in which the latter forms and activities might affect the former.

In part, this administrative and behavioral preoccupation reflects the widespread managerial bias of organizational inquiry at the time, but it also reflects a strong orientation to practice and the absence of a Weberian past in the educational field. Earlier work on the social organization of education had been primarily Durkheimian. Lacking the structuralist inheritance that the broader field had received from Weber, there was no secure intellectual framework to fix scholars' attention (as Blau's had been fixed) on structural interrelationships among elements of production and administrative organization— and, therefore, on the entire organization, if not on the organization-environment system.

Organization and Environment

The absence of a structuralist inheritance has meant that in the educational field neither the sociotechnical nor the contingency theoretic attempt to account for the covariation of environmental and organizational structure and composition has had much effect. Thus, some of the most striking recent work on educational organizations has continued in the behavioral vein. Indeed, as part of the growing two-way traffic between general and educational organizational studies, Weick's well-known essay on "loose coupling" (Weick 1976) has substantially broadened the behavioral approach by holistically considering organizations (educational and others) as more or less complex and decomposable information systems (compare Simon 1962).

As a consequence of Weick's holistic approach, we are taken a considerable distance toward thinking about organizational regulation as a *function* of an entire organizational system rather than as a *unit* of that system (that is, an administrative or a managerial unit). The environment remains essentially a source of information, but it is seen as more differentiated in its scrutability and informational stability and composition than it was in earlier behavioral work. Therefore, it can become a prime explanans of the complexity of the organizational information system.

Nevertheless, organizations as Weick depicts them do little beyond processing information and making decisions. What else may be done in an organization and how an organization acquires structure (so that these things can be done) are peripheral.

A second direction of education-based organizational theory building is attributable to Meyer and his colleagues (for example, Meyer and Rowan 1977; Meyer and Scott 1983). Meyer makes technology an essential part of the explanatory apparatus. However, it is more a constant than a variable; it is theoretically significant because it is organizationally trivial. Bypassing the problems addressed by the Weberian and sociotechnical theorists, Meyer in effect gives Thompson's notion of the necessity of a stable technical core an interesting, but not entirely satisfactory, theoretical reorientation.

Like Thompson, Meyer let the diverse, unstable, or uncertain environment serve as a primary source of nonrandom disturbance to the technical core of production. However, Thompson saw the technological imperative as so powerful that the buffering task of management is essentially to preserve the fit between technological requirements and production organization. For Meyer, who appears here as a Thompsonian cynic, the technology of instruction is so weak and unproductive that the buffering work of school administrators at root is a work of mystification and concealment.

The threat of environmental disruption is posed more by interest-driven school politics than by the complexity, instability, or uncertainty of technological or other inputs to production. Buffering means guarding against the potential adverse reaction of a constituency or an external controlling agency, lest it discover that what is done in the classroom will almost certainly have little bearing on what students learn or on what schools accomplish. Despite Meyer's cynicism about the work of instruction, note that he remains firmly in the control-system camp. It is just that in his view organizational regulation centers more on managing appearances than on the rational business of the organization.

PROSPECTS FOR AN OPEN, TECHNOLOGY-EMBRACING SYSTEM

As is true of general organizational theory, each of the various theoretical accounts of educational organizations has tackled a portion of what might become a full open-system formulation. It remains to assemble the pieces—a task that may be quite difficult if the pieces prove not to belong to the same puzzle.

How, then, can one say that we are poised for a major step toward understanding educational organizations and, through them, organizations generally? For many years in sociology there has been a radical separation of "shop floor" sociology (for example, Dalton 1959; Burawoy 1979) and organizational analysis. Perrow and the other sociotechnical theorists pointed toward an integration, but their success was partial and the separation largely remains. This separation has reinforced the organizational theorists' preoccupation with management and has contributed to their failure to surpass control-system thinking.

A truly open-system formulation will build upon advances in control-system theorizing and especially the notion of regulation as a system function. It will also employ the definition of organizational dynamics as a process of structural change in which regulatory and production activities interact to give form to the units and higher-order structures of an organization.

It will show that these processes operate under three principal sets of environmental opportunities and constraints. First, there is an array of resource suppliers (organized in markets or their functional equivalents). Second, there is an array of social controls and controllers and of political supporters and adversaries (organized as states and polities). These environmental components have been well described in general analytical terms, especially by students of interorganizational networks and interorganizational action (compare Laumann, Galaskiewicz, and Marsden 1978). Here power and its exercise throughout an organization (as envisioned by Abell) must surely be key variables if we are to understand the dynamics of educational or other organizations.

Third, there are the resource inputs themselves—the labor, materials, and technological elements (knowledge, procedures, and tools)—that are combined in production. Certain of these phenomena and their relationships to interworker social ties have been described with much richer detail by the shop-floor sociologists than by the sociotechnical or other organizational analysts—although with no greater analytical scope or clarity. The comprehensive, general analytical treatment and concomitant taxonomy of technological and materials properties is only now underway (Bidwell and Kasarda 1985). This analysis, which finds sources of organizational differentiation in the diversity and interdependence of the resources used in production, remains to be linked to a conceptual armamentarium concerning interpersonal ties that is of increasing power and precision.

The taxonomy required on the technological side must offer terms that are distinctive of properties of organizational structure before we can proceed to study the dynamics of organizational systems. In short, the systematic study of work in many organizational settings is required. Fortunately, we now see a strong movement in educational research in precisely this direction—toward a taxonomy of instructional variables and their analysis as components of classroom social systems (Bennett 1976; Barr and Dreeben 1983). Rebecca Barr and Robert Dreeben most notably have begun a research program that relates instructional technology and the social organization of instruction, each described in analytically distinct terms. For example, they have demonstrated that the resource-distributing effects of elementary school organization (such as ability grouping) interact with how teachers teach to influence the breadth and depth of pupils' exposure to knowledge.

Theorists of school organization now must have the imagination to incorporate and build upon such work to present an account of the dynamics of the organizational systems found in schools, school districts, colleges, and so on. If they are successful, they will have moved the entire field of organizational studies forward. At the least, they will have provided for the first time more than impressionistic evidence concerning (1) the degree to which and the sense in which instructional technology is in fact "weak" or "strong," productive or unproductive, (2) the observed extent of connection or disconnection between instruction and the organizational structures and processes of schools, and (3) the sources of variation in such relationships. Even this more modest contribution will be a substantial gain in our understanding of the structures and activities of formal education.

REFERENCES

Abell, P., ed. *Organizations as Bargaining and Influence Systems*. New York: Halsted Press, 1975.

Allison, G. T. *Essence of Decision: Explaining the Cuban Missile Crisis*. Boston: Little, Brown, 1971.

Barr, R., and Dreeben, R. *How Schools Work*. Chicago: University of Chicago Press, 1983.

Bennett, N. *Teaching Styles and Pupil Progress*. London: Open Books, 1976.

Bidwell, C. E., and Kasarda, J. D. *The Organization and Its Ecosystem: A Theory of Organizational Structuring*. Greenwich, Conn., and London: JAI Press, 1985.

Blau, P. M. "A Formal Theory of Differentiation in Organizations." *American Sociological Review* 35 (1970): 201–218.

Boulding, K. E. "General Systems Theory: The Skeleton of Science." In *Modern Systems Research for the Behavioral Scientist*, edited by W. F. Buckley. Chicago: Aldine, 1968.

Burawoy, M. *Manufacturing Consent: Changes in the Labor Process under Monopoly Capitalism*. Chicago: University of Chicago Press, 1979.

Chandler, A. D., Jr. *Strategy and Structure: Chapters in the History of the Industrial Enterprise*. Cambridge, Mass.: MIT Press, 1962.

Coase, R. H. "The Nature of the Firm." *Economica* N.S. 4 (1937): 386–405.

Crecine, J. P. *Governmental Problem Solving: A Computer Simulation of Municipal Budget Making*. Chicago: Rand McNally, 1969.

Cyert, R. M., and March, J. G. *A Behavioral Theory of the Firm*. Englewood Cliffs, N. J.: Prentice-Hall, 1963.

Dalton, M. *Men Who Manage*. New York: Wiley, 1959.

Durkheim, E. *Moral Education*. New York: Free Press, 1961.

Etzioni, A. *A Comparative Analysis of Complex Organizations: On Power, Involvement, and Their Correlates*. New York: Free Press, 1961.

Getzels, J. W.; Lipham, J.; and Campbell, R. F. *Educational Administration as a Social Process*. New York: Harper and Row, 1968.

Hall, R. H.; Haas, J. E.; and Johnson, N. J. "Organizational Size, Complexity, and Formalization." *American Sociological Review* 32 (1967): 903–912.

Halsey, A. H.; Floud, J.; and Anderson, C. A., eds. *Education, Economy, and Society*. New York: Free Press, 1961.

Klatzky, S. R. "Relationship of Organizational Size to Complexity and Coordination." *Administrative Science Quarterly* 15 (1970): 428–438.

Laumann, E. O.; Galaskiewicz, J.; and Marsden, P. V. "Community Structure as Interorganizational Linkages." *Annual Review of Sociology* 4 (1978): 455–484.

Lawrence, P. R., and Lorsch, J. W. *Organization and Environment: Managing Differentiation and Integration*. Boston: Graduate School of Business Administration, Harvard University, 1967.

Levy, F.; Meltsner, A. J.; and Wildavsky, A. *Urban Outcomes: Schools, Streets, and Libraries*. Berkeley: University of California Press, 1974.

Litchfield, E. H. "Notes on a General Theory of Administration." *Administrative Science Quarterly* 1 (1956): 3–29.

Lortie, D. C. *Schoolteacher.* Chicago: University of Chicago Press, 1975.

March, J. G., and Olsen, J. P. *Ambiguity and Choice in Organizations.* Bergen, Norway: Universitetsforlaget, 1976.

March, J. G., and Simon, H. A. *Organizations.* New York: Wiley, 1958.

Meyer, J. W., and Rowan, B. "Institutionalized Organizations." *American Journal of Sociology* 83 (1977): 340–363.

Meyer, J. W., and Scott, W. R. *Organizational Environments: Ritual and Rationality.* Beverly Hills, Calif.: Sage, 1983.

Meyer, M. W. "Size and the Structure of Organizations: A Causal Analysis." *American Sociological Review* 37 (1972): 434–441.

Parsons, T. *Structure and Process in Modern Societies.* Glencoe, Ill.: Free Press, 1960.

Perrow, C. *Organizational Analysis: A Sociological View.* Belmont, Calif.: Wadsworth, 1970.

Pugh, D. S.; Hickson, D. J.; Hinings, C. R.; MacDonald, K. M.; Turner, C.; and Lupton, T. "A Conceptual Scheme for Organizational Analysis." *Administrative Science Quarterly* 8 (1963): 289–315.

Pugh, D. S.; Hickson, D. J.; Hinings, C. R.; and Turner, C. "Dimensions of Organization Structure." *Administrative Science Quarterly* 13 (1968): 65–105.

Pugh, D. S.; Hickson, D. J.; Hinings, C. R.; and Turner, C. "The Context of Organization Structures." *Administrative Science Quarterly* 14 (1969): 91–114.

Simon, H. A. "The Architecture of Complexity." *Proceedings of the American Philosophical Society* 106 (1962): 467–482.

Swidler, A. *Organization without Authority.* Cambridge, Mass.: Harvard University Press, 1979.

Thompson, J. D. "On Building an Administrative Science." *Administrative Science Quarterly* 1 (1956): 102–111.

Thompson, J. D. *Organizations in Action: Social Science Bases of Administrative Theory.* New York: McGraw-Hill, 1967.

Waller, W. *The Sociology of Teaching.* New York: Wiley, 1932.

Warner, W. L.; Havighurst, R. J.; and Loeb, M. B. *Who Shall Be Educated?* New York: Harper, 1944.

Weber, M. *The Theory of Social and Economic Organization.* Edited and translated by A. M. Henderson and T. Parsons. Glencoe, Ill.: Free Press, 1947.

Weick, K. "Educational Organizations as Loosely Coupled Systems." *Administrative Science Quarterly* 21 (1976): 1–19.

Williamson, O. E. *Markets and Hierarchies: Analysis and Antitrust Implications.* New York: Free Press, 1975.

Woodward, J. *Industrial Organization: Theory and Practice.* London: Oxford University Press, 1965.

Woodward, J., ed. *Industrial Organization: Behavior and Control.* London: Oxford University Press, 1970.

10

On Economics

Mary Jean Bowman

Today's frontiers in the economics of education have their foundations in both a far distant and a comparatively recent past. They have early foundations in the concept of "human capital," which initially had no direct connection with schooling but came gradually,[1] and most fruitfully in the past quarter century, to be closely associated

---

1. In fundamental respects, the modern concept of human capital and its measurement was anticipated in the eighteenth century, by predecessors of Adam Smith. This was also before formal schooling had come to take the important place in economic life that it occupies throughout the world today. The early approaches, like aggregative assessments in recent decades, started from two distinct orientations: (1) evaluations of the human capital stock based on its "yields" in the contributions of working people, and (2) evaluations based on the costs of rearing children. To Sir William Petty, in the seventeenth century, labor was the "father of wealth" and a valuation of labor must therefore be included in any estimate of the national wealth (Kiker 1966, p. 52). The value of human capital was thus assessed by its yield, as it is today in Edward Denison's modern national accounting. Petty went on also to emphasize the importance of human capital for the economic strength of the nation, which led him in turn to a mercantilist's concern with what became in a later era (two centuries later) a concern with "brain drain."

The earliest cost-based valuation of human capital of which I am aware also goes back to a predecessor of Adam Smith—in this case a Frenchman, Richard Cantillon. Cantillon was concerned about the relationships between land and the principal produced factor of production—human labor. He asked how much land was required to rear a child and support working adults. Today, cost-based assessments have been

with analyses of investment in the formation of human resources. That analysis has focused not only on formal education but also on postschool learning and on-the-job training. It has drawn more recently from general economics, in the development of benefit-cost accounting. Beginning to emerge in some current work is a synthesis of human capital theory with the economics of information and "signaling,"[2] which draws also from work in other disciplines on "communication fields."

Many, perhaps most, of the major contributions over the past twenty-five years have incorporated either explicitly or implicitly the idea of opportunity cost, which leads in both the economics of education and the economics of the family to an emphasis on the allocation of time, whether the time spent is children's or adults'. Time spent by youth in school is time that cannot be spent at work, and thus time spent in school entails potential foregone earnings, which can constitute a major part of the costs of secondary education and especially of higher education. Similarly, time spent by women in child rearing may entail high costs in foregone earnings when that time is *not* spent in the labor market—a fact that has led to the emphasis on the rising education of women (and hence rising potential earnings) as a factor in the decline of fertility in economically advanced nations.[3] Meanwhile, a new and profoundly important frontier faces us in the treatment of time and perceptions of time as they relate to human development and the utilization of human resources in less developed countries (LDCs).

Some of the past seminal contributions in human capital theory

---

introduced into national income accounting, primarily by John Kendrik, and cost measures take a prominent place in one of the principal economic models used in analysis of relationships between education and fertility.

T. W. Schultz drew initially on a Fisherian yield-based definition of human capital, which is independent of the costs of human capital formation, but he turned quickly also to a cost-based definition. It is the combination of yields and costs that is needed for any assessment of investments, though not simply for national accounting. (On conceptual and other differences between the Denison and Schultz treatments of education in aggregate economic growth, see Bowman 1964.)

2. The term "signaling" as used here refers to the role of formal educational attainments as a signal of potential productivity of the individual—whether simply through screening of individuals for their initial traits or through what schooling has added to their productive potentials. See pages 207 to 208.

3. Becker's seminal treatments of time run through most of his work on education, on consumption, and on the family and fertility. For a comparatively nontechnical discussion of fertility and demographic transformation, see Bowman 1985.

have made steady-state simplifying assumptions. Others have stressed the effects of education in adaptation to and the fostering of techno-logical change. Emerging at the frontier in this research may be a new and more sophisticated concern with the processes of institutional change as they affect and reflect economic development and changes in postschool human resource formation and utilization.

I can hope to touch only a few of the many facets of research on the economics of education. Regretfully, I ignore altogether three fields of research in which I myself have recently been engaged and on which I have just published or am writing for publication. These are (1) relationships between education and fertility; (2) research on the spread of schooling, using an integrated framework that combines economic decision theory with a modified version of Torsten Hager-strand's theory of "information fields" (which Phyllis Goldblatt and I have redefined as "communication fields");[4] and (3) uncertainty, expectations, and educational choice. Also ignored, with equal regret, are contributions on relationships between education and the beha-vior of consumers, the still tentative but continuing sorties into the economics of collective choice in education, the expanding research on education and the roles of women in the labor force, the quite extensive roles of economists in studies of the performance of pupils in the schools, and new developments in the analysis of conditions and effects of students working while they are enrolled in school and the transition from school to full-time employment.[5]

THE RECENT PAST

My own definition of the *recent past* is that part of the past in which I have been an active, presumably mature, participant—which means that it begins with the 1930s. Neither in that decade nor in the 1940s had the time come for a flowering of the economics of education. On the contrary, the economics of education was at an exceptionally low ebb. Among other things, economists were far too absorbed in macro-economics, Keynesian and otherwise. Nevertheless, isolated new beginnings foreshadowed a future healthy economics of investment in human beings. Ray Walsh (1935) addressed the question of whether the benefit-cost results of training in various professions (or for the

---

4. For a discussion of this framework, see Bowman 1984.
5. This is of fundamental importance for the reassessment of treatments of the Mincer "overtake point" in empirical studies.

bachelor of arts degree) were consistent with rational and informed choices made by students. Though Walsh's methods were faulty, the question he posed remains relevant today. A few years later C. A. Anderson was running an interdisciplinary social science seminar for faculty and graduate students at Iowa State University. Seeking to build links among participants from the various disciplines, he pursued the theme of "investment in human capital." Although Schultz, who later was to win a Nobel Prize partly for his work on human capital, was chairman of the Iowa State University Department of Economics and Sociology, he did not pick up this theme at that time. Anderson and I pursued it in a joint seminar course at the University of California at Berkeley in 1948–49, by which time the 1946 book by Milton Friedman and Simon Kuznets entitled *Income from Independent Professional Practice* had been published. Like Walsh, they estimated values of discounted net income streams,[6] in this case of doctors and dentists, but they asked whether the returns to investments in the training of doctors and dentists were consistent with relatively open access or implied monopolistic constraints on entry to those professions. More than a decade was still to pass, however, before the "human investment revolution" in economic thought would arrive.

Meanwhile, sociologists had been at work on the 1940 and 1950 censuses of the United States. Ready at hand for the economists were the first systematic census figures relating schooling, age, and sex to earnings. This encouraged empirical explorations of long-standing questions about the associations between schooling and earnings, including associations between the age paths of earnings with experience and the distribution of income, which were followed up by a few economists in the 1950s. These data were to provide a base for the first benefit-cost assessments of investments in education and the first empirical incorporation of education in growth accounting—both took place in the 1960s.

The 1950s brought also the Russians' Sputnik, which shocked America into concern about the state of scientific and mathematical

---

6. The net income stream is the series of income differentials over the life span between, in this case, the bachelor of arts graduate and the physician. The "discounted net income stream" is the sum of the values of those differentials each of which is discounted back to a decision point—in this case to age at graduation from college. The discount rate is selected on the basis of interest rates on alternative investments with which comparisons are to be made. These alternatives need not be, and usually are not, investments in human capital.

competence in this country and precipitated studies of "shortages"—
especially of engineers. This set off studies of short-term adjustments
in the labor market to shifts in skill demands and supplies, a line of
work that remained independent of human capital theory and continued to lie largely dormant for another decade, but which is again
important today.

Of more immediate impact in economics was the demonstrated
inadequacy in the 1950s of the then prevailing aggregative econometric models designed to illuminate the sources of economic growth.[7]
Efforts to explain the "unexplained residual" opened the way for the
inclusion of adjustments for educational composition of the labor force
in aggregative growth accounting.

By the end of the 1950s the time had come for education to take a
more central place in economics; it was already an important part of
public budgets and of many aspects of economic life.

A NEW ERA

Despite what may seem in retrospect to have been heralding a
new and much enlarged place of education in economic thought, the
seminal contributions of T. W. Schultz and of Gary Becker in the
early 1960s came as an explosion, and they generated a new era in the
analysis of investments in human beings.

Schultz's initial interest in "human capital" came primarily from
his concern with economic growth. How far and in what ways might
investments in people contribute to growth? His perspective was
essentially dynamic, and it is no accident that some years later
Schultz wrote an article on the importance of the "ability to deal with
disequilibria" (Schultz 1974). From the start he emphasized the
broad scope of investments in people to include not only schooling

---

7. A series of papers on the "unexplained" sources of economic growth exploded in
the late 1950s and early 1960s—along with much argumentation about the assumptions and the "aggregate production functions" involved. An important landmark in
debates concerning the contributions of education to growth was the OECD study
group of May 1963 and the ensuing publication, edited by John Vaizey, entitled *The
Residual and Economic Growth.* See the reference, however, under Denison 1962.
Denison's national accounting model and that of followers has continued through the
past two decades, with applications to most of the industrialized nations. Results
have been mixed. For a particularly optimistic summarization of the situation today,
see Psacharopoulos 1984, and the appreciative but more qualified comments on his
paper by T. W. Schultz.

and various sorts of postschool training, but also investments in migration as a way of enhancing potential productivity and investments in health (which were already being examined in a benefit-cost framework in the late 1950s). Nor was this all. In a tour de force, Schultz explained his thesis in the book entitled *Transforming Traditional Agriculture* (1964). While he looked with the utmost respect on the shrewd intelligence of the traditional peasant, Schultz saw education as a factor that could undergird an agricultural transformation. Education offered a newly inexpensive "investment in the acquisition of a permanent income stream," and took a prime place in the dynamics of economic development.

Gary Becker's principal interests were quite different; he drew more from questions related to income distribution.[8] His seminal contributions in the early 1960s were two-fold. First, he developed a theory of investments in human beings that encompassed in one tidy model both investments in schooling and subsequent investments in the further acquisition of skills or competencies in the postschool years. Those who remain unaware of this accomplishment miss a major part of the essence of modern human capital theory.

Second, in an analysis that has much in common with the brilliant article by Walter Oi (1962) entitled "Labor as a Quasi-Fixed Factor," Becker drew the distinction between "general" and "specific" human capital. That distinction is between the aspects of the accumulation of skills (human capital) that have "general" applicability in the economy, wherever they may have been acquired, and "specific" skills, the value of which depends largely or wholly on their use in the firm or agency in which they are acquired. This distinction can have profound implications for the functioning of labor markets, including those "internal" to the firm. In Becker's work, and even in Jacob Mincer's subsequent analysis (1974), the learning processes in the internal labor markets remain empirically unspecified, however, and the extensive literature on internal labor markets has not yet contributed coherently to filling that gap. This remains a challenge.

SCHOOLING, INFORMATION, AND THE HETEROGENEITY OF HUMAN CAPITAL

Even if we ignore the distinction between Becker-general and Becker-specific human capital, it is clear enough that human capital

---

8. Becker's initial work on education (1962, 1964) was stimulated by the discussion of associations among schooling, on-the-job training, and life cycles of earnings in Mincer's doctoral dissertation. (See the 1958 article by Mincer on this topic.)

(like physical capital) is in fact heterogeneous. Simplifications that ignore this heterogeneity can be useful up to a point, but that point is reached quickly. Just two major sorts of heterogeneity are discussed in this section: differences in curricula or types of formal education (at any given level) and differences in individual traits. It is primarily the latter that underlie debates over schooling as a screening device versus schooling as a source of higher potential for an individual to be productive—which is a subject I discuss briefly at the end of this section. I defer discussion of some closely related questions concerning learning and earning in the postschool years to the later section on schooling and postschool years.[9]

Curricular Heterogeneity

From the start, empirical researchers such as Walsh (1935), Friedman and Kuznets (1946), and W. Lee Hansen (1963) estimated private (and in Hansen's case, social) benefit-cost relationships with respect to investments in various professional skills. Economic analyses of the effects of higher institutions attended and of types of curricula pursued in secondary schools on subsequent earning patterns required data that were generally less available. Probably the first research to focus attention on relationships between secondary curricula and the *time paths* of subsequent earnings was done by E. S. Todd (1969), who studied graduates of various curricula in a large Chicago secondary school. In an analysis that defined curricula with scrupulous care and covered the first seven postschool years, he showed that for graduates of some curricula the earning streams were much flatter than for others and some paths crossed over others, from lower starting points to higher earnings, at the seventh year in the labor market. More recently, economic studies of investments in vocational education and in various curriculum mixes have been vastly enriched through exploitation of data from the "National Longitudinal Study of the High School Class of 1972" (see especially Robert H. Meyer 1982). Still more material is now available with the "High School and Beyond" survey, which was carried out in replication for Japan as well as for the United States.

Meanwhile, a study of costs and benefits of diversified secondary curricula in three less developed countries has been sponsored by the World Bank and conducted by staff in its department of education.

---

9. The question of differences in "school quality" as these may affect the heterogeneity of human capital is bypassed but by no means unimportant.

This research (Psacharopoulos and Loxley 1985) is something of a breakthrough in empirical work on curriculum questions in the Third World. It is also a reflection of rising interest in careful empirical examination of economic issues involved in debates over curriculum policies.

Underlying Individual Characteristics as Components of Human Capital

When we look at human capital from a yield (rather than an investment-cost) perspective,[10] the importance of variation in individual characteristics must be obvious, but that is not all. There are also questions about how those characteristics interact with education and the joint associations of schooling and personal traits with various indicators of economic success—earning paths, the incidence of unemployment, occupational status, and so on. There are persistent questions also, perhaps more in the domain of educational and social psychologists than of economists, about how and to what extent individual traits shown to be of critical importance in a lifetime perspective can be modified.

The first challenge to both estimates of rates of return to schooling and treatment of education in growth accounting came from the proposition that those who go further in school are different from those who stop sooner in ways that affect their earnings and careers. Initially the response to this was to introduce an arbitrary adjustment coefficient into both the estimates of contributions of education to growth and the estimates of private rates of return. This modified the estimates, but it told us nothing about the interactive effects of ability, noncognitive traits, and more schooling on subsequent careers. Recent and current work has begun to open up some of these questions along at least two lines.

Robert Willis and Sherwin Rosen (1979) explored econometrically the question of self-selection in relation to what individuals of greater or lesser measured ability may gain from more education. Their findings suggest that those who continue through four years of college are not only the more able but also gain more from the full four years than would those who in fact stop their education after junior college; these are rational choices.

Meanwhile, it is becoming possible, through the use of newly

10. On a yield-versus-cost perspective, see note 1.

available panel data, to identify some of the unmeasured individual characteristics associated with schooling and postschool performance. Preliminary results indicate, for example, that those who are irregular in school attendance are irregular also in attendance at work and are prone to high job turnover (see Meyer 1981 and Weiss 1984).

Screening, Certification, and the Economics of Information

A major part of the uncertainties and gaps in information that must be faced by both individuals (or families) and employers in making decisions about the formation and utilization of human resources derives from the heterogeneity in supplies of and demands for skills and the differences among individuals in abilities and other traits that affect performance. A world of costless information about people would have no place for a "screening debate," and labor markets characterized by full costless information would have no place for the "economics of information" as applied to human resource formation and utilization. But the real world is characterized by wide human variability, large gaps in information, and continuing change.

In the 1970s the theme of individual characteristics and their associations with educational attainments was taken up not merely to suggest that unadjusted estimates of effects of schooling on productivity were biased upward, but to suggest (in the most extreme variants) that schooling was primarily (if not solely) a selection mechanism or *screening* device that signaled prospective productivity, not an instrument for the formation of human capital.[11] A considerable literature has tried to sort out this issue, which may in any case be a false one. Few people would argue that schooling does *nothing* beyond selecting those who will be more productive; at the same time, few would argue that schools have no selection effects.[12] What is abundantly clear, however, is that the relative importance of selection

---

11. The challenge is a double one. First, how much does schooling in fact contribute to productive potential? And if the answer to this first question is "not much," then we have a second question: Is education a socially inefficient signaling system? The societal need for a signaling device is not challenged. On this, see Arrow 1973 and the seminal work on signaling by Spence 1974, summarized with respect to education in his 1973 article.

12. Particularly relevant among recent studies are those that address empirically the relationships between schooling and incomes in nonwage and in private versus public employments. See, for example, Jamison and Lau 1982 and Cain 1976.

differs greatly from one society to another, and that these differences are bound up with the relative importance of certification and the formalization and bureaucratization of labor markets (see Ronald Dore's *The Diploma Disease* [1976]). The debates over screening per se have stimulated a more active interest in the processes by which information about capabilities and performance evolves and in the relation of those processes to schooling and to students' subsequent careers in the United States.

Meanwhile, applications and extensions of the "economics of information" and job search theory, another seminal forward leap of the 1960s (see Stigler 1962) cuts into these questions with special relevance at the transition from school to labor market and on into promotions and job shifts in the postschool years.[13]

SCHOOLING AND POSTSCHOOL LEARNING

Up to this point I have considered the heterogeneity of human capital primarily as a matter of individual genetic and social heritage and as a function of kinds of formal schooling. We may view heterogeneities on many other dimensions, however, and several dimensions in the mixes of learning and earning in the postschool years are extremely important. Taking a broad swathe, I distinguish here just two of these dimensions: (1) learning to earn versus learning to learn and (2) the complementarity (or substitutability) of schooling and human capital formation at work.

Learning to Learn and Learning to Earn over the Life Cycle

If the acquisition of enhanced ability to learn and of earning power are interchangeable, we would have what has sometimes been labeled "neutrality" in the formation of human capital. Assuming homogeneity of human capital in this dimension, Yoram Ben-Porath (1970) undertook an econometric experiment to test whether the observed concavity of postschool earning paths could be explained by a Becker-based theory of investments in human beings together with the fact that working life is finite.[14] He came out with negative results.

---

13. Recently, growing numbers of labor economists have been exploring some related issues by applying contract theory, which can illuminate some aspects of the processes that determine patterns of human resource formation and utilization in postschool employment.

14. This refers to Becker's treatment of "general" human capital and his application of the "foregone earnings" concept to analysis not only of costs of schooling but also of formation of human capital in the postschool years.

Although the ability to learn contributes directly to earning power, the neutrality assumption could not be fully maintained. Ben-Porath's findings could imply also that over time the learning-to-learn component in postschool learning (formal or informal) shrinks in importance relative to a more immediately job-focused training. This is an intuitively appealing hypothesis. But would we expect it to carry over to the school years as well, which would imply a gradual shift from maximal learning-to-learn components during the early school years toward combinations with more narrowly focused learning to earn in the later years? The fact that curricula become more differentiated at more advanced levels does not give us the answer, since greater emphasis on mathematics, for example, can still constitute predominantly learning to learn. Moreover, we cannot assume that existing practices are optimal. Also, school and out-of-school environments have distinctive characteristics, and there could be many situations in which comparative advantages shift rather sharply at the transition from school to work. If so, this underlines a proposition that is too little heeded in many comments about schooling—a major part of what schooling does, and perhaps *should* do up to some fairly advanced level, is to prepare for subsequent learning at work. This would imply that the quality of schooling should be assessed primarily by how far it raises the ability to learn. Who learns best in what environments, learning which things, in what ways? This is largely unploughed country, with open frontiers that are just beginning to attract systematic research by scholars of many stripes, from economists to psychologists.

Complementarity Between Schooling and On-the-Job Learning

Are schooling and on-the-job learning predominantly substitutive or complementary? The evidence for the United States, at least, and from my reading of it (without any econometric tests) for Japan, strongly suggests, in fact, a strong complementarity between these two phases of human resource formation. The few relevant studies in LDCs manifest a clear complementarity at lower levels between schooling and postschool progress in the acquisition of journeyman skills and modest managerial competence. But there is at the same time the serious problem in the LDCs of the limited conditions and opportunities for learning on the job. Under some circumstances, this can force substitutive strategies back toward earlier "vocationalism" in the schools. In other words, we are dealing here with an important set of problems, the answers to which will differ with the particular context. Nevertheless, some principles relating to what schools can do best and how other agencies and schools may best be combined can have great pragmatic generality. (On this theme see Bowman, Sabot, and collaborators 1981.)

CHANGING SKILL DEMANDS AND SUPPLIES, HUMAN CAPITAL UTILIZATION, AND ECONOMIC GROWTH

The more rapid is the pace of technological and organizational change, the greater is the need for people with the ability and attitudinal readiness to adapt to change—or in the terminology used above, with the ability to learn rapidly. This can be critical both for relatively quick adjustments in the face of change and for the generation of technological and economic progress. So broadly stated, this is the main theme of both this section and the preceding one, in which I address the most direct bits of micro-economic evidence on the effects of schooling on innovative behavior.

In the present section I discuss three topics: (1) the nature of jobs and educational expansion in the LDCs, (2) the organization of production and the utilization of schooled human resources in economically advanced countries, and (3) complementarity among human capital, physical capital, and research and development.

The Nature of Jobs and the Political Economy of Frustrated Expectations

In the 1950s concern about skill shortage prevailed; in recent years, however, more concern has been voiced about the alleged "filtering down" of individuals into lower-status jobs because of the expansion of schooling. Especially with reference to LDCs, such allegations must immediately raise the questions, What does a job label mean? and How are job requirements related to skill availabilities? These are critical matters that cut into almost every facet of the economics of education in its relation to labor markets. They can take on special importance, however, in periods and situations in which there are major changes in the educational composition of the labor force.

Some of the dilemmas are most easily observed in Africa, where primary-school leavers can no longer gain entry to the white-collar job that such schooling had opened up for an older brother, and often the secondary graduates can no longer get one of the cherished jobs that had been open to such graduates in the past. Yet anyone who tried a decade or so ago to work with an African primary-school leaver as a secretary can attest to the fact that the job of secretary or even of clerk will be quite a different job when it is filled by a person with secondary schooling than by a person with only primary schooling. This is an unduly simplified example, of course, but it illustrates with special clarity the fact that an alleged "filtering down" of people may be due to approaching a more reasonable match between the presumed job content and the capabilities of the job holder. In such cases no one really went down; instead, jobs went up. This does not, however, dispose of the problem of individual reactions to the changing situation, nor does it imply that job requirements will always rise in line with rising capabilities. When and at whatever levels expectations are frustrated, the political impact can and often does lead to dyseconomic public policies.[15]

The Enlistment of Human Capabilities

Often, those who speak of "overeducation" refer not to reduced monetary rates of return (as did Richard Freeman 1976), but rather to a "mismatch" in which many people are in jobs that demand far less than their levels of education—sometimes with actual negative effects on productivity. The proposition that "overeducation" so defined may depend more on how work is structured or on investments in research and development than on the educational composition of the labor force has been receiving increased attention recently. Again, we come back to the nature of a "job," but now in another context.

Some of the faculty and graduate students at Stanford University have been addressing the problem of using worker capabilities in ways that may encourage group commitment to improved quality standards and may raise job satisfaction and self-respect. They bring work of industrial psychologists on job dissatisfaction together with economic assessments of experiences in various forms of worker partici-

---

15. Richard Sabot and some of his associates have recently completed important research on education and labor-market developments over a decade in Tanzania and Kenya. While this research refers only to the "modern" sector, it includes low-level jobs in that sector, with some probing into job content and into relationships between measured ability and the occupational attainments and responsibilities of workers. These data can be cross-classified against formal schooling. It is hoped that such work may be carried out in other countries and other settings. The promise for enrichment of the economics of education is substantial.

pation and collective management. (See Rumberger 1981; Levin 1984; Tang and Levin 1985; and, by contrast, Weiss 1984 and references therein on "job enrichment.")

Elsewhere, concern about Japanese competition is stimulating pragmatic and discriminating analyses of the lessons to be learned from Japanese practices that have (and have not) proven to be transferable to other cultural settings. Nowhere is there clearer evidence than in Japan that the personnel and development policies of the firm can build well on high levels of per-capita human capital.

This leads not only to the matter of better utilization of human capabilities, but also, coming full circle, to how skills of the labor force can be enhanced during the postschool years. Whatever the position taken on over- or undereducation in terms of schooling, there can be no question about the importance of human resource development in the postschool years—a problem that should be much easier to resolve in the United States and even in the middle-income countries than in Sub-Saharan Africa.

Complementarity Among Human Capital, Physical Capital, and Research and Development

This brings me to another matter—the importance for economic growth of complementarities among human capital, physical capital, and research and development—and with this the importance of reserves in the human capital stock.

Great as the contributions of conventional national income accounting methods have been, they still have not accommodated satisfactorily the dynamics of growth processes. To illustrate, Edward Denison and W. K. Chung (1976) and others have found by their measures that education contributed comparatively little to Japanese economic growth in the 1960s. These findings were despite the rapid expansion of education in that country, a high quality of schooling, and extensive on-the-job training. Rapid and extensive investment in new, technologically advanced physical capital was important, to be sure. But Japan's strong human capital base was indisputably a necessary condition for the success of the new investments. And this is not the end of the problem. How should we interpret econometric findings of complementarity between human and physical capital? Neither the injections of the Marshall Plan's physical capital in postwar Europe nor the rapid pace of investments in physical capital in Japan were merely replications of old capital; new technologies were involved. Econometrically observed complementarities between human and physical capital pick up relationships between education and Schultz's "ability to deal with disequilibria." They may reflect also the more direct embodiment of advances in knowledge in new human capital. A recent article by W. W. McMahon (1984) pursues this theme.

EDUCATION AND INNOVATIVE BEHAVIOR

Schultz has never been alone in his emphasis on the importance of looking at education in a context of change. Indeed, Frederick Harbison was writing and talking many years ago about educated people as agents of change, and Richard Nelson has long argued the close relationship between technological change and the value of education. This is not just a matter of adaptive behavior, or of abilities to deal with change. Education can also generate change. It can do this both indirectly, as through effects on how people perceive the world, and more directly, through effects on abilities to add new knowledge and to apply it. The latter idea has often received resistance, since it is obvious enough that most highly educated people are not notably creative, and relatively uneducated people can display outstanding ingenuity. It is clear, nevertheless, that education opens opportunities for innovative and creative contributions by people whose special potentials would not otherwise be realized. Research on this theme has taken two main directions.

Schooling and Innovative Behavior in Agriculture

Research on relationships between schooling and innovative behavior in agriculture has been extensive. Evidence is accumulating that schooling is important for agricultural progress *where research and experimentation have demonstrated the superiority of new practices*—and, of course, where the means for adopting those practices are available. Meanwhile, investigations of the kinds of qualifications associated with different levels of education among farmers in the United States (and also in India) have set "allocative" apart from "worker" behavior[16]—

---

16. "Worker" behavior refers to skills employed in the various day-to-day tasks involved in operating a farm. "Allocative" behavior refers to making decisions about such things as product mix, combinations of inputs (in land, equipment, seeds, fertilizers, and so forth), marketing procedures and timing, and so on.

an analysis that has applications well beyond agriculture. (For an overview of the research in agriculture, see Lockheed, Jamison, and Lau 1980.)

Education and Nonfarm Entrepreneurial Behavior

Of special interest must be the unique research by T. K. Koh (1977) on the innovative behavior of Japanese independent and family enterprisers. He was able to distinguish clearly three types of innovative behavior reported by respondents who were asked what had been the "most important" change they had made in their business in the past five years. Relating these responses to the entrepreneur's schooling, Koh found that technological or processing changes were most often reported as the most important by men with only compulsory schooling, which, in his sample, was usually through eight years. Changes in buying or selling practices were the most frequently cited as most important among those in the middle education ranks. Only the college men reported important structural or organizational changes. These last sorts of innovation were unmistakably the most demanding educationally.

Meanwhile, economic journalists have begun writing of *intrapreneurship*, which refers explicitly to efforts to decentralize responsibilities in big firms; such efforts thereby seek to encourage active and independent entrepreneurial behavior that is financed under the umbrella of a big organization. Also, in both Japan and the United States individuals have sometimes spun off into independent enterprise from positions in large corporations—although the Japanese and American approaches to this seem to be quite different.

Large or small, and with whatever linkages, the exploration of innovative behavior and of the role of education in it is clearly a challenging frontier for research in the economics of education—and for social scientists of all stripes.

REFERENCES

Arrow, Kenneth. "Higher Education as a Filter." *Journal of Public Economics* 2 (1973): 193–216.

Becker, Gary S. "Investment in Human Capital: A Theoretical Analysis." *Journal of Political Economy* 70:5, part 2 (1962); supplement on *Investment in Human Beings*, edited by T. W. Schultz, pp. 9–50. Chicago: University of Chicago Press, 1962.

Becker, Gary S. *Human Capital: A Theoretical and Empirical Analysis, with Special Reference to Education*. New York: National Bureau of Economic Research, 1964.

Becker, Gary S. *Human Capital.* 2d ed. New York: Columbia University Press, 1975.

Ben-Porath, Y. "The Production of Human Capital over Time." In *Education, Income, and Human Capital,* edited by W. L. Hansen. Studies in Income and Wealth. Vol. 35, pp. 129–147. New York: NBER, 1970.

Bowman, M. J. "Schultz, Denison, and the Contribution of 'Eds' to Economic Growth." *Journal of Political Economy* 72:5 (1964): 450–465.

Bowman, M. J. "An Integrated Framework for Analysis of the Spread of Schooling in Less Developed Countries." *Comparative Education Review* 28:4 (1984): 563–581.

Bowman, M. J. "Education, Population Trends and Technological Change." *Economics of Education Review* 4:1 (1985): 29–44.

Bowman, M. J.; Sabot, R.; and collaborators. "Human Resources in Africa." A background World Bank paper prepared for the 1982 Conference of African Governmental Experts on Technical Cooperation among African Countries on Human Resources Development and Utilization, 1981.

Cain, G. "The Challenge of Segmented Labor Market Theories to Orthodox Theory: A Survey." *Journal of Economic Literature* 14 (December 1976): 1215–1217.

Denison, E. F. *The Sources of Economic Growth and the Alternatives before Us.* Supplementary Paper No. 13. New York: Committee for Economic Development, 1962. A paper based on this book, but concentrating attention primarily on education, was presented at a session of the Economics of Education Study Group of OECD in May 1963 and published in *The Residual Factor and Economic Growth,* edited by J. Vaizey. Paris: OECD, 1964.

Denison, E. F., and Chung, W. K. *How Japan's Economy Grew So Fast.* Washington, D.C.: The Brookings Institution, 1976.

Dore, Ronald. *The Diploma Disease.* Berkeley: University of California Press, 1976.

Freeman, Richard. *The Over-Educated American.* New York: Academic Press, 1976.

Friedman, M., and Kuznets, S. *Income from Independent Professional Practice.* New York: National Bureau of Economic Research, 1946.

Hansen, W. Lee. "Total and Private Returns to Investment in Schooling." *Journal of Political Economy* 71: 2 (April 1963): 128–140.

Jamison, D., and Lau, L. *Farmer Education and Farm Efficiency.* Baltimore: Johns Hopkins University Press, 1982.

Kiker, B. F. "The Historical Roots of the Concept of Human Capital." *Journal of Political Economy* 74:5 (October 1966): 481–499.

Koh, T. K. "Education, Entrepreneurial Formation, and Entrepreneurial Behavior in Japan." Ph.D. dissertation, University of Chicago, 1977.

Levin, H. M. "Improving Productivity through Education and Technology." Institute for Research in Educational Finance and Governance, Stanford University School of Education, Project Report No. 84–A25, 1984.

Lockheed, M. E.; Jamison, Dean; and Lau, Lawrence. "Farmer Education and Farm Efficiency." *Economic Development and Cultural Change* 29:1 (1980): 37–76.

McMahon, W. W. "The Relation of Education and R & D to Productivity Growth." *Economics of Education Review* 3:4 (1984): 299–314.

Meyer, R. H. "The Effect of Personal Attributes and the Labor Market on School Choice and Attendance Behavior." Harvard University, working paper (February 1981).

Meyer, R. H. "Job Training in the Schools." In *Job Training for Youth,* edited by R. E. Taylor, H. Rosen, and F. Pratzner, pp. 307–344. Columbus: Ohio State University, 1982.

Mincer, Jacob. "Investment in Human Capital and Income Distribution," *Journal of Political Economy*, August 1958, pp. 281–300.

Mincer, Jacob. *Schooling, Experience and Earnings*. New York: National Bureau of Economic Research, 1974.

Oi, W. "Labor as a Quasi-Fixed Factor." *Journal of Political Economy* 70:6 (December 1962): 538–556.

Psacharopoulos, G. "The Contribution of Education to Economic Growth: International Comparisons." In *International Comparisons of Productivity and Causes of the Slowdown*, edited by J. W. Kendrik, pp. 335–360. Cambridge, Mass.: American Enterprise Institute, Ballinger Publishing, 1984.

Psacharopoulos, G., and W. Loxley *Diversified Secondary Education and Development*. Baltimore: Johns Hopkins University Press, for the World Bank, 1985.

Rumberger, R. W. *Overeducation in the U.S. Labor Market*. New York: Praeger, 1981.

Schultz, T. W. "Education and Economic Growth." In *Social Forces Influencing American Education*, edited by Ralph W. Tyler. Chicago: National Society for the Study of Education, 1961.

Schultz, T. W. *Transforming Traditional Agriculture*. New Haven, Conn.: Yale University Press, 1964.

Schultz, T. W. "The Value of the Ability to Deal with Disequilibria." *Journal of Economic Literature* 13:3 (September 1974): 827–846.

Spence, Michael. "Job Market Signaling." *Quarterly Journal of Economics* 87:3 (August 1973): 355–374.

Spence, Michael. *Market Signaling*. Cambridge, Mass.: Harvard University Press, 1974.

Stigler, G. H. "Information in the Labor Market." *Journal of Political Economy* 70:5, part 2 (1962); supplement to *Investment in Human Beings*, edited by T. W. Schultz, pp. 94–106. Chicago: University of Chicago Press, 1962.

Tang, M. C., and Levin, H. M. "The Economics of Over-education." *Economics of Education Review* 4:2 (1985): 93–104.

Todd, E. S. *Some Economic Implications of Secondary School Curricula*. Ph.D. dissertation, University of Chicago, 1969.

Walsh, J. R. "Capital Concept Applied to Man." *Quarterly Journal of Economics*, February 1935, pp. 255–285.

Weiss, Andrew. "Determinants of Quit Behavior." *Journal of Labor Economics* 2:3 (1984): 371–387.

Willis, R. J., and Rosen, S. "Education and Self-Selection." *Journal of Political Economy* 87:5, part 2 (1979): S7–S36.

11

On Historiography

Geraldine Jonçich Clifford

In 1915 Frederick Bolton of the University of Washington surveyed course offerings in university departments of education. He found that the history of education was one of the leading subjects in the curriculum (Bolton 1915, p. 838). He suggested three reasons for its prevalence in the curriculum: (1) tradition, (2) the lesser objection to history than to other branches of education on the part of faculty in other departments, and (3) history's frequent inclusion in statutory requirements for the licensing of teachers. Bolton might have added a fourth reason: the absence, at that time, of much codified knowledge in potentially competing fields. Subsequently, however, the competition asserted itself, with educational psychology and measurement courses becoming widely taught. The history of education lost what remained of the "benign favor of the scrupulous academic gods" when Committee Q of the American Association of University Professors, reviewing required courses in education, reported in 1933 that few teachers thought history a worthwhile study; the committee wondered whether it was being taught by "first-rate scholars" and whether it might not be postponed to graduate schools where advanced students could better appreciate its significance (Committee Q 1933; Williamson 1936, p. 43). Meanwhile licensing authorities expanded subject-matter, special methods, and practice requirements at the expense of traditional theory courses. There is evidence, then, for Edgar Wesley's assertion that the history of education experienced its "golden age" about 1911 (Wesley 1957). *Alas!* As with other golden ages, it had come—and gone—before we realized it.

In the last two decades there has, however, been a revived interest in the history of education. While the subject has not won a larger place in the curriculum during this period and not, therefore, in the writing of textbooks, much scholarly activity and theoretical debate have taken place. Monographs, new surveys, and critical essays have contributed something to "a hard core of facts, however much it may be concealed by the surrounding pulp of disputable interpretation" of those facts—to borrow the words of Sir George Clark (in Silver 1983, p. 11). This period has illustrated what Harold Silver calls "the complexity of the levels at which the history of education needs to be written." He goes on to say, "If it is about pioneers and their reputations, it is also about ideas and movements. If it is about ideologies, it is also about the interactive nature of popular expectations and attitudes. If it is about policy on the grand scale, it is also about experience" (Silver 1983, p. 281).

WHAT HAVE WE LEARNED?

I am happy I have been asked to write about *"historiography"* (the writing of history, the written product), and not *"history"* (the character and significance of past events). I say happy because I believe that the overshadowing insights of the past twenty years concern what the historian creates rather than what the historical actors have created. By examining what American historians of education have written, we can learn as much or more about the present than about the past. We can see, more clearly than before, how events in the historian's present will motivate, shape, and color the search for the story and its assigned meanings. These biasing influences, once implicit, have been made explicit in polemical written exchanges among historians of education, in reviews, in conferences, and in the gossip chain. Many American historians would, I think, largely agree with the view of us reportedly held abroad: that our recent historiography has "more to do with American politics than [with the] history of education" (Silver 1983, p. 285).

In a critical review of the use of social science research in courts of law, economist Henry Levin argues that the social scientist is substantially the product of that which she or he studies. One's social origins and engrained experiences help select certain problems for study and produce particular "understandings" of the results (Levin 1975, pp. 232–233). While hardly a new idea, consideration of this possibility played little part in the training offered by schools of education to my generation of historians of education. We would contribute to the picture of education's past by *adding* detail; today's student is accustomed to thinking of *revising* or overturning the received wisdom.

In part this new stance derives from changes of focus in the historiography of education discipline itself and from greater interdisciplinary contact. Social history has grown to challenge the intellectual and political history of education, as it has challenged the larger profession of history. I am not certain whether social history is potentially more inherently critical, but there is little doubt that the historiography of education has altered with the consideration of such topics as changing family roles, group life in America, and the intersections of institutional agendas with race, class, and gender. As contemporary geography went beyond looking at how the land appears to surveyors or aerial photographers to consider how Earth appears to ordinary people who daily move across its surface, so historiography became less a story of leaders and sacrosanct institutions and more one of their interplay with ongoing social forces. What was lost in clarity was made up for by colorful diversity. Meanwhile the humanistic studies of history and philosophy made contact with the sociology of education, an area that burgeoned after World War II. Comparative education was growing and becoming less historical with the interest in the "development" of the Third World. Before the funding balloon burst, schools of education were also employing political scientists, economists, and cultural anthropologists in their social foundations or policy departments (Powell and Sizer 1969, pp. 69–70).

The transformation of public education from a "growth industry" to a depressed sector of the nation's psychic and political life is, I think, another and crucial factor in explaining the historiographic upheavals of the later 1960s and 1970s. Public support—characterized by one school superintendent as being like a Florida river: one mile wide and an inch deep—turned unfavorable toward public schools and their teachers. Educational researchers contributed to a mood of deepening skepticism about the cognitive and social effectiveness of schools; for example, the Coleman Report (1966) and Christopher Jencks's study, *Inequality: A Reassessment of Family and Schooling in America* (1972). Taxpayers' revolts and demographic changes weakened the fiscal and political support for schools in their competition with other public services for funding. The schools were failing, it was said, and were inadequate to the tasks they had once performed so well.

When in 1960 Bernard Bailyn spoke against the preoccupation with schooling as the primary theme of educational historiography, I do not know that many saw it as much more than another sour and overstated indictment, by an academician, of the educationists' products. It now seems to have become an early salvo in a wider war on the *public* historiography of education. Popular and intellectual repudiation of such American institutions as public schools flourished in what Michael Kirst has called the "age of the querulous"—polarized and quarrelsome. Relations among historians of education partook of that general spirit.

The conventional wisdom had linked opportunity to education. Disappointment with the slow progress in bettering race relations and gaining scholastic equity worked against the optimistic tradition in the historiography of American schooling. The civil rights movement aroused other groups—various minorities and the presumably assimilated descendants of European immigrants (the "white ethnics")—who captured the attention of scholars as well as politicians; the Left and the Right both gained adherents, at the expense of the Center. Urban riots, strikes by public employees, defiance of military policy, disruptions of city council and school board meetings, and well-publicized campus revolts all shook the comfortable status quo, even as the poor sought empowerment. Business leaders saw urban schools unable either to police their students or to teach them marketable skills.

The battle in inner cities for community control of schools extended beyond issues of control over textbooks or, even, teacher selection; it was "an aspect of the larger struggle to redistribute life chances between blacks and whites" (Katznelson 1981, p. 118). Concerned friends of public education were beginning to protest that the schools were being asked to do too much, and that the assault on social problems must be fought on other fronts. If our national confidence in *present* social arrangements was shaken, perhaps our *past* was not all that we had formerly been taught either. A corrective historiography could be used to make schools a smaller target. Lawrence Cremin's recasting of the history of American education, which reduces schooling to the status of one of many agencies of education, can be understood as a defense of the public school (Clifford 1985).

SHIFTING TIDES: FROM LIBERAL TO RADICAL THEMES

While not the first important historian of American education, Ellwood P. Cubberley, whose *History of Education* sold over 100,000 copies, was so unabashed a proponent of the progressive perspective that he became the chief target of latter-day revisionists. His authorship of textbooks on the history of education aimed to impress upon students of education the proper appreciation of the magnitude of an inspiring victory on behalf of public education. The transfer of schooling from private and church sponsorship to public control represented "the most important constructive undertaking of the state" (Cubberley 1923, p. 545). The Great Depression stimulated reassessments, like Merle Curti's *The Social Ideas of American Educators*. But the war effort and the postwar economic boom supported renewed self-congratulation as Europe finally appeared ready to emulate American expansiveness in school provisions. In the 1950s, despite the attacks from the Council for Basic Education, which was perceived to be a reactionary and elitist fringe group, there was essential confidence in the past and present American system of education. Many liberals were jubilant when the Supreme Court, in its 1954 decision against segregation by race in public schools, finally gave the public schools the opportunity to redress the one obvious unmet challenge of democratic education. After 1963 the assistance of the federal government, through President Johnson's Great Society education and training programs, would help schools to remove race and chronic poverty as obstacles to full participation in the "good life."

The intractableness of these barriers did not so much create doubters—some were always there—as it energized them and readied an audience. Where there had been historiographic silence, there was now clamor (Silver 1983, p. 12). The linking of educational to capitalist development began to seem less alien, as did the framework of class struggle long employed by European historians of education. The concepts of "social control," "imposition," and educational "colonialism" became familiar themes in discussing American minority groups and immigrants' experiences with schools. Arthur Jensen's writings on racially influenced IQ became a catalyst for younger historians wishing to trace "Jensenism's" roots to their eugenic origins; the search led even to Britain: to Francis Galton, Karl Pearson, and Cyril Burt. Previous reform efforts, from progressive education to the junior high school and community college, were reinterpreted as manipulative strategies or efforts to forestall the only avenue of real change: political and economic revolution. Rather belatedly the "radical revisionists" discovered women and added gender politics to their analyses. In sum, schooling was revealed as profoundly reactionary, an agency of false consciousness, the principal impediment to the necessary revolution.

Among the revisionists the work of Michael B. Katz was especially cited. (For example, see Katz [1971].) Economists Samuel Bowles and Herbert Gintis employed it in making their case in *Schooling in Capitalist America* (1976). Enrollments in the now-"sexy" history of education courses went up for a while, at least at Berkeley. Yet, even as this historiography was being widely disseminated, a reaction was setting in. Some thought the revisionists arrogant—for all their identification with the underclasses. Harold Silver (1983) found them inadequate in meeting the test of a historian's ability to conduct a "dialogue with the dead." He states, "It means a constant effort to lower the historian's own voice and the stridency of his own time. It means a constant diminution of his sense of knowing the outcome, of the arrogance of his own judgment after the event" (p. 299).

"The stridency of the historian's own time" was obvious enough in the revisionists' historiography to subject them to charges of presentism and anachronism. A group response to these charges was made in the preface to *Roots of Crisis* (1973), by Clarence Karier, Paul Violas, and Joel Spring. They quoted Nietzsche's "You can only explain the past by what is highest in the present." As the liberal progressive culture of twentieth-century America—with its "ideas of progress, rationality, community, science, and technology"—constituted the world view that guided former historians of education, so the revisionists' historiography represents their own attempt to add meaning to the present. Their assumptions were of a present society that is "racist, fundamentally materialistic, and institutionally structured to protect vested interests"; consequently, schools function as agencies of control and repression. The authors concluded, "People prefer one history over another because it is that history which most *satisfies* their quest for meaning" (pp. 1–5).

In the collection *Historical Inquiry in Education: A Research Agenda*, published by AERA in 1983, one finds a range of largely lukewarm allusions to the satisfactions of radical historiography (Best 1983). Michael Katz himself did not retreat from the central role that he assigned to conflict in generating pressures for educational change (Katz and Hogan 1983, p. 285). Henry Johnson (1983) found the revisionists' historiography wanting for being rooted not in "actual inquiries about schools" but in "vast hypotheses generated . . . by approved social scientists" (p. 19). William Reese (1983) thought that historians studying the experiences of American ethnic groups had progressed beyond social-control interpretations and that the complex interactions of ethnicity and social class awaited more careful analysis (pp. 230, 242). But the "policy implications" had *already* troubled others. Samuel Bowles and Herbert Gintis, and Martin Carnoy in *Education as Cultural Imperialism* (1974), were proclaiming that liberal social policy had been discredited by critical social science, historiographic revisionism, and evaluations of federal education programs. In her extended review, *The Revisionists Revised* (1977), Diane Ravitch worried that the new body of radical writings, using history wrenched from its context to make political points, gives comfort to reactionaries: "To argue, against the evidence, that meaningful change is not possible is to sap the political will that is necessary to effect change" (p. 34). *Revisionists Respond to Ravitch* (Feinberg et al.) was published in 1980, but interest in the debate had already subsided—in part, at least, because the United States was turning its back on the intense questioning of itself that had characterized the previous fifteen or so years. In the 1960s the political language of the cities was of "power and powerlessness, internal colonialism, repression, poverty, racial and ethnic discrimination, participatory democracy, and community control." The terminology switched to defining action "in terms of balancing budgets, bondholder confidence, service cutbacks, wage freezes, municipal employee layoffs, the erosion of the tax base, and making do with less" (Katznelson 1981, p. 4).

FROM KATZ TO KATZNELSON: A NEW SYNTHESIS?

One of the questions I have been asked to consider is "What can we no longer believe as a result of the recent developments in your field?" We can no longer say that Americans never think in class terms, as Louis Hartz concluded in *The Liberal Tradition in America* (1955). The "consensus" school *had* fostered the false view that Americans belonged to "one big happy family"; it usually treated conflict with "patronizing afterthought" (Katznelson 1981, p. 14). If the revisionists are much of the time wrong about the motivations and impulses behind the establishment and expansion of public education, they are largely correct about the failures to realize the liberal dream—although they may also have underestimated the democratic achievements of the system for many Americans, especially the descendants of diverse immigrant groups.

The image of the common-school movement, associated with Horace Mann and his followers in the mid-nineteenth century, has undergone important shifts. This work, pursued also by historians sympathetic to the radical revisionists but not firmly identified with them, like David Tyack and Carl Kaestle, has shown that widespread use of schools, especially in rural areas, antedated the changes associated with Mann and his fellow reformers. It now appears that what happened in the nineteenth century was less a flowering of interest in schooling than a *transfer* of educational responsibility from private to public hands; school attendance was a popular phenomenon. The substitution of public for nonpublic sponsorship was *not* led by nascent capitalists seeking to socialize a docile labor force and protect property from the children of immigrant mobs (Angus 1983, p. 81; Kaestle and Vinovskis 1980). Instead, the leaders were self-styled "Christians and patriots," a "Protestant-civic" cultural group rooted in rural and small-town America (Gordon 1978). Social control and bureaucratization have, thus, been downgraded as key themes in nineteenth-century school development. Ministers, temperance workers, and local elites tapped sufficient common values and shared interests to persuade countless communities to build public schools, patronize them, and start the processes of expansion, bureaucratization, and internal differentiation that reached their culmination in large urban systems in the twentieth century (Tyack 1980).

James Sanders (1983) thinks that the battle between the liberals and the radicals "has ended in a stalemate for the protagonists and boredom for the less ideological bystanders" (pp. 217, 224). I am not, however, persuaded that their "mutually exclusive positions" do not allow other historians ample room to maneuver—to go from Katz to Katznelson. There are numerous indicators of work that represents some synthesis of the progressive thesis and the revisionist antithesis.

The urban studies of two political scientists perhaps best illustrate emerging syntheses in action. Paul Peterson and Ira Katznelson have looked both at school politics today and in several nineteenth-century cities (Peterson 1985; Katznelson et al. 1982). Peterson accepts social stratification and conflict as givens, in the radical tradition. But, consistent with liberalism, which considers access and participation crucial to democratic possibilities, Peterson shows how American political traditions of a widespread franchise and highly contested politics empowered successive groups to wrest concessions from public school educators.

Taking the idea he developed in his study of a New York City neighborhood during the community-control struggles of the 1960s, *City Trenches*, Katznelson (1981) and his colleagues looked at late nineteenth-century Chicago and San Francisco to see whether the working class then manifested the same "split consciousness" in its political lives that he sees in the present: Did those American workers also think of themselves in class terms only around the work place, and act on the basis of ethnic-, partisan- and neighborhood-based self-identifications in their other dealings with capitalists and institutions? He concludes that they did so, and he appears to agree with William Issel (1979) that capitalists with their "capital-logic" and noncapitalists with their "democratic-logic" were increasingly sharing the stage with a powerful third "logic"—that of state building by public-administration professionals and bureaucrats:

State-building educators were more significant in pressing for school expansion than were workers or businessmen. Workers did not act in the school arena as a class. Instead, they selectively attended to educational issues, sometimes as labor, at other times as ethnics. This pattern of participation reflects not only the peculiarities of American class formation but also the early entry of workers into the public schools [when compared to the pattern in other industrialized societies]. [Katznelson et al. 1982; p. 125]

Thus it seems that no matter how sensitive scholars have become to issues of economic class and to the intense conflicts waged by ethnic and other groups in a divided America, it appears as if our historiography of education will continue, into the indefinite future, to be framed by the sense of *American exceptionality*—more than it will pay obeisance to the transsocietal "laws" of social science.

REFERENCES

Angus, David L. "The Empirical Mode: Quantitative History." In *Historical Inquiry in Education: A Research Agenda*, edited by John H. Best. Washington, D.C.: American Educational Research Association, 1983.

Bailyn, Bernard, *Education in the Forming of American Society*. Chapel Hill: University of North Carolina Press, 1960.

Best, John Hardin, ed. *Historical Inquiry in Education: A Research Agenda*. Washington, D.C.: American Educational Research Association, 1983.

Bolton, Frederick E. "Curricula in University Departments of Education." *School and Society* 2:50 (December 11, 1915): 829–841.

Bowles, Samuel, and Gintis, Herbert. *Schooling in Capitalist America: Educational Reform and the Contradictions of Economic Life.* New York: Basic Books, 1976.

Carnoy, Martin. *Education as Cultural Imperialism.* New York: Longman, 1974.

Clifford, Geraldine Jonçich. "An Historical Account of the Shifting Relations Between School and Non-School Education." In *Education in School and Nonschool Settings,* edited by Mario D. Fantini and Robert Sinclair. Eighty-fourth Yearbook of the National Society for the Study of Education. Chicago: University of Chicago Press, 1985.

Coleman, James S., et al. *Equality of Educational Opportunity.* Washington, D.C.: U.S. Government Printing Office, 1966.

Committee Q. "Required Courses in Education." *Bulletin of the American Association of University Professors* 19 (March 1933): 173–200.

Cubberley, Ellwood P. "The College of Education and the Superintendent of Schools." *School and Society* 17:438 (May 19, 1923): 538–545.

Cubberley, Ellwood P. *History of Education.* Boston: Houghton-Mifflin, 1948.

Curti, Merle. *The Social Ideas of American Educators.* Totowa, N.J.: Littlefield, Adams, 1978.

Feinberg, Walter; Kantor, Harvey; Katz, Michael; and Violas, Paul. *Revisionists Respond to Ravitch.* Washington, D.C.: National Academy of Education, 1980.

Gordon, Mary D. "Patriots and Christians: A Reassessment of Nineteenth-Century School Reformers." *Journal of Social History* 11:4 (Summer 1978): 554–574.

Hartz, Louis, *The Liberal Tradition in America.* New York: Harcourt, Brace, 1955.

Issel, William. "Americanization, Acculturation and Social Control: School Reform Ideology in Industrial Pennsylvania, 1880–1910." *Journal of Social History* 12:4 (Summer 1979): 569–590.

Jencks, Christopher, et al. *Inequality: A Reassessment of the Effect of Family and Schooling in America.* New York: Basic Books, 1972.

Johnson, Henry C. "Rescuing Clio: Philosophy of History." In *Historical Inquiry in Education: A Research Agenda,* edited by John H. Best. Washington, D.C.: American Educational Research Association, 1983.

Kaestle, Carl, and Vinovskis, Maris A. *Education and Social Change in Nineteenth-Century Massachusetts.* Cambridge: Harvard University Press, 1980.

Karier, Clarence J.; Violas, Paul C.; and Spring, Joel. *Roots of Crisis: American Education in the Twentieth Century.* Chicago: Rand McNally, 1973.

Katz, Michael B. *Class, Bureaucracy, and Schools.* New York: Praeger, 1971.

Katz, Michael, and Hogan, David. "Schools, Work and Family Life: Social History." In *Historical Inquiry in Education: A Research Agenda,* edited by John H. Best. Washington, D.C.: American Educational Research Association, 1983.

Katznelson, Ira. *City Trenches: Urban Politics and the Patterning of Class in the United States.* Chicago: University of Chicago Press, 1981.

Katznelson, Ira; Gille, Kathleen; and Weir, Margaret. "Public Schooling and Working-Class Formation: The Case of the United States." *American Journal of Education* 90:2 (February 1982): 111–143.

Levin, Henry M. "Education, Life Chances, and the Courts: The Role of Social Science Evidence." *Law and Contemporary Problems* 39:2 (1975): 217–240.

Peterson, Paul. *The Politics of School Reform, 1870–1940.* Chicago: University of Chicago Press, 1985.

Powell, Arthur G., and Sizer, Theodore R. "Changing Conceptions of the Professor of Education." In *To Be a Phoenix: The Education Professoriate*, edited by James S. Counelis. Bloomington, Ind.: Phi Delta Kappa, 1969.

Ravitch, Diane. *The Revisionists Revised: Studies in the Historiography of American Education*. Proceedings of the National Academy of Education. Vol. 4, 1977, pp. 1–84.

Reese, William J. "Neither Victims Nor Masters: Ethnic and Minority Study." In *Historical Inquiry in Education: A Research Agenda*, edited by John H. Best. Washington, D.C.: American Educational Research Association, 1983.

Sanders, James. "Education and the City: Urban Community Study." In *Historical Inquiry in Education: A Research Agenda*, edited by John H. Best. Washington D.C.: American Educational Research Association, 1983.

Silver, Harold. *Education as History*. London: Methuen, 1983.

Tyack, David B. "Reformulating the Purposes of Public Education in an Era of Retrenchment." *Educational Studies* 11:1 (Spring 1980): 49–64.

Wesley, Edgar. *NEA: The First Hundred Years*. New York: Harper, 1957.

Williamson, Obed Jalmar. *Provisions for General Theory Courses in the Professional Education of Teachers*. Contributions to Education No. 684. New York: Teachers College, 1936.

12

On Political Science

Paul E. Peterson

The politics of education hardly existed as an identifiable field of study twenty years ago. The most important works on the topic had been written by individuals such as Richard Fenno, Robert Salisbury, and Robert Dahl, who only happened to discuss educational topics in the course of developing much more general arguments about political processes and institutions. Today the field is organized, specialized, and quite self-conscious about its identity.

If a clerk from the State Department were hired to write a brochure on the politics of education for distribution overseas, I am sure that he or she would be able to quantitatively demonstrate extraordinary progress. The number of journal articles devoted to the topic, the number of professors teaching full time in the area, the number of papers presented at professional meetings, the number of books published, the size of government and foundation grants awarded, and the frequency of literature reviews have almost exponentially increased over the past two decades. The very size, vigor, and continuing strength of the Politics of Education Association testifies to the organizational significance of the enterprise.

But what do we in this field *know* now that we did not know when

Previously published in *Politics of Education Bulletin* 12 (1984): 1, 3, and 7. Reprinted with permission.

Fenno, Salisbury, and Dahl put pen to paper on educational topics? When the issue is posed in these terms, it makes us all a bit uncomfortable. We like to believe in progress, in the accumulation of knowledge, and in the usefulness of applying scientific methodologies to social and educational phenomena. After all, it is the belief in progress—in linear development along a definable course—that separates us moderns from the ancients, who saw only cyclical change in the "great wheel of history." And it is the belief that scientific inquiry can enhance progress that has justified our profession's call for resources from society.

Now, maybe, it is unfair to ask for indicators of success after a mere twenty years. Maybe it is as inappropriate to ask social science for signs of progress as it is to ask postmillenarianists to state the time and place of the Second Coming. Maybe a thousand years is but a day not only in the sight of the Lord but also in the eyes of the social scientific disciplines. In due course we shall sort out the competing paradigms, refine the appropriate methodologies, recruit the pathbreaking Newtons and Einsteins, and produce the nonfalsifiable propositions of broad and compelling significance. But in an age that demands a "new idea" if not every week at least every quadrennium, such a lofty position is likely to leave a profession in the dungheap of history. The profession thus needs an answer to the question posed by George Washington Plunkett, the Tammany Hall Democrat who was himself the quintessential modern: "What have you done for me lately?"

To answer this question, I will first describe the analytical lenses, the questions posed, and the conventional answers given two decades ago. Then I will describe the analytic perspectives, dominant questions, and new orthodoxies that pervade the field today. That will at least tell us what changes have occurred in the politics of education. Then we can ask whether change is progress or whether we are merely in a new phase of the historical cycle.

The major perspectives that shaped much of the politics of education literature a generation ago included decision-making theory, group theory, systems theory, and social-psychological concepts. Decision-making theory provided an answer to such questions as: Who has the power? What is the balance of influence between school board and superintendent, between City Hall and school system, between administrators and teachers, between school professionals and the lay public? Power relations were estimated by calculating the relative impact of various participants on decisions.

Group theories supplemented theories of decision making by providing a framework for understanding the bases of political interest and the processes by which coalitions were formed. From this perspective the following questions were asked: When do groups in education coalesce? Why do they split in disarray? What groups seem to have the most continuous impact on policy? Why? Group theory was most often applied at national and state government levels. It said that conflict among races, religions, and ideological groups prevented the federal government from giving more than limited support to education. At the state level, it showed that educators were most successful when they moderated their differences and worked together.

Systems theory focused attention on the entire policymaking process—from the formulation of demands to the way in which policy outputs generated a new cycle of demands. Systems theory allowed political scientists to ask the following questions: Does politics make a difference? Are school politics primarily the product of broad social and economic conditions? Do political processes act, at best, as a set of mediating variables? In general, studies undertaken within this framework found a puzzlingly small amount of independent political effort.

Finally, political scientists drew on social-psychological theories to explain citizen participation. They showed that those most involved in school affairs were the better-educated, higher-status, more socially integrated members of society. Whenever the less involved, more alienated members became activated, they voted against the schools. But this happened infrequently, because school issues were usually not salient to most people.

A COHERENT PICTURE

In retrospect, it can be said that these analysts painted a more or less internally coherent picture of educational politics. Power was exercised primarily by education professionals, who usually operated in a relatively consensual decision-making system in which leaders deferred to the expressed preferences of well-organized groups. An apathetic public generally acquiesced to low-visibility politics at the local level because educational groups worked cooperatively. Nationally, the federal government was prevented by group conflict from contributing to education.

But, you say, this was about 1964, the year after the Kennedy assassination, the year of Martin Luther King's March on Washington, the year of the Hanoi bombing, and the year Lyndon Johnson won by a landslide. How could educational research be so blind to the world around it? The answer is to be found in the words of Mister Dooley: Educational research, like the Supreme Court, follows—it does not lead—the "election" returns. Books and articles published in 1964 reflected the wisdom gathered in a prior decade, not the passions gathering steam in the early sixties. However, it must be acknowledged that educational researchers were beginning, in their papers and proposals, to focus on questions of educational equality. Were fiscal resources equally allocated among districts, among schools, within classrooms? Were school systems so isolated from politics that they were impervious to minority-group influence? Was citizen non-participation due to exclusion instead of apathy?

In the ensuing two decades the politics of education discipline has been profoundly altered by changes in the world it studies. The civil rights movement, the war on poverty, Title I, the political awakening of minority groups, judicial activism, the appearance of strong public-sector unions, the reinvigoration of neoconservative thought, the revival of nonpublic schools, the new energy of the Moral Majority, and the election of the first frankly conservative President in fifty years. The ebb and flow of the political tides have been too profound not to have shaped the contours of this discipline.

THREE NEW CONCEPTUAL FACES

Where have these changes left the study of the politics of education? Do we now have a new body of knowledge that allows us to explain what we have experienced? Since it is easier to describe than assess what has happened, I will do that first. Quite clearly, the political storms all but swept away the concepts, questions, and agreed understandings that guided research two decades ago. Instead of decisions, groups, systems, and perceptions, analysts now write of markets, collective action, loose coupling, and capitalism. Instead of asking who governs or which group participates, analysts ask how choices are made and whether policies can be implemented. Instead of a broad consensus on the overall shape of educational policy, analysts now disagree vigorously about the very units of analysis to be employed. Three types of analyses now seem dominant: *economic theory*, *organizational theory*, and *Marxist historical analysis*.

The first, economic theory, is both currently and potentially the most influential of the three. Its assumptions are simple, can be widely applied, and permit the construction of complex but elegant models. The analytical unit is the autonomous individual acting rationally to maximize his or her self-interest. In the politics of education, economic analysts ask: What are the conditions under which individuals will act together? Are public school systems quasi-monopolies? Or do they compete with one another—and with the private schools—for teachers, pupils, and fiscal resources? How do changes in educational markets affect school board decision making? What are the consequences for local school expenditures of increased federal or state aid? Does it substitute for—or supplement—local revenue sources?

Organizational theory takes the social role as its fundamental unit of analysis. From its vantage point, individuals in their social roles are constrained by inadequate information, biases, perceptions, and limited time. As a result, they and their organizations act in standardized ways. New problems are treated in the same way as old problems. Change occurs slowly and on the margins. In the politics of education, this theory has been applied most frequently to the questions of implementation. How are decisions executed? What happens at the bottom of an organization when policy is made at the top? Why is it that educational symbols change rapidly while educational practice changes slowly, if at all?

Finally, a variety of Marxist analyses have been used to interpret and characterize educational systems more generally. Here, the unit of analysis is the social system as a whole. The most successful attempts are either studies of historical change or comparative analyses of educational systems in countries at various stages of economic development. These theorists ask: What are the connections between educational institutions, economic development, and political change? How are schools used by elites to perpetuate existing patterns of domination and subjection? What are the patterns of discrimination that can be observed? Do schools help resolve—at least temporarily—the contradiction between the need for continuing capital accumulation and the necessity of preserving popular legitimacy?

RESEARCH DIRECTIONS SPLINTERED

Needless to say, these three perspectives have little in common. As a result, research on the politics of education has splintered in diverse directions. A unified agenda, always difficult to realize, seems an even more distant goal.

But have we at least progressed beyond the naiveté of research twenty years ago? To some extent, the answer must be yes. To give just one example, consider the question of political power. Twenty years ago it was thought that this issue could be resolved by looking at who made decisions, or who was thought to be influential, or who held key positions of responsibility. Now, we realize the context for choice is much more important than the background or character of the choice maker. Economists want to know whether choices are individual or collective and whether the decisions are made in a monopolistic or competitive context. Organizational theorists want to know the information available to the policymaker and whether he or she is able to direct those for whom the policy is made. Marxists want to know the broad economic and political constraints under which policy is formulated.

But loss of innocence is not necessarily progress. It may only be a sign of aging, or even worse, mortality. Our pictures of the politics of education are today more varied, more subtle, and more provocative, but do even the photographers themselves believe them to be more accurate?

Surely, to the consumer the pictures are nothing but a blur. The most recent spate of education commission reports provide a dramatic example of the way in which the supposed scientific knowledge of the politics of education profession is regarded by informed policymakers. Instead of drawing on the subtle, sophisticated understanding of the economist or organizational theorist (to say nothing of the Marxist historian), the new educational reformers have proceeded along lines virtually indistinguishable from their genre in past generations. To be sure, the watchword now is quality, not equality. But they pursue quality by the well-worn but flawed political approaches of the past.

To the economists' chagrin, virtually no changes in educational markets are proposed. Even the notion of merit pay is only remotely related to the economists' concept of market price. To the chagrin of the organizational theorist, quality is mandated by legislative fiat or regulated by means of a new Washington grant-in-aid program. To the chagrin of the historian of reform, Marxist or not, little attention has been paid to whether reforms of the past have had the intended consequences. Instead, the present commissions of education think existing educational organizations will change their behavior either if leaders exhort or command them to do so or if more money is thrown at the problem. The ancients' view of history as a cycle repeating itself seems disquietingly apt.

We do not know if schools have failed to teach Johnny how to read. But we do know that those conducting research on politics of education have failed to teach political practitioners. But we shall not despair. In our sight, as in that of the postmillenarianist believer, a thousand years is but a day.

BIBLIOGRAPHY

Altbach, P. G.; Kelley, G. P.; and Weis, L. *Excellence in Education: Perspectives on Policy and Practice.* Buffalo, N.Y.: Prometheus, 1985.

Bailey, S. K., and Mosher, E. K. *ESEA: The Office of Education Administers a Law.* Syracuse, N.Y.: Syracuse University Press, 1968.

Bowles, S., and Gintis, H. *Schooling in Capitalist America: Educational Reform and the Contradictions of Economic Life.* New York: Basic Books, 1976.

Callahan, R. E. *Education and the Cult of Efficiency.* Chicago: University of Chicago Press, 1962.

Cronin, M. *The Control of Urban Schools.* New York: Free Press, 1973.

Dahl, R. *Who Governs?: Democracy and Power in an American City.* New Haven, Conn.: Yale University Press, 1961.

Eliot, T. H. "Toward an Understanding of Public School Politics." *American Political Science Review* 53 (1959): 1032-1051.

Grubb, W. N., and Michelson, S. *States and Schools.* Lexington, Mass.: Lexington Books, 1974.

Hochschild, J. *The New American Dilemma: Liberal Democracy and School Desegregation.* New Haven, Conn.: Yale University Press, 1984.

Iannaccone, L. *Politics in Education.* New York: Center for Applied Research in Education, 1967.

Iannaccone, L., and F. Lutz. *Politics, Power and Policy: The Governing of Local School Districts.* Columbus, Ohio: Charles Merrill, 1970.

Katz, M. B. *The Irony of Early School Reform: Educational Innovation in Mid-nineteenth Century Massachusetts.* Boston: Beacon Press, 1968.

Katz, M. B. *Class, Bureaucracy and Schools: The Illusion of Educational Change in America.* New York: Praeger, 1971.

Kerr, N. "The School Board as an Agency of Legitimation." *Sociology of Education* 38 (1964): 34-59.

Kirp, D. L. *Doing Good by Doing Little: Race and Schooling in Britain.* Berkeley and Los Angeles: University of California Press, 1979.

Minar, D. "Community Basis of Conflict in School System Politics." *American Sociological Review* 31 (1966): 822-835.

Munger, F. J., and Fenno, R. F., Jr. *National Politics and Federal Aid to Education.* Syracuse, N.Y.: Syracuse University Press, 1962.

Murphy, J. T. "Title I of ESEA: The Politics of Implementing Federal Education Reform." *Harvard Educational Review* 41 (1971): 35-63.

Oates, W. E. "The Effects of Property Taxes and Local Public Spending on Property Values: An Empirical Study of Tax Capitalization and the Tiebout Hypothesis." *Journal of Political Economy* 77 (1969): 957-971.

Olson, M. *The Logic of Collective Action*. Cambridge, Mass.: Harvard University Press, 1965.

Orfield, G. *The Reconstruction of Southern Education*. New York: Wiley, 1969.

Peterson, P. E. *School Politics Chicago Style*. Chicago: University of Chicago Press, 1976.

Peterson, P. E. *The Politics of School Reform, 1870-1940*. Chicago: University of Chicago Press, 1985.

Peterson, P. E. *City Limits*. Chicago: University of Chicago Press, 1981.

Pressman, J. L., and Wildavsky, A. *Implementations*. Berkeley and Los Angeles: University of California Press, 1973.

Ravitch, D. *The Great School Wars: New York City, 1805-1973*. New York: Basic Books, 1974.

Ravitch, D. *The Revisionists Revised: A Critique of the Radical Attack on the Schools*. New York: Basic Books, 1978.

Rogers, D. *110 Livingston Street*. New York: Random House, 1968.

Salisbury, R. H. "Schools and Politics in the Big City." *Harvard Educational Review* 37 (1967): 408-424.

Tiebout, C. M. "A Pure Theory of Local Expenditures." *Journal of Political Economy* 64 (1956): 416-424.

Tyack, D. *The One Best System: A History of American Education*. Cambridge, Mass.: Harvard University Press, 1974.

Zeigler, H.; Jennings, M. K.; and Peak, W. *Governing American Schools: Political Interaction in Local School Districts*. North Scituate, Mass.: Duxbury Press, 1974.

Zeigler, H.; Kehoe, E.; and Reisman, J. *City Managers and School Superintendents: Response to Community Conflict*. New York: Praeger, 1985.

13

A Philosopher Looks at the Social Context

Maxine Greene

Philosophy does not accumulate knowledge nor add, in any substantive way, to the development of a "knowledge base." To "do" philosophy is to pose questions about the nature of knowledge itself, to look critically at claims to knowledge, to clarify such assumptions as those underlying the conception of "foundation" or "base." No matter what the orientation, I would suggest, philosophers of education are generally committed to doing battle, as Ludwig Wittgenstein once said, "against the bewitchment of our intelligence by means of language." More often than not, they are concerned with, to use John Dewey's words, "thinking what the known demands of us—what responsive attitude it exacts." They want to provoke people to disclose their major premises when they talk about the role of education in society, when they make prescriptions for the school as a social institution, when they make class and other distinctions in their classrooms. They want to make it possible for practitioners to articulate their own vantage points as thoughtfully and coherently as possible with respect to the social and political roles they play. As significantly, they try to integrate insights from the various social sciences (for instance, anthropology, sociology, social psychology) as they affect the study of education. Conscious of the normative dimensions of educational processes, they work to overcome long-standing splits between facts and values, to probe untapped possibilities in the moral and political domains.

Social philosophers like Hannah Arendt, Jurgen Habermas, and Richard Bernstein have become influential in the fields of educational philosophy, as have Peter Berger and Thomas Luckmann with their notion of the "social construction of reality." Educational philosophers like Harry Broudy, Jane Roland Martin, Betty Sichel, and Kenneth Strike, among others, seem interested in theory in its classic sense. In other words, they pay less attention to explanatory theory than they do to the kind of theory that might enable them to think about what might constitute a more rational and humane society. Jonas Soltis is among those who write of a "sociocentric" approach to knowledge, meaning a communal approach to knowledge making and a conception of knowledge as something more than what is contained in books. It is conceived to be inherent also, as Soltis puts it, "in hands and actions as we take part in social living."

Although I am aware that not all practicing educational philosophers share these views, they do suggest the interests and projects at the center of my own thinking. My views are also specifically affected by social phenomenology and critical theory, as developed by certain members of the Frankfurt School, particularly Theodor Adorno, Walter Benjamin, and Habermas; and I know I am not alone in this. It is important for the reader to hold this orientation in mind, however, because in this chapter I try to locate what I believe to be the crucial aspects of the "social context" of education today and try, at once, to pose some useful questions.

Indeed, the questions are multiple. Many of them spring from our long habit of conceiving of educating as a social process carried on through structured interactions in classrooms, and of acknowledging (often vaguely) that community values in some manner have determined or affected what has been taught. We have acknowledged certain of the interfaces between the microsystems of schools and families and the macrosystems of the socioeconomic order; but we have often reduced what we have seen to cost-benefit considerations. Preoccupied with measurable achievements, we have thought often in terms of inputs and outputs, relatively seldom about human distinctiveness and human worth in a changing, variegated social world. Similarly, we have thought relatively little about the problem of special interest groups (fundamentalist, "free Christian," and others) or the crying need to reconstitute what Dewey called an "articulate public."

We were informed about poor children and immigrant children; but we paid little heed to their lived lives, to the stresses of those lives, to the strengths and weaknesses to which they gave rise. We knew theoretically about the impacts of social and economic class; but, from our middle-class standpoints (which we often confused with a universal standpoint), we could not infuse into our notions of class membership much existential reality. Even when we began pondering the range of cognitive learning "styles" (and tried to do justice to those that were not ours), we tended ordinarily to think of a generic schoolchild—a client, a case, an object of well-meaning ministrations. It was rare to hear someone wondering about a child's family, a child's life history. He or she was "kid," a "pupil," a decontextualized "child," whom we—in our dutifulness and benevolence—were asked to socialize.

As late as the 1960s, most people in our field presumed the existence of an open-opportunity system in which the properly skilled would find a place, if our teaching (or training) were effective enough. Most educators, I am convinced, thought of children as deficit systems, whether the children were disadvantaged or advantaged. Even when attention was turned to spontaneity or expressiveness, the child was viewed as anonymous and in need of just those stimuli, just those ideas the teacher *in situ* was equipped and ready to provide. We had learned that children were social organisms; we even knew that persons became human only by means of communication and in the context of communities. Nevertheless, few educators posed questions with any sense of the worlds children lived in or with any curiosity about how children constructed their social realities.

I believe that it was the civil rights movement and the abrupt emergence of the "invisible poor" in the 1960s that led many of us in philosophy, as well as in the social sciences, to pay attention to economic and political issues we had ignored up to that time. In many cases it was the surge of critique of the schools' presumed inability to solve problems of inequity and inequality that made us doubt what we had taken for granted for so long. Even for philosophers (who should have known better) "equal opportunity" had meant open doors for all, a fair shake for each, a "democratic" solution for the problems of mass education. Actually, it took a number of analytic philosophers like James R. McClellan, Jr., and Jerrold Coombs to draw attention to the fact that equality did not mean sameness, that an insistence on equal opportunity for differentially endowed (and privileged) children led to blatant inequities. Slowly recognizing that justice entailed making relevant distinctions, humane distinctions, philosophers had to confront the impacts of poverty and discrimination, crippling consequences now being revealed by social scientists of different persuasions. Many of us recall the effects of these revelations on our expectations of schools. We recall the impact of a book like John Rawls's *A Theory of Justice*, which forced us to realize that analytical philosophy, at its most rigorous, could penetrate to the heart of the social context, in which the questions of equality and fairness were being fought.

From many of our vantage points, the educational reforms were undertaken in response to social predicaments we were, in any case, first beginning to identify. Compensatory and remedial measures aroused hope for a brief time; then philosophers, like so many others concerned about education, began to recognize the full complexity of the damage that had been done over the years and the damage still being done. Given the nature of the economic system, given the stratification of industry, given the prevalence of bureaucratic structures, how could a just society (and a just school) be guaranteed? How could the schools overcome the effects of family dislocation or indigence or ineffectuality? How could the schools guarantee fulfillment for all the children? How could they reconcile the needs of so many different children with the demands of an expanding, technologizing, war-oriented society?

So much had been hidden, submerged in taken-for-grantedness, smothered in pieties. Many of us were astonished by what we had never seen before, by lurking questions we had never before thought to ask. When asked to say what we know in the mid-1980s that we did not know in the mid-1960s, I can only respond by thinking of the questions we did not pose two decades ago, questions that are inescapable today. We were made aware of some, I think, during the days of desegregation and the struggles in the South. Robert Coles' tapes, like his book *Children of Crisis*, heightened the meanings of the images of Little Rock, New Orleans, and the other cities where children braved brutal opposition to integrate the schools. *The Autobiography of Malcolm X* gave us insight into what it must have been like to be black, brilliant, and deeply frustrated in America. The Reverend Martin Luther King's addresses and, later, his *Letter from a Birmingham Jail* introduced us not only to a prophetic voice but to the painful particularities of racism, to the experience of what Dr. King called "nobodyness." Claude Brown's *Manchild in the Promised Land* told us something about existence in the northern ghetto, in this case the existence of a young man who transcended and survived. We learned something about Puerto Rican life from Piri Thomas's *Down These Mean Streets*, something more and from another perspective from Oscar Lewis's *La Vida* and other works.

Perhaps strangely, it took us somewhat longer to attend to the predicament of girls and women within the schools. We had long known about classroom discrimination, about the channeling of female students into traditional female roles, about the shutting off of options through taken-for-granted emphases on what presumably had to be. We knew Virginia Woolf's work and Simone de Beauvoir's; we were beginning to read women's literature. We needed such works as Nancy Cott's *Roots of Bitterness: Documents of the Social History of American Women* to find out something of the lived lives of such women as the Grimke sisters, Catherine Beecher, and Lucy Larcom, who was a factory worker at the Lowell Mills. Soon there were Adrienne Rich, Tillie Olsen, Toni Morrison, Maya Angelou to communicate the sense of suffered inequities, limited opportunities, and resistance to the comforts of the "domestic sphere." Today, the sources have multiplied remarkably; and we look back from Carol Gilligan's work and Nancy Chodorow's and Jean Baker Miller's with an incredulity at our relative silence twenty years ago.

There were other revelations in other human domains; but I mention these because they educated me, sensitized me to the ways in which people constructed their own meanings in the contexts of their actual lives. Like others, I began paying more attention to the demographic and ethnographic studies that began to emerge. I became fascinated, rather early, by the sometimes autobiographical accounts of life within public schools by people like Jonathan Kozol, Herb Kohl, George Dennison, James Herndon. They helped us to understand the pressures, the confusing signals, the occasional instances of liberating teaching. They made clear the degree to which social relations within classrooms often created the contexts in which learning occurred. They sometimes made it possible to discern how different people related to the world of the school, and how their selective interactions were affected by daily life outside the institution. Many, of course, were libertarian or romantic anarchist in belief; and, along with Marxist critics of the schools (like Samuel Bowles and Herbert Gintis, for instance), they exacerbated the political and philosophical difficulties confronting people trying to make sense of the school's social roles. Their critiques, however, contributed to the posing of further unasked questions. It became less and less possible to assume that the public schools, by their very nature, nurtured the growth of children and contributed to an ongoing development of democracy.

The consciousness of such questions may have helped philosophers with an existential-phenomenological orientation like my own to find studies of everyday life taking on new philosophical significance. We became aware of the one-dimensional social science filters, of the quantitative lenses through which we had been asked to look at schools; and now we felt ourselves drawn as much to confrontations with the everyday, commonsense world. We found ourselves trying to imagine ourselves into the minds and bodies of children who were strangers, trying to fuse something of ourselves with something in them. It may well be that we understand far more about cultures and their symbol systems than we could have before, far more about how cultures are actually lived. Without quite realizing it, some of us were beginning to engage in interpretive modes of inquiry. We were working to pose our philosophical questions with respect to meanings and perspectives and the ways in which they mediated learning. We were influenced by Hans-Georg Gadamer, Paul Ricoeur, Clifford Geertz, Charles Taylor, and others opening up the pathways of hermeneutics; and, in cases like my own, the works of Martin Heidegger and Alfred Schutz, a social phenomenologist, took on a new relevance. Neighborhood structures, street lives, family patterns: all became aspects of our philosophical subject matter where social life and social relations were concerned. Work such as Valerie Polakow Suransky's on the "phenomenology of childhood" also began feeding into and diversifying some of our thinking about teaching, learning, and possibility.

Aware, now, of multiple human realities and points of view, we are aware that no single reform or mode of practice can tap the capacities and intelligences of the diverse young persons in American schools. Yet we confront demands for the cultivation of predefined "basics," "common learnings," excellence equated with measured achievement. Certain of our questions cluster around the purposes of public education today, around the meaning of a "public" and the role of the school when it comes to the education of what Dewey called an "articulate public." How do we meet the expectations of parents who want, above all else, to see their children become what Hannah Arendt called "jobholders and consumers"? How do we reconcile our concern for critical thinking and expanded perspectives with the demands of special interest groups who want the schools to train

God-fearing, docile, acquiescent individuals? How, at a moment when equality has become problematic as a value, do we serve the cause of justice and equity? How do we justify the special attention given to the affluent and the talented? How do we meet the nation's professed needs for proficiency in science and technology and at once release the energies of the excluded, at least to the degree that some will learn to learn? How can we, as educators, deal with the problems of dislocated workers and their families, suddenly rootless, suddenly lost? How do we educate so that the young can cope with the destructive possibilities of the atomic bomb and become informed enough, committed enough to stave off nuclear war?

Looking back for two decades, we cannot but be conscious of the ways in which ordinary benevolence resulted in the demeaning of children who were different, in the disconfirming of their experience. So many of us simply assumed the higher value of the languages we spoke, the things we cherished; we found it almost impossible to ascribe worth to other cultures, other ways of being in the world. Today, even while we acknowledge the importance of initiating the diverse young into the mainstream of cultural life, more of us are able to respect (if not always to understand or do justice to) the cultures of the newcomers. The questions, however, about particularism and universalism, about plurality and community, remain open, as do the urgent questions about what it signifies to be an individual and what it means to be free. We can no longer demand that the young screen out the Sicilian overtones, the Colombian memories, the Haitian concerns, the Jamaican traditions, the Greek forms of life. At once, even as we affirm and reaffirm the worth of the traditions in which we are embedded, the art forms we love, the symbol systems that structure our experience, we have to keep grounding and seeking justification for our efforts to usher the young into what we think of as the common world.

These are, to a large degree, moral issues, ethical issues, at the center of every philosopher's primary concerns. We have to deal as well with the meanings of technology, the fact of bureaucracy, the problem of living in an administered society, an information society, a "high-tech" society, a post-industrial society. It becomes clearer and clearer that the schoolroom will play a relatively minor role in the construction of shared social realities; and we are bound to pose all sorts of new questions now that we realize that all knowledge is socially constructed. How do we overcome relativism? How do we allow for multiple provinces of meaning? How do we engage students in such a fashion that their own distinctive voices can be heard even as they are moving toward one another in what we still hope will be a norm-governed world, a nonracist and nonsexist and equitable world? How do we meet the resistance of those young people insistent on creating their own enclaves and cultures, sometimes to secure values we despise?

Our questions multiply along the paths already opened by Elizabeth Cohen. I am preoccupied with technicalization and with militarist logics and with budget cuts—and with the ways they put so many of the young at risk. The questions we have to raise must not be repressed; if they are, energy and desire are repressed, as is the sense of what might be. Any effort to retreat and take comfort in the benevolence of the past or the calculativeness of the present can only damage the young and diminish our profession. We are faced with incompleteness, as we are with mystifications. Now, in the mid-1980s, it is time for new initiatives, new beginnings. It is time to resist and to imagine—to move toward what we believe to be desirable, toward what might be.